# THE ALMIGHTY DOLLAR

## A PSYCHIATRIST LOOKS AT MONEY

### EUGENE L. LOWENKOPF, M.D.

Copyright © 2022 by Eugene L. Lowenkopf, M.D.

ISBN 978-1-960063-07-6 (softcover)
ISBN 978-1-960063-08-3 (hardcover)
ISBN 978-1-960063-09-0 (ebook)
Library of Congress Control Number: 2022923067

All rights reserved. No part of this book may be reproduced or transmitted in any form or by any means, electronic or mechanical, including photocopying, recording, or by any information storage and retrieval system without express written permission from the author, except in the case of brief quotations embodied in critical reviews and certain other noncommercial uses permitted by copyright law.

Printed in the United States of America.

Book Vine Press
2516 Highland Dr.
Palatine, IL 60067

This book is dedicated to the memory of Jp. M. (1961-1994)

# CONTENTS

Introduction: What This Book is About and Why I Wrote It ............. vii
1   Kid Stuff ........................................................................................ 1
2   Growing up ................................................................................. 17
3   Marriage ..................................................................................... 39
4   Having too Little ........................................................................ 57
5   Taking Other People's Money ................................................... 75
6   Having too Much ....................................................................... 91
7   Hoarding and Collecting ......................................................... 109
8   Giving it Away ......................................................................... 127
9   Playing Around with Money ................................................... 145
10  Money Transactions in Everyday Life .................................... 165
11  Parenting and Grandparenting ............................................... 189
12  Breaking up .............................................................................. 209
13  Retirement ................................................................................ 231
14  Getting Old .............................................................................. 249
15  To the Grave and Beyond ........................................................ 267

Appendix A: How Much is Enough? ................................................. 287
Appendix B: Becoming Rational About Money ................................ 293

# INTRODUCTION:

# *What This Book is About and Why I Wrote It*

Money is one of the most important concerns we have to deal with as we go through life. If we have only a small amount, we are restricted in what we can do, we have to make hard choices about what we absolutely must have and what we can dispense with, and we may even suffer from unfulfilled needs of such basics as food, clothing and shelter. If we have enough, life is much easier, and if we have lots of it, then life may even approach the blissful.

It is, therefore, only natural that money is of enormous interest to just about everyone but it's almost invariably looked at from the viewpoint of how to get more of it right now and how to keep on having more of it for the rest of our lives. The many books that deal with money are about just these subjects and don't pay attention to any deeper meanings money has for people over and above being what "makes the world go round".

Inevitably such an important concrete commodity becomes psychologically important in every stage of life, taking on many other meanings in addition to what it can purchase. These meanings vary widely depending upon who you are, what culture you live in, and what your background and experiences are, both personal and familial.

Money and these other meanings enter into almost every interpersonal transaction which makes it all the more surprising that the subject has been given so little consideration by psychiatrists and psychologists in their professional writings as well as in what they write in books and articles addressed to the general public.

Some years back, when a colleague (Sheila Klebanow, M.D.) and I were planning a symposium on "Money and Mind" sponsored by the American Academy of Psychoanalysis, I reviewed the professional literature on the psychology of money, and I turned up only a handful of books and articles, all covering limited aspects of the subject and most very much out of date in their contents and approach. Dr. Klebanow and I subsequently organized the papers presented at the symposium as well as several additional ones into a book, also called "Money and Mind", published by Plenum in 1991, but that book was directed to a professional audience and would probably not be very helpful to a layperson in answering whatever questions he or she might have about the psychology of money. The book focused primarily on the uses of money in psychotherapy, only one of many possible transactions and, while it did touch on money in the life cycle, it did not go very deeply into the great number of meanings of money with which people endow it.

I can only speculate on why there has been so little written about money by professionals who have written so extensively on sex, on violence and on a variety of other subjects. One possible explanation is that some of the earliest writings on money were so far-fetched that they not only did not hold up under scrutiny but put a damper on further explorations into the subject. Another possible explanation that has been suggested is that the psychology of money is too abstract, too ethereal, to really grab hold of and study but that doesn't seem very valid since money is about as concrete and as substantial as anything in this world, and maybe more so. Yet another possible explanation about why professionals don't go into the subject is that we're afraid of revealing too much about ourselves and our own attitudes and philosophy of life. I personally feel that this last explanation is probably the most important since, as I began to write this book, I realized that I was often talking about my own values and my own experiences, opening myself up to criticism by colleagues and to public criticism as well. People might say that thinking and speaking so much about money is inappropriate for a psychiatrist and reveals a disturbed and disturbing obsession.

Even today, several years after I first reviewed the literature on money, when I go into my local bookstore to check out the titles and contents of over twenty-five feet of shelves containing books devoted to either money or psychology so that I can see what's been written on the subject recently, I come up with the same conclusions as I did the first time round, hardly anything, and what there is is very limited in its coverage. A computer search only serves to confirm this impression. Rarely do the two subjects appear together and even then the book that does consider them together focuses on an examination of one or another very specific issue rather than providing an overall perspective, let alone an examination of money's changing but always important psychological significance throughout life.

Money is simply not examined as the vital psychological entity it is, whether this meaning is considered neutral or is considered from the point of view of its use to do good or the contrary, its use to do harm.

From early on in the history of civilization, money has played this dual role of being both good and evil. Probably the earliest writings known to archeologists are records of business transactions. Such records became cumbersome, not only because they had to be carved on rocks or scratched into clay before it was baked, but also because it was hard to measure one piece of merchandise against another in terms of their values. Eventually, someone got the idea that the value of everything could be translated into some generally agreed upon rare substance, and what we know as money was born; this happened in many different cultures around the world and, as far as anyone can tell, it occurred more than five thousand years ago.

Money was initially some precious metal; gold, silver, bronze and copper were used, but other materials were used as well including shells, salt, beads, cocoa beans and semiprecious stones. Women and cattle also served as media of exchange, the women part may be offensive to some but it is historical fact and even turns up in some societies these days. Actual coined money appeared later on, the earliest known dating to about 2700 years ago. Paper money arrived on the scene much later on, and plastic only very recently, and what will be the next development in this age of the internet remains to be seen. Because of its role in facilitating business transactions and the spread of commerce, money can without exaggeration be described as essential to civilization. There's an old saying that "money is the measure of all things" which means that money is the one thing that can be used both to set a comparative value on almost everything else and, once that's done, to obtain them: food, clothing, shelter, appliances, jewelry, vacations, cars and so forth. Why then is it called the "root of all evil"? Because money has another side since it can be used to get all kinds of things for someone. Throughout history, it has been the wish to obtain more of what it could buy that has resulted in wars, persecutions and other horrors. That's the evil in terms of societies but, on a more personal and individual level, it stimulates desires, represents feelings and comes to mean so many things that people literally kill others for it. Every one of us can think of examples, many, many of them, in which people we personally know did strange and dreadful things because of money, and perhaps we too are aware that we ourselves have also been guilty to some extent of misdeeds all in an effort to acquire more money.

While I speak of money in our human situation, that is a kind of shorthand since other possessions come to represent money to different people, but in a different way than money was measured in ancient times. Misers hoard money but there are others who hoard objects, sometimes valuable ones (like jewelry, furs, antiques and artworks, among others) and sometimes things with no obvious worth (like pieces of cardboard, old newspapers, broken toys and rags, among others). All of these objects can become loaded down with symbolic significance and sentimental value, there may be people who regard them as precious, being willing to fight and even to kill to obtain additional ones or merely to hold on to what they already have. Such objects may be thought of as money equivalents.

In my career as a psychiatrist, now over thirty-five years long, I have come to recognize that money, perhaps more than sex, perhaps more than violence, is one of the most essential subjects I have to deal with as I treat patients. Indeed, I have come to feel that I have not truly completed treatment of a patient until I have helped him or her clear up whatever problems with money he or she has. I say this from the viewpoint of having worked with rich people and with poor people, with criminals and with law- abiding citizens, with psychotic patients and with people who are quite sane, and with children, with adolescents, with mature adults and with geriatric patients. I have consistently uncovered monetary issues that get in the way of my patients' mental health and happiness, and that significantly alter their relationships with others.

What this book is about, then, is what I have learned about the many psychological issues relating to money in a large cross-section of the population. I have arranged these issues, for the most part in a sequential fashion, starting with childhood and extending through the many phases of the life cycle up to and including death (even when one dies, psychological problems with money abound even though the deceased, not being present any more, is spared the pain and upset of what's going on). I have also described some special situations in which psychology plays an enormous, probably the principal, role in dealing with money; these include stealing, gambling, hoarding, poverty, wealth and philanthropy. In each chapter, I report on what I have learned over the years, not only from my patients but from people I have met in all sorts of relationships. One of the things that I find most striking is that, in spite of new technological and social developments which have so changed society, people's reactions to money have pretty much gone on unchanged, still creating the same old problems as always. In other words, while the world changes, people and their problems, with or without money, persist.

I also, in this book, criticize psychological theories and psychiatric diagnoses and treatments which I believe are not only not inaccurate but also not helpful in understanding personal involvements with money, and I have provided abundant case illustrations to help the reader understand the points I am making. Cases are of course disguised so that the confidentiality of my patients is preserved. I have used as well examples that are part of the public record or which have been covered by the media in addition to illustrations borrowed from history and from literature.

Why have I written this book? First and foremost, I like to teach, something I have done throughout my professional career. I enjoy communicating information which I possess and which is unknown to someone else. In the case of this book, it's not my students and not my patients whom I wish to educate but the public at large. The information that I am imparting here is interesting in and of its own right, and is of daily concern to almost everybody.

Second, I have written this book in the hope that people will be able to take away from it knowledge and understanding which will help them deal with their own personal problems with money. It will make them more aware of what they are doing in their own money transactions and will perhaps help them to eliminate or reduce the troubles that money contributes to their lives, and let them enjoy the benefits of its positive side. Reading this book is no substitute for a full-fledged psychotherapy but it should give readers enough facts about money for them to think about and examine to see which ones apply to them. This in turn should help them to modify those attitudes which give them grief.

There is yet another reason I am putting my thoughts into print, and that is the wish that it will help to stimulate further studies about money in the fields of psychiatry and psychology by awakening my co-professionals to the importance of the subject. Hopefully, I can do my share towards ending what looks like a conspiracy of silence about money that pervades the mental health professions even though I doubt that there is a true conspiracy, rather more an embarrassment about the subject.

There are some words of caution, though. While many of the chapters describe in broad terms what money issues people encounter as they work their way through life, not everyone's development or personal experience is the same, and things that are true for one person are not necessarily true for another. Some of the experiences with money that I describe are practically universal, occurring in almost everyone; I can, therefore, generalize although each person's experience is unique. In those chapters that deal with poor people or wealthy people, collectors or philanthropists, thieves or gamblers, I describe what I have learned from the patients I have seen and from people I have met who fit into these categories. The number of people in each category is so great that what is true for some is not necessarily true for others. It is truly impossible to come up with explanations that fit every single one of millions of people. Therefore, when you read this book, recognize that not every theory or example applies to everyone. Try hard to see what applies to you but be aware that not everything may be relevant to your particular case.

There are also many differences from one culture to another. What is true in the United States may not be exactly the same in other industrialized countries which, even though they usually have fairly similar social structures and family arrangements, also have their differences. Things may be even more different in people living in countries with totally different social structures and religions. Even in our own society, there are many subcultural variations since we are not a homogeneous people; Americans from different ethnic backgrounds or from different social classes are bound to have different ideas about money in the same way that people who belong to different religions have different ways of approaching money and different philosophies about it. Single people will look at it differently than married people without children, and they in turn will be different from married people with children. Men and women may have different approaches to the handling and management of money and different realities concerning income and expenditures and, of course, people with large incomes will feel different about it than people who are barely getting by. These factors influence what people experience in regard to money and what, as a consequence, they do about it.

I have, in the chapters dealing with phases of life, grouped problems with money along the pathways in a person's life, putting certain issues in the age categories where they generally arise. However, not everyone develops at the same pace and, for example, some things that one person experiences in childhood another experiences in adolescence. Similarly, some issues that arise as one gets older affect people at different ages, and you might find them covered in the chapter on Getting Old or in the chapter on Retirement.

It is my hope that you will enjoy reading this book and learn from it how to live your life with money more successfully. By success, I do not mean acquiring more and more money and money equivalents. I mean that you will achieve less storminess and conflict, both in your own internal feelings and in relation to others, and will feel greater satisfaction and harmony in those areas of your life that relate directly to money and which overflow the boundaries of that subject to influence other areas of your life as well.

# 1

# Kid Stuff

There is universal agreement that attitudes towards money begin in childhood as do attitudes to almost everything else and as do personality traits. People also agree that attitudes and traits change over the years as one matures. What is more controversial is just how these attitudes are formed, what factors in childhood influence them, and in what ways they develop or change.

About the very earliest period of childhood, there is little that can be said about money and its relationship to psychology. The newborn infant is primarily concerned about getting fed and feeling comfortable, and has no awareness that any such thing as money exists. It lacks the thinking capacity to even begin to conceptualize what money is about. Nevertheless, while the infant may look like an eating, pooping and crying machine, it is gradually learning much about the world around itself and, even in the first few days of life, relates to others with eye-to-eye contact, soon supplemented with smiles added on to the tears. It very quickly comes to recognize its major caretakers, its parents, while rejecting others who come too close. With time, it ability to relate to others increases and it is at about six months of age (most mothers naturally will disagree with this, seeing it earlier) that it begins to show some individuality and personality, at least to outside observers. By the time it gets to be one year old, it is quite a social creature, knows who are its nearest and most important people, and has begun to master all kinds of physical skills.

This growing mastery continues at a rapid pace into the second year (and further on into the rest of its life) and includes the acquisition of such abilities as walking and talking while also developing skill in the use of its hands. There is also an increasing awareness of itself and its own wishes separate from the wishes of those around it which is expressed in its ability to refuse what parents request. Indeed, every parent learns to dread the repeated "nos" told to them by their formerly compliant babies. By the time the age of two is reached, the question of bowel and bladder training has arisen, and successful accomplishment of control of these functions is well on the way to completion by its third birthday. During this period, there are many other accomplishments as well: improved speech, greater awareness of others, and an immense growth of knowledge about things occurring around it at home, in nursery school and in other familiar locations. After three, the child's horizons continue to expand as it masters and fine tunes more skills, gets acquainted with more people, and learns more and more about its own body.

It is tempting to tie in experiences in these early phases of life with personality features that appear later on but it's still controversial how personality develops and what contributes to the eventual outcome. Is it a genetic phenomenon, something that one is born with that will show up as specific characteristics that an individual is saddled with for as long as he or she lives? Or are adult personality traits the outcomes of events that occur as the normal developmental processes unfold, because of traumatic or other special events which occur at strategic times, because there is no positive reinforcement for what the infant does or because there is absolute neglect? A definitive answer to these questions is hard to come by since it takes years of observation from childhood to adulthood to prove anything, even whether a child has any inborn characteristics at all, traits such as being sluggish, relaxed, happy, irritable, friendly or whatever. Many wise people take the stance of straddling the fence in this controversy over nature (inborn genetic disposition) vs. nurture (early childhood experiences) by saying that both contribute their share, and that it takes the right situation for a genetic tendency to emerge and flourish. Without that, potential characteristics may simply not appear and the potentiality is forever lost.

The reason I mention this dispute which has not so far even touched upon money is because one has to know about it in order to understand what has been the major psychiatric theory about money, one that was formulated by Sigmund Freud, the great Viennese founder of psychoanalysis. Freud, whose work dominated psychiatric thinking during the last years of the nineteenth century and the first half of the twentieth, continues to be an influential figure, even though many of his theories have been rejected or superceded with time and with the accumulation of more knowledge and more actual observation of children. Nevertheless, there are still many who accept his word as Gospel while there are others who reject the whole of psychoanalysis and any influence of outstanding experiences during development on personality because of some of Freud's less logical theories which seem to go against what we can see for ourselves. There are those who see these theories as more an intellectual game than a serious scientific explanation of events.

Freud believed that childhood personality development unfolds against a background of a set pattern of biologically pre-determined phases in which each phase emphasizes one particular part of the body. He characterized the earliest period of life as oral; during this time, the infant relates primarily through its mouth, incorporating food and, somewhat later when teeth appear, using them to bite all sorts of things and people. Trauma or some other emphatic experience at this phase might produce an orally fixated individual who, as an adult, is primarily concerned with satisfactions coming through the mouth whether they be from food, drugs, alcohol, tobacco or words; sexual urges may even be channeled into oral pathways.

The next phase of development is the anal one, in which the parents attempt to train the child to have bowel and bladder control, the word anal referring to the bowel part of that. Emotional trauma or other stressful experiences occurring during this period might produce a need to hold back or to accumulate, and this in the future might lead to problems with money, which Freud saw as an adult representation of feces. He also believed that anally oriented people were stubborn, stingy and excessively orderly, and had anal preoccupations which influenced their sexual activity as adults. While little infants may play with their own stool and may even briefly highly esteem it as a toy, there is absolutely no proof that this behavior turns into a need to accumulate money or into problems with money as life goes on. It is also difficult to prove that such experiences determine lifelong sexual practices although it's easy enough to speculate that that is the case.

The next phase in development is the sexual which occurs at age five or six, and it is to Freud's credit that he advanced the theory of childhood sexuality progressing into and influencing adult sexuality in spite of major resistance to such ideas in the late Victorian era in which he lived and in which he first propounded his scheme of personality development. However, as interesting as the theories about sexuality are, I will take a pass on discussing them and return to his thoughts about money representing feces.

One of Freud's followers, Otto Fenichel, a man who took Freud's theories yet further and who attempted to explain peculiar personality pictures named neuroses, suggested that money could symbolize many other important things that could be given or taken away such as body parts like the breast or the penis, body products like semen and milk and babies, and various abstract entities such as power, protection, anger or degradation, in other words a fairly wide variety of things.

Today, most people would regard Freud's concept of money and Fenichel's extension of the concept as the end-result of wild thinking or even of psychosis, forgetting the historic context in which these ideas were formulated. This brand of psychoanalysis attempted to understand both ordinary and unusual patterns of thinking and behavior that people lived, and they used symbolism and imagination in order to do so. After these two thinkers, other creative and thoughtful psychoanalysts came along and developed yet more ideas that helped one to understand (and sometimes to make more mysterious and impenetrable) human personality in any number of its presentations.

Unfortunately, over the years, psychological theories about money, by and large, have not departed too far from equating it with feces, and this has proved crippling for current-day understanding, leaving the literature on the subject and the role it plays in the lives of children (as well as adults) sparse and not particularly enlightening. More's the pity because, as a result, the study of one of the most important elements of life, one of the major entities in human interactions, has been neglected, and psychiatry and psychology are the poorer for it. Even though today there are many psychiatrists and psychologists who still are true believers in some of the theories I've mentioned, a lot of others, including myself, prefer to look at the subject in less speculative terms and in ways that can more easily be seen and proven.

Let's move back to what is happening to the child. Children begin to have favorite objects which we psychiatrists call transitional objects, like blankets or dolls or almost anything else, but usually something soft and cuddly. These objects are very much their property and the children drag them around with them, becoming angry and tearful when they are not available or when they are lost. Nothing else will substitute for these objects which have been labeled "transitional" to suggest that they help the child make the transition from physical closeness to the mother and her many attentions to getting along without them. Transitional objects soften the sense of loss that the child feels at the growing separation from its mother.

Although it's usually the separation from the mother that makes the child hold a transitional object so dear, the person may well be anyone who assumes the mothering role, a grandmother, a sibling, a nanny or even a father.

At about age two or three, the child still has no concept of money although it does begin to have a sense of what is its own property. All you have to do is see a child whose toy is touched by another, and I don't mean its transitional object, let alone by a younger sibling, and you will see, with no doubt about it, the outrage that child feels about someone else using what belongs to it with or without permission. Sometimes the child doesn't understand what it means to give permission, and it will say yes when asked if it's okay, then howl when the toy is used.

Between a child's need for transitional objects and its growing sense of property, one can well observe the beginnings of some attitudes to money which the child later one learns is so important in life.

As far as real money goes, a bright youngster may realize, when he or she accompanies mother or father to the store, that the parent gives over to a store worker some pieces of paper and some metal pieces. The idea that this is a universal commodity, money, is certainly not clear to the child and it's not at all certain that it has the intellectual ability and the capacity for abstract thinking to recognize such a concept at this early stage. With repetition, though, the child begins to get the idea that money is something that can be exchanged for other things. In these days of credit cards, the idea that gets communicated is a bit more complicated. One shows a card, the clerk does something with it and then the parent writes something. This process requires a still greater ability to abstract and delays by a short while the child's appreciation of what money is. And, if the parent shops on the internet, the degree of abstract thinking required is even greater and it takes the child even longer to develop the concept of money and its value for buying things.

Nevertheless, the child does get the idea that you can change this paper and these metal objects, and later on the plastic card, into things it wants for itself, and the idea of money is born. Naturally, the child wants a lot of things, and realizes that a lot of this material called money is needed in order to acquire these things. At first, it thinks in terms of quantities it can see and feel; it's amusing to see how the child prefers a lot of coins to even a large denomination bill since, according to the child's logic, the coins are more plentiful and they are heavier, and that means that they should be able to buy more things. Of course, a bit later on, it recognizes that different coins have different values and that paper is worth a whole lot of coins. Later on, when it learns to read, it realizes that even paper money has different values and the larger the number on the bill, the better.

The use of paper money is somewhat more easily understood by children in foreign countries where the bigger the banknote, the greater its value; in addition to that, bills of different values are different in color. It's harder in the United States where all bills are the same size and the same color, and the child really can't tell the difference until it learns some elements of reading, and can distinguish numbers such as 1, 5, 10, 20, etc. There is some talk in government circles of remodeling our currency so that different amounts will come in different colors which would make it easier for children who can't read but changes tend to be talked about long before any action takes place.

At the same time that the child is learning what money is and that you need it to buy things such as toys as well as favorite foods, it is also learning that its parents may not always want to use it the way the child does or may not always have enough to do everything it wants. Parents sometimes appear stubborn and argumentative when the child expresses a wish, may disagree between themselves, and may even deny the wish completely. Tears may be used to express the child's disappointment and anger, and this sometimes produces a change in parental attitudes, resulting in their giving in rather than in continuing to deny their child's wishes. In these simple transactions, repeated time and again, the child learns a number of things: that money is not always there for the asking; that parents are not always in agreement about it; and that parents can often be influenced by crying. The child may be told that "money doesn't grow on trees" and it will be instructed that the parents have to work hard for the money, a new concept for the child who previously saw this as something that was always there and the parent simply took out of a purse or wallet.

What the child starts learning at this phase is that money does not come in unlimited supplies and that one reason that its parents have to leave home every day to go to work is to obtain it. The idea of working for pay to be able to exchange it for worldly goods begins to be born in the child although it is still a long way from realizing what the concept of making a profit is all about. Except in rich families and sometimes even then, the child begins to realize that the world imposes some limitations on it and that its wishes are not necessarily going to be fulfilled. These ideas become part of the child's future understanding of money and contribute to a number of adult personality traits (such as ability to accept limitations on desires, and understanding something of the needs and limitations of others) in addition to contributing to future career choices such as which jobs can provide them with the largest amounts of money.

But perhaps more important, the child begins to learn a method of coping in situations where money and other goods that money can buy are in short supply, and that is how to influence others, in the first instance its parents, to get more than others are willing to give. This influencing of others may become a forerunner of manipulation which, while initially for money and whatever it might buy, becomes part of the child's method of operation in dealing with others when it is denied its wishes, even in matters having nothing to do with money. Obviously, tears only work with close relatives and only at an early stage of the child's development. As it becomes older, the nature of what it wants inevitably changes and other methods of manipulation are substituted for tears, but the concept that you can get what you want through playing upon others' feelings, whether it be by tears, by pouting, by creating problems or by inducing guilt, gradually infuses the child's personality, and may, with sufficient repetition, contribute to personality traits in adulthood.

Noah, for example, was a much wanted only child born into a working class family with mother and father often at odds with each other but united in their devotion to their son. Throughout his early years, he was deluged with all sorts of toys, sometimes more than the parents could comfortably afford; yet they always placed his needs and wishes first. When he reached four years old and became fascinated with television, he proved to be a highly desirable consumer (that is, from the manufacturer's viewpoint) who was very much influenced by the ads. His requests for new toys became very frequent and involved much more expense than his parents could afford and they were forced, as a consequence, to deny his wishes. Prior to this, he had never heard the word "no" when it came to buying him something, and he became outraged at the denial, starting in on a series of tantrums until his parents finally threw in the towel just to satisfy Noah even though it meant having to deny themselves some treats and on occasions some near necessities.

Noah had learned quite competently how to influence others to do as he wished although this is not a technique that would work if he tried it on people outside of his family and would certainly not be too highly regarded by others when he got older. Even though he would eventually discard the technique of throwing tantrums, what remained in his personality was the idea that he could manipulate others to do his bidding even though the style of manipulation would change with the circumstances. In other words, he learned to sense what would influence people and then would push the right buttons to get his way.

Not every child is inevitably damaged by a parent saying no and it helps to explain to the child within the limits of its understanding why that no has to be spoken. It also is helpful not to respond to the child's attempts to manipulate parents into giving in since not going along tends to discourage the use of manipulation as a way of getting what it wants. Parents who want their child to have everything may be unrealistic if they never refuse requests, and this imposes a burden on themselves. They may feel guilty about not giving the child everything, they may resent the requests, and may feel inadequate that they must deny for practical reasons what their child wants. The child, innocent as it may be, can still pick up and respond to such parental reactions. Remember that the child is incredibly attuned to every emotional response on the part of its parents, the two most important people in its life. This sensitivity tends to lessen as the child ages, whether it's because there are so many other influences on it or because needs move on to larger and larger grounds.

Speaking of the child's response to parents, it tends to absorb almost by inhalation parental attitudes towards money. In an extreme example, if the family is into stealing and regards all money as fair game for it to take, the child is likely to pick up this technique rather than see it as dishonest. The word "dishonesty" has no meaning to such a child. What comes across to it is that you take money and its equivalents any time you can do so and safely get away with it. These parental attitudes do not have to be expressed directly or out loud but the child perceives and adopts them on its own, entering into the family scheme of things.

At another extreme in attitudes towards money is a comment ascribed to Sara Delano Roosevelt, the mother of Franklin Delano Roosevelt, who was President during World War II and is generally considered one of the most outstanding presidents in our history. Mrs. Roosevelt, a lady of the old school and a woman of great personal dignity, reported that his parents never discussed money in front of Franklin, not wanting to expose him to such a vulgar subject at an early age. Whether this was indeed the situation we'll never know, but such an approach to money can render the child growing into adulthood naive and incompetent in monetary matters with little understanding of this very real material and its ability to influence human affairs. However, even if the story is true, it does not seem to have harmed Roosevelt or impaired his ability to lead the country through very trying times.

There are other attitudes to money that the child picks up without much conscious thought. Parental priorities and preferences as to how money is used become part of the child's style of handling it as well without having to be spelled out. For example, in a family that values lavish displays of expensive objects, the child will tend to place importance on these objects as well. Conversely, a family that counts its pennies may produce a child who is cautious about spending whatever money comes its way and is likely to save rather than spend even when it really wants those toys or that candy.

In other words, the child is learning all sorts of ways of dealing with money as it goes along without actually taking classes from its parents. It observes, it thinks about things and develops its own conclusions which usually don't depart too far from those of its parents. This is not to say that some children do not develop ideas on their own that sometimes are the reverse of what they have seen their parents do. This may appear as being spoiled or being difficult, sometimes as being rebellious. Curiously enough, some of the things that the child rebels about, it eventually comes to accept and follow on its own as it enters adulthood and gets ready to pass on to its own children its own approach to money.

One of the key issues that occurs between parents and children in the handling of money is the setting up of allowances; this of course occurs at an age when the child is able to appreciate the relative value of different coins and differently denominated paper money. When children can tell the difference and have some idea of the value of money, they want to have some of their own so that they can buy things independently of whatever their parents provide them. There is something about being able to choose for yourself and plunk down the money that gives everyone of us, including children, a feeling of being in charge of things. The problem for a parent is deciding what level of allowance to provide, in other words how much. I can't give you a definitive answer to this question but it has to be some amount that allows the child to buy things it wants, an extra piece of candy or an ice cream or a simple toy. The amount should rise as the child gets older and it wants and needs more expensive items, but the line must be drawn at some point. Some parents feel that whatever is bought should have some useful value and encourage their children to buy clothes or school materials with their allowances, while others give the child free rein to do whatever he or she wishes with the money.

Another issue that comes up is whether the child should be given an allowance free and clear or whether it should receive money only if it performs some household chores like raking the leaves, mowing the lawn, taking out the garbage or straightening up the garage, representing a sort of salary. Again, there's no one answer since parents who want a child to enjoy itself with the money it has on its own do not accept the idea that the child must work for this privilege. Parents who want a child to work for an allowance argue that it is being taught a lesson for life; that one must work to gain privileges. If they have this approach, they believe that any other way of handling the question of allowances does not serve the purpose of equipping the child for life but instead spoils it and gives it no real concept of how the world operates. These attitudes are expressed not only in the giving of allowances but in almost any activity of family life.

Another way of going about teaching that money matters and that the child has to be careful in its spending is to set up a small bank account in its name, make regular deposits instead of giving cash, and then go with the child to the bank on a regular basis to withdraw money. This certainly helps the youngster to understand something about how banks operate but seems to be expensive in terms of parental time as well as keeping the child very much under the parents' control with little freedom to use its money in the ways it might prefer. In fact, it does communicate to the child that it itself can't really be responsible in money matters but needs its father or mother to help it along the way. While this may be the reality of the situation, it's not a good idea to keep a child on such a tight leash that it has no freedom of choice or independence at all.

Allowances may be used as a reward-punishment system with something like good grades in school resulting in a continuing payment of the allowance or in a bonus payment while doing poorly in school, arguing with parents and refusal to do assigned chores result in non-payment. Overall, it's better to keep the allowance going on a regular basis without introducing the concept of punishment since, as the saying goes, "you catch more flies with honey than with vinegar", and it's just as well not to use negative measures, either by taking away the allowance, withholding privileges like watching television or going to the movies, or slapping it around.

Children can also become aware that there are times when parents do not feel much interest in what they are doing, being too involved in their own affairs to bother about the kids. At these times, the parents may well give generous gifts to a child just to keep it busy and occupied on its own rather than having it make demands for attention or interest that the parents don't feel at the moment or want to be bothered with. With some parents, that's only an occasional situation but, with others, that may be the regular state of affairs. Parents don't have to be eternally at the mercy of their children and their needs, drowning their own needs in the process. But children are capable of realizing that some of the gifts they're getting are substitutes for real attention and sometimes for real affection. This sets the scene for future problems because the child may grow up feeling unloved and uninteresting. This happens only after repeated constant ignoring of the child and does not happen when its needs are passed over only occasionally in an overall atmosphere of love and warmth.

It's also not a very good idea to promise a child a reward for some accomplishment or even to promise that something the child desires will be delivered at a later date, and then not come across with the present, whether it be money or something else. The child responds to the promise with the desired behavior and acts "good" but, in the meantime, the parent has either forgotten that the promise was made or had no intention of ever fulfilling it. While the child can tolerate, even if impatiently, a delay in getting what it wants, it finds it difficult to accept that the whole situation was a lie meant to fool it. The result is not only a loss of faith in the parent but also a loss of faith in promises from others. It may sound like a very large consequence, losing faith in other people's promises for the rest of one's life and it surely does not happen if it's only a one-time breach of faith.

When the lack of results becomes an ongoing business, then it does have a significant influence on the future adult's sense of trust in others.

In the same way, using money and its equivalents to bribe children is not a very helpful way to bring up children. They see the commodity aspect of what they do and how they behave, and learn to conform to their parents' wishes in the most effective way to obtain whatever they regard as the good things of life. Much too early in their own lives are they exposed to the corrupting aspects of money rather than to its beneficial aspects, and too much of this makes them much more likely to be involved in bribery of one sort or another as they get older, whether this be in their personal dealings with others or whether it be in a larger business or political context. Let's look again at the case of Noah and see what happened to him several years after he was four years old and learned about manipulating others.

When Noah was nine, his parents finally decided that the marriage wasn't working and, in view of the fact that they both had other romantic interests, decided to get a divorce. Noah was a bone of contention between them since they each wanted custody with the other contributing some money to child support. Noah was devastated at the divorce and very worried about what would happen to him since he disliked his parents' new romantic interests. Nevertheless, as the question of custody progressed through the courts, he used his sad status to get his parents to buy, not only the latest toys and computer games but, since he was now older and into new things, the latest sneakers and high status clothing. They competed with each other at great expense to buy his devotion, and he was alert enough to the situation to coldly and calculatedly use it for his material advantage, even though he was by no means happy at developments. Here we see an evolution of a child's early experiences at manipulation of parents to a more sophisticated exploitation of them, a kind of forced bribery.

It is impossible to leave the subject of familial influences on a child's perception of money and its meanings without discussing the question of sibling rivalry. Anyone who has seen in action a family with more than one child is aware that the children compete with each other for parental affection and attention with this also happening in relation to grandparents, friends and neighbors and virtually all other adults to whom the child is exposed, even including older children. The rivalry extends from wishes for attention and approval to wishes for money and monetary equivalents, which so often substitute for attention and approval. It would be nice to think that children are so pure that they will accept a totally fair share of whatever it is that they want but they usually seem to want their fair share plus a bit more. It takes really thoughtful parents to deal with this issue so fairly that their children are not scarred with excessive competitiveness for the rest of their lives.

Persistent sibling rivalry is a well known fact of life and has provided many a therapist with a field day as he or she approaches a patient's problems, the sibling rivalry and the competition with the rest of the world being so prominent a part of what makes them unhappy as adults.

Kate was the older of two children whose brother Clay was born when she was two and a half years older. She was very conscious of the loss of her parents' attention even though they made every effort possible to give her a lot of their time and to interest her in her baby brother. She disliked him and things that belonged to him and suggested, as often happens, that her parents throw him out. As he grew a bit older, her parents wanted to use some of her old clothes and toys, things that were no longer suitable for her, for him but Kate wasn't having any of that and protested loud and long. Her parents tried to explain matters to her but that didn't help much and they went ahead and did what they had to without her approval. A child can sometimes be helped to feel a participant in rearing the younger one but that doesn't always happen, and it didn't happen here. As they grew older, Kate remained resentful of Clay and criticized him for being a baby all through the time they were children. They finally became more friendly but, even in their adult years, Kate felt little warmth for him and watched carefully what her parents did for him, making sure that they did at least as much for her.

Sibling rivalry is aggravated all the more when there is overt parental favoritism. What causes such favoritism is something I'll go into in the chapter on parenting but it is undeniable and extremely prevalent. Many times, there are alliances in the family with mother and son aligned against father and daughter but, no matter how these situations come about, they are destructive and are seldom limited to the giving of financial benefits or toys. They too have life-long consequences in terms of personality traits and relationships with others.

Things change for a child as it reaches later childhood, the time at which it enters a world larger than its home, that is when it starts school, makes non-family and non-neighbor friends, and begins to have a social life of its own somewhat independent of its family. It is at this time that new factors enter the situation and the child sees how money is used in other families and how they handle it. The new world the child is entering brings with it other new aspects of the money situation and contributes in its turn to future developments in personality.

Every child enters this phase of life with a considerable experience of money and its meanings, and carries with it some attitudes that have already become part of its permanent personality structure. Nevertheless, it is still in a formative period of life and the experiences it undergoes at this stage may add to, modify or totally change some of these attitudes.

It's not that the child who reaches school age has not already been exposed to money situations outside its own home; it has, unless the family lives in a desert or on a mountaintop or unless the parents have specifically prohibited contacts with others. The child has already interacted with neighbors, has made some friends and has visited back and forth with aunts, uncles, grandparents and cousins. But entering school marks a major advance in its development, an increase in the amount of time spent outside the home and a significant broadening in the number and variety of people it knows. This results in exposure to many different styles of dealing with money.

What happens now is not unrelated to what went on before. For one thing, the competition with siblings for parental attention and monetary rewards is now a basis for new relationships with classmates in school, even when the teachers, the new parent substitutes, are not giving out monetary rewards. Children who are competitive with brothers and sisters are competitive with fellow students; hopefully, the competition may be directed by a knowledgeable teacher into a desire for learning rather than into more material channels.

There is, however, a new dimension to the competition, something of which the child was not previously aware, and that is the transformation of money and what it can buy into measurements of prestige and social standing. Children, even at the tender age of six or seven, learn that it is better to have one brand of sneakers than another, one kind of jacket than another or one type of watch than another. Wearing the better brands means that they are better than their classmates if their classmates don't have anything that measures up. On the other hand, if they themselves do not have the best, they end up feeling less worthwhile than their classmates, and the situation may actually lead to their being made fun of, worsening the challenge to their self-esteem. While I've mentioned some of the status symbols (children may not understand this term but they sure do feel its effects), there are others and they all contribute to the establishment of a status ladder which all the children in the class are aware of. Other possessions that fit into the ladder include what bicycle you ride, what T- shirts you wear, what kind of a backpack you have, and on and on. Children who wind up low on the status ladder are often classified as nerds or dorks, and this condemnation becomes something that they feel for the rest of their lives is their fate. That's a pretty large consequence for what rational adults may regard as just nonsense.

Worse than the hierarchy that has been established is that some children steal status objects from others, and there are plenty of cases on record of children who have killed others in order to take over their high status items. Some schools have reacted to this by establishing uniform dress codes so that all children look the same and there would be, as a result, no sense in stealing something you already own. Yet, there always remains some item which gives status which is not controlled and the crimes continue.

It's in the early years of school that in-groups tend to form and, while it's nice to think that these groups are based on merit such as intelligence or consideration of others, that is rarely the case. Group formation tends to be based on what you have, first and foremost, with what you look like and athletic prowess being additional considerations.

Not only is the child exposed to these distinctions in school but it also starts making new friends from a much wider social and economic background, not only in school but also in extra-curricular activities. These friends' families are bound to have a wide variety of attitudes towards money and will likely be different in the priorities they have for spending money as well as in the amounts of money they have. Trust the child to want to imitate those friends whose families have lots of money and who spend it on prestigious purchases such as luxury cars, summer homes and exotic vacations in addition to what they provide for their children. The child in a middle class home can probably rank cars by cost from the most expensive down to the cheapest even at the age of seven. That part is okay but the problem arises when it starts asking its parents why they don't have a better car or, even worse, when it starts criticizing them for having such a cheap car that no one else would want. Even parents who have tried to explain to their kids the limitation of their income find themselves stressed by the children's expressions of disappointment at their parents' failure to do better.

While criticizing parents is usually considered a characteristic of adolescence, there is a period of criticism, a milder form which occurs in childhood. Mild as it is, there may be battles over the parents' failure to provide the child with sufficient status in its group. Parents are overwhelmed and may respond by trying to limit their child's friends to fellow-students who come from the same income group and whose families' purchases and status symbols they can match, but any such restriction of friendship usually backfires. The children can do pretty much as they please when they are out of their parents' sight and control most of the day, and they can get away with not following their parents' instructions. Even when they do accept restrictions on friendships, feelings of anger and disappointment in their parents are likely to continue. It sounds like a hopeless situation for parents but what they have to do is remain patient, not impose social limits on their children, and explain time and time again the truths that not everyone can earn a lot of money and that the value of a human being is not based on the amount of money he or she earns or spends, not such bad truths to carry with them throughout life.

Doing without is more destructive in terms of setting up negative personality traits with some children than with others, and they may develop a kind of self-defensive snobbery about the whole thing, debunking the value of money and emphasizing instead the qualities that they have. This sounds like a good, realistic approach to take, and it is just so long as the child does have real appreciation of its own personal value instead of starting from the position of feeling negative about itself and having to defend itself against that picture the whole rest of its life. This is one of those cases where the same characteristic in adulthood might stem from two different and opposing causes, one case being a good adjustment and the other a denial of the negative and a bad adjustment. You can tell the difference when they reach adulthood by just how vigorously they hold onto the characteristic and what happens when it's challenged. The unhealthy one tends to fall apart, get angry or get vicious and attack the challenger while the other, the healthy one, just reacts with a shrug.

What I have described in this chapter is the progress of a relatively normal child as it goes through the stages of learning about what money is and the early problems that arise in handling it. I have presented some of the challenges it faces and some of the consequences of these challenges not being well handled. I have not discussed the problems of what is called the exceptional child, he or she who has serious psychological problems or who is retarded or who has that poorly understood, but frequently diagnosed and overmedicated condition called variably attention deficit disorder or hyperactivity disorder. All of these pose severe problems for parents in teaching them how to deal with money, problems which may seem overwhelming and insurmountable. The retarded child has difficulty learning about money and is usually unable to conceptualize its meaning, requiring a greater degree of protection on a parent's part and the attention- deficit or hyperactive child may appear to understand but shows such instability in money matters as to require, in its turn, greater parental supervision and control. There will no doubt be resentment of the parents whose controls add insult to injury and further complicate the handicapped child's life, but it is necessary, as always, to assert the realities of the situation and act within these realities.

So much is going on in childhood and all at the same time. It can make the conscientious parent worry whether he or she is really instilling healthy attitudes in children in relation to money as well as in relation to so many other things. The good news is that most parents, in spite of the challenges, manage to do quite well, if not perfectly, and children emerge from this formative phase of their lives with constructive approaches to life which providing a solid building block for the influences of adolescence and other future phases in the life cycle.

# 2

# *Growing up*

Adolescence is a turbulent time, generally considered the most difficult stage of life. There are problems which arise inside the individual himself or herself and are inevitable aspects of the growth process, and there are problems which arise in relationships with parents and with others. Negotiating one's way through all of them and coming up with good solutions mark the successful passage from childhood to adulthood. As is the case all through life, difficult situations often find expression in terms of money and the things that money can buy, and the more difficult the situation, the more complicated its effects on what one does with money. With all the storms inherent in adolescence, it would be impossible for anyone to get through these years without there being a significant number of problems involving money.

    The most important event occurring in adolescence is, of course, puberty, the appearance of defined sexual characteristics with a resulting change in the way the adolescent sees himself or herself, becoming a fully fledged sexual adult. Adolescents have to contend with changing body images as their bodies develop, and they also have to deal with overwhelming sexual impulses, learning how to channel them into appropriate expressions. Not to be minimized are such incidental by-products of the maturational process as the appearance of pimples and the resulting anxiety about their effect on looks. The physical process of puberty takes about two to three years and usually begins in the early teens although it may start earlier or later. Getting psychologically adjusted to the changes may take considerably more time.

Adolescence is of much longer duration, however, than puberty and entails many other issues on the road to maturity. From a protected home and family, the adolescent ventures out into the wider world and is exposed to many new situations for which he or she has not been sufficiently prepared. Intellectual capacity enlarges enormously, as does the amount of information that adolescents learn in school and from friends. As they go along, they are exposed to different family structures, to different ways of doing things, to different social values and to different ethnic and social class approaches to life. They learn that their parents, no matter how wonderful, practice only one of many ways of dealing with the world. As they realize this limitation, adolescents begin a process of separation from their parents as well as from their more extended families, and add to their childhood identities new characteristics learned from these new influences which include friends, friends' families, religious leaders, teachers and entertainment idols.

In addition, adolescents, as they progress through the teen years, have many choices to make on which their futures depend, increasing the stressfulness of this phase of life; careers must be planned for and the appropriate education obtained, romantic partners must be chosen and adult relationships developed. Going to college extends the period of adolescence since, typically, adolescents remain dependent on parents economically and frequently emotionally during this phase even though they may strenuously deny this. Continuing one's education beyond college results in an even longer adolescence, a statement that will no doubt outrage most postgraduate students. Some individuals never achieve real adulthood, remaining hung up for the rest of their lives on problems that should have been settled during this period and never being able to face the world on their own.

Separation from parents and parental values, although necessary for future individuality, causes problems at home with parents often in violent disagreement with what they see as their children's turning away from them and their ways. Parents also complain of their children's secrecy about what they're doing, but their children see the very same silence as a right to privacy. There are good reasons for this secrecy/

privacy. One is that adolescents feel uncomfortable with their burgeoning sexuality and are reluctant, sometimes embarrassed, to discuss details of their experiences with their parents. Another is that, as early adults, they want to develop their own opinions and ideas, and resent intrusion on the process, sometimes even when they expressly ask for advice. While shutting out their parents, they turn to their friends with whom they can go on for hours discussing the most intimate details of feelings and sexuality and, in these relationships, they are very open. Privacy also extends to how the adolescent uses money, and most teenagers feel invaded when their parents want some accounting of how funds are being handled. At this point, adolescents often become closed-mouthed about where the money is going, although they may not have been particularly private or quiet when their demands for it were being made.

In a similar vein, what parents view as rebelliousness is seen by their adolescent offspring as the establishment of their own personal identity. Conflicts are even worse when the adolescent is taller than his or her parents and makes the assumption that size indicates worldly wisdom. In addition, the adolescent is aware that he or she belongs to a different generation, not only different than their parents, but also different from brothers and sisters who may be only a few years younger or older. The adolescent experiences a need to identify with its own generation and tends to reject anything that came before as ridiculously old-fashioned, hopelessly out of date, and silly both in ideas and in behavior. Anyone younger is considered to be infantile and simply not smart enough to deserve much attention.

Another conflict that arises in adolescence is that, at the very same time that the adolescents are running away from parental values and arguing with them, often savagely, there is a need for an ongoing relationship with their parents and with the security of the parental home. One of the more confusing aspects of adolescence, at least to parents, is how their children may avow one set of values one month and a totally different one another month. What is happening is that members of the younger generation are trying on different identities in their search for who they are. Frequently enough, they often end up with the same values as their parents after having gone through a number of changes along the way. Almost as often, they wind up with totally different attitudes to life and to money, and then there are many cases that fall in between. Indeed, it sometimes seems that almost anything can happen as far as how the adult personality will eventually turn out.

With all of these issues going on simultaneously, there is great potential for major disagreements about money and the way it is used. Even when the child, now the adolescent, has been educated about the proper use of money and how to deal with it, it often seems that all that education goes out the window and that the youngster has to learn these things for himself or herself all over again. The important thing, though, is for parents to recognize what their adolescent children are going through during this phase and acknowledge that it finds expression in money matters. By viewing the money situation as a learning and developing process, they are much more likely to help things along rather than to aggravate them.

Some of the issues I have mentioned came up in the case of Caitlin who was 13 when she started high school, having previously gone to an elementary school a short walk from her home. Her parents were warm, involved people who were active in community affairs. They were protective of Caitlin and had rarely let her leave home by herself, but now they had to let her travel to high school on a city subway alone since they were unable to arrange their work schedules to accompany her going there and coming home every day. They did escort her to school the first few days and did pick her up, and they also gave her the standard lecture about not talking to strangers or going with someone she didn't know, but just coming straight home. They also tried to find other students who lived nearby so that they and Caitlin could travel together for security.

However, what they didn't think of in their warnings and what Caitlin was not prepared for was the presence of beggars in the subway. She was overcome with pity for these poor souls and started out by giving them her lunch and then went on to give them her loose change, going on to give them every bit of money she could honestly lay her hands on. She told her parents about these needy people and asked them to help her look after them but her parents refused to do more than they were already doing by giving to charities; they were aghast to learn that Caitlin was giving away her own food and her allowance. At first, they kept cool heads and tried to convince her that other channels were available for helping the poor, but she didn't accept this and accused them of copping out. This precipitated a crisis in which she went on to attack them verbally for their lack of generosity and to criticize their whole way of life. For the first time ever, there was a major rift in the parent-child relationship, which extended for several weeks. Caitlin's parents eventually managed to channel her charitable impulses into other, less personalized, directions and they also increased their own involvement in charitable causes, allowing peace to reign in their family once again.

This case illustrates one of the money problems that arise in adolescence and where it stems from. There is exposure to new situations and new problems that goes along with the wider horizons that open up to the adolescent. There is the beginning of ideas and actions that may have some relationship to what the parents did before (they were substantial givers to charities, both of time and of money) or may be at odds with it, and there is independent action and criticism of parents to an extent not seen before. There is also the desire to use one's money (even if the adolescent didn't actually earn it) according to one's wishes. As part of the process of separation, there is an increasing awareness that parents are not the center of the world and may even be less than perfect. Once the adolescent realizes this, parents are fair game for criticism; their style of life, their financial limitations and their personality flaws are all subject to attack.

Within the larger world now open to the adolescent, there is greater scope for whatever problems have appeared concerning money. The rivalry that was previously experienced with siblings about who got more now extends to friends, classmates and peers in clubs and social events while still continuing with brothers and sisters. Of course, there are some changes since the rivalry outside the home has to do with winning the attention of adults other than their parents, the original givers of approval. The rivalry may now include approval for athletic achievement, good school grades or demonstrations of special skills.

Sometimes, the rivalry may appear in situations that are less than constructive and sometimes even destructive, such as who can get away with what, including petty crime, bullying and sexual abuse of others. There are even some cases where an adolescent, in an effort to beat out others, may invite the sexual attention of an adult, especially when it's accompanied by gifts, in order to prove that he or she is more attractive and more desirable; sometimes, it's a question of needing love, no matter how it's obtained and no matter who the competition may be. The adolescent who suffered from severe sibling rivalry as a child usually becomes a highly competitive person in other areas of life, and this trait of trying to beat out others usually becomes part of one's lifelong personality.

As I already mentioned, some attitudes learned in childhood concerning the usages of money may be challenged by the new situations in which the adolescent finds itself, and may change, while some attitudes that started out in the family setting may be confirmed and strengthened during this phase. For example, in those homes where money was used in a manipulative fashion by parents to obtain good behavior from their children and where children responded to such bribery, they are likely to use money in the same vein now that they are more independent. Where parents gave gifts of money and objects to compensate for their lack of interest, attention and affection, the adolescent may be inclined to have the same expectations in dealing with others. It will also tend to doubt that others are sincerely interested in what it is doing, and will often demand that its insecurity be soothed by something material, whether that be money or presents.

Gary was a 16 year old who was brought in for treatment by his parents because he couldn't seem to hold on to his money and refused to discuss anything with them. They wondered whether he was concealing illegal expenditures and, in particular, worried that he might be involved with drugs. Gary was angry at his parents' suspicions and even more angry that they forced him to come into psychiatric treatment, and he was a reluctant patient, as are most adolescents. Once a friendlier relationship between him and me had been established, he brought a cup of coffee and a Danish pastry for me to our early morning session. I was somewhat hesitant about accepting this since there should be no material exchanges in a therapeutic relationship except for the fee for professional services, but I did accept this time with thanks. He again brought coffee and Danish to our next session and I told him we would have to talk about this since, though I appreciated his generosity, the nature of psychotherapy made it impossible for me to accept any gifts.

He was initially surprised at my reaction but then told me he was relieved because it meant that he didn't have to take any extra steps to get me to like him, something he felt obliged to do with just about everyone he knew; this accounted for his disappearing money. We quickly went on from there to an extensive history of family gift-giving to obtain favors and to cover up lack of involvement or interest in what the others were doing.

Adolescents coming from such a background believe they have to buy off new friends and classmates by giving gifts, even when these may be ill afforded. While the recipients may feel flattered and may enjoy the gifts, they are not always aware that they are incurring obligations to the giver, mostly to like him or her but sometimes to do more than that. When these "debts" are called in, the recipients don't always come through as expected, creating disappointment and anger in the givers and puzzlement on the recipients' part as to what has produced such a reaction. It's a case where the styles of the two parties to a transaction are different and are not always that easy to bridge. Trying to buy friends and expecting them to pay back favors on demand often become lifelong personality traits.

Another attitude also frequently found in adolescents is the contrary of gift giving and receiving, and that is a willingness to do without, to accept minimal material circumstances. Youngsters in this category feel there is strength in self-deprivation and that whoever can manage with less is the better off for it. Sometimes such an attitude is a direct consequence of a negative family attitude toward material objects and, at other times, it is a reaction against the materialism that the adolescent grew up with. Parenthetically, some of the most violently disposed terrorists and defenders of the poor come from wealthy homes where they could have literally anything their hearts desired. However, they rejected material goods and went on to choose what they felt were idealistic plans to rectify the wrongs of the world as they saw them. Rejection of the pursuit of material objects as a way of life is also seen in people who choose a religious vocation and become nuns or monks.

Kevin was 15 when we first met and, like Gary, saw no reason for coming to my office even though his parents were upset because he refused all the material things that they offered him, things they believed were part of the good life. He told them that he was not materialistic and had no interest in such things, being more concerned about his spiritual welfare and inner peace. This language sounded to his parents as if he was headed in the direction of joining a cult and they were in a panic. As we talked, Kevin said he was tired of being drowned in possessions and felt that his parents were more concerned about their own giving and their status in the community than they were about what he really wanted out of life. He talked about his own goals, goals which were hardly fixed at his age, and he said that he wished to choose for himself what direction he would follow. After a while, he admitted that some of the material goods did indeed appeal to him but not all, and he began to focus on what he himself wanted. It was easy to gain his parents' cooperation in no longer being so forcefully generous since they were tremendously relieved that he wasn't going off on a religious extreme and they could still maintain their relationship with him. They still tended to be too generous but they did exercise some self-control and Kevin helped to channel their generosity into things that he really wanted rather than allowing himself to be a showpiece for them to demonstrate their wealth to the rest of the community.

Kevin's case is hardly typical. In later childhood, one is already becoming more and more aware of the many material goods that our society provides, and this process of learning about the abundance the world offers and what it means to have lots of good things only accelerates in adolescence. Through television and magazines as well as through education at school and the influence of friends, the adolescent learns about the extensive variety of consumer goods on tap, and starts having a wish list of what he or she wants. Adolescents also develop intellectual interests and search out those things that satisfy and stimulate their curiosity about the larger world. This is the period of life when people begin to collect things such as coins, stamps, baseball cards and so forth, over and above all sorts of prestige-giving items.

All of this costs money, and the child or adolescent needs more than it previously had. Parents tend to increase the amount of the allowance given to their child in recognition of its need for more possessions of its own and its need for a certain degree of freedom from parental control to accomplish these purchases. In spite of having a larger allowance, the adolescent still feels the financial limitations imposed upon it. When one was a child, these limitations didn't matter so much but, now that one is in the larger world and realizes what the world offers and what is beyond its reach more clearly, there is much more pain and much more anger at those who impose limits, the parents. Even when parents struggle to provide what their children want, there may be a feeling of insufficiency and resentment in the younger generation and a belief that they are being cheated. Some adolescents go so far as to check up on what parents buy for themselves, asking why the money is going in that direction and not in their own. They are very much aware of their own needs and wishes, and less tolerant of the needs and wishes of their parents, another source of friction between the generations.

At times, this leads to stealing from parents, from siblings and from others outside the family. Most people tend to keep a small supply of ready cash around the house, hiding it or even leaving it out in the open, an amount that keeps them from having to go to the bank or the ATM more often. The deprived-feeling adolescent sees the stash and helps himself or herself to some of it, hoping that the theft will not be discovered. Eventually, the stealing is found out and it's not that hard for parents to figure out who took the money; at times, they might even set a trap to catch the culprit red-handed. The parents experience hurt and anger for a number of reasons; one is that their child has been dishonest with them. Their own flesh and blood has taken things from them and they feel that they can no longer trust him or her. Another reason is that they feel the youngster lacks any understanding of how hard they are working to give it the good things of life, to make its life and future better than their own, and is instead more concerned about meeting its own desires than having a sense of family feeling. They also fear that it may be showing the first signs of starting on a life of crime and that they have failed somehow in their rearing practices.

The adolescent in turn usually feels ashamed of what it has done, whether impulsively or calculatingly, and is embarrassed to face its parents. It also may wonder if it has a criminal streak and is doomed to a life of antisocial behavior. Sometimes, in defense of itself, it attacks its parents, accusing them of starving it of enjoyments and possessions, comparing its situation to the situations of its wealthier friends. An altogether messy state of affairs arises which can only be solved by all parties sitting down and discussing the "crime" calmly and realistically, trying not to let anger dominate and trying not to say things that are hurtful and not easily retracted. This is a mistake of adolescence from which a great deal can be learned if the matter is handled in an atmosphere of warmth and understanding rather than one of punishment for crime.

Adolescents may also steal from grandparents with the same angry results when the theft is discovered. These thefts should be handled in much the same manner as they are handled with parents. There are also thefts from siblings which produce less storminess, but still plenty of parental involvement. However, siblings usually are all pretty much in the same financial fix so there is less likelihood of theft of any great value; what we usually see here are conflicts over "borrowing" the valuable and the not-so- valuable possessions each one may have; however, the importance of what is "borrowed" is not usually its worth in money but rather a question of one sibling violating the property rights of the other.

The real problem is when adolescents steal from people outside the family or from stores. Matters are not so easily handled once they hit the larger world, and a sit-down open discussion does not necessarily prevent an angry storekeeper or friend's parent from reporting the matter to the police or initiating legal action.

This should be avoided at all costs since it would be tragic to apply a criminal label to a youngster who did this just once. However, repeated stealing suggests that there is a real problem and calls for some kind of professional intervention.

At times, the criminal activities of the adolescent go far beyond what a therapist can handle. Stealing cars may be something done once on a dare, but repeatedly doing so means that the adolescent is getting into real crime, and this may be more a matter for the legal system, only involving a mental health worker if some specific psychological problem can be demonstrated. Also, when a youngster steals money in order to buy drugs, this too suggests problems that are beyond the scope of an ordinary therapist and perhaps beyond the scope of any therapist at all, even a drug counselor.

Mixed in with other things that the adolescent wants are items that confer upon it status and prestige among its peers, things that give it a special ranking within its group. Virtually every adolescent yearns for acceptance and tries to win it, sometimes through fair means and sometimes through foul. One way of being admired is to have objects that are considered desirable: the right sneakers, a certain kind of jacket or the correct kind of neck chain among others. He or she who can afford these things gains respect from others and may become part of the "in" group as a result. This is a very materialistic view of the world in an age group that so often vigorously disdains materialism, but the adolescent wants whatever it takes to give itself distinction in its group. Seeking out distinction and status among one's peers on the basis of certain kinds of possessions is something that is not unique in America or western countries but occurs everywhere, even though the nature of what gives status may be vastly different from one place to another.

Adolescents live in a world which centers around themselves and their friends, and in which parents and such considerations fade in importance compared to what goes on with people their own age. Each adolescent has a standing in its own group, a status position, which may be higher or lower but which is merciless because, if you don't place highly enough, you aren't even worth looking at. This is in contrast to the much gentler hierarchy that exists at home and in the family where you may matter less than someone else, perhaps being the least preferred child, but you still count for something. It is not surprising that adolescents go to extremes to gain a position in that hierarchy for, not to be important in this group of friends means to the adolescent that it will forever be a failure as a human being. Even many years later, no matter what a person has accomplished in life, the feelings of inferiority that not being in the "in" group engendered in adolescence persist to color one's self-image.

Paula was a bright and pretty adolescent who came from a poor, immigrant family. Although she did well in high school, her parents couldn't afford the clothes or the life style of the wealthier students who were the recognized class leaders, and she felt left out and disliked. She went on to a first-rate university on a scholarship and did well there too although she was not very sociable, being considered a bookworm and not a highly desirable date for anyone. Eventually, she obtained a Ph.D., became a professor and a nationally recognized expert in her field, winning awards for her contributions. She also married and had two children who grew up to assume responsible positions. In spite of all her achievements, Paula always felt that she had done poorly in life and was less adequate than most of the people she worked with. She only realized how important her high school experiences were in contributing to her low self-esteem when she returned there for a reunion many years later and had a chance to catch up with the career achievements of all her classmates; she was clearly an outstanding performer but that new self-image was very hard for her to accept and she kept trying to argue it away.

Sometimes, those who can't afford to buy status objects simply bully others into giving away these items as "presents", which then confer status and prestige on the new owner; the bullies are also letting their small corner of the world know that they are people who get what they want. Adolescents who have had things stolen from them, or who lose valuable goods (they tend, as a group, to be less careful in keeping track of their belongings than older age groups), are reluctant to talk about their losses or to confide in their parents for fear that their parents might either blame them for the loss, lose trust in them or punish them, additional reasons for the secrecy we see in adolescence. They are also afraid that their parents might intervene against the thieves, which would make even more public the fact that they were unable to take care of things on their own. Not only would this prove that they lack the capacity to protect themselves and announce it to the world at large, but it might lead to more bullying at the hands of others since they are now on record as being easy marks.

Frequently, the nature of what their children want is too expensive for parents to afford, and they simply can't keep up. Youngsters are not always realistic in their understanding of the cost of things and the limitations of their own and their parents' finances. What is the solution for their increased financial demands as they want more and more to purchase all the things they feel they need? Sometimes grandparents step in to foot some of the bill but this solution is not always available and is not always sufficient and, even when it occurs, it certainly does not help the adolescent to learn the realities of financial limitations. One logical step is for the adolescent to take on some kind of job. Initially, this may be doing something on a regular basis for a parent's business but that doesn't last long, and the youngster looks for some more financially rewarding work outside the home. Every adolescent who starts a "real" job has the feeling that he or she is doing something important and the amounts of money involved, while small in terms of buying power, seem to be enormous since that money continues to come in week in and week out, in a sense constantly replenishing itself. It takes a while for reality to set in and for the typical adolescent to realize that whatever he or she earns will not go very far if it is spent too freely.

Yet spending freely also seems to be another characteristic of this age group. Adolescents are quite expansive in their wishes to take care of themselves and to treat their friends, often shooting the whole paycheck in one evening on foolish purchases. Most adolescents demonstrate unrealistic thinking about financial affairs, not really having had to earn their own living and balance their own accounts. There is also a tendency to act impulsively, doing things on the spur of the moment and wanting to express their warmth and friendship in the fullest sense towards those they feel close to, that is, those in their own social group. It's also part of the prestige system to appear to have so much money that you simply don't have to worry about spending it.

Benjy was in his late teens and had just gotten a part-time job at a local franchise of a nation-wide fast food chain. His salary was not very impressive but was a useful supplement to the money that his parents could give him as they struggled to keep up with the tuition and living expenses of their three children. When he received the paycheck for his first two weeks of work, he felt that he had really entered the national economy and he invited his girl friend, as well as his best friend and his girlfriend to dinner at a local restaurant. Benjy's money barely covered the cost of the good dinner they had, and he received the thanks and admiration of his guests for his treat, which was great for his status. The next day, though, he had to approach his father for the money he needed to get through the next two weeks. The one good thing about Benjy's big splurge was that it helped him to learn fast that he had to exercise caution and good budgeting in his handling of money.

Another aspect of Benjy's overspending so foolishly was his wish to impress his girlfriend with his willingness to spend money on her. Even at his young age, he was already aware that many potential romantic and sexual partners are turned on by lavish spending. People like Benjy believe that nothing is good enough for the one they love. This trait often persists into adulthood but is more frequently seen in adolescence where boys feel so much in love that they are blinded to monetary realities.

For the first time in their lives, adolescents like Benjy have what are called discretionary funds, that is money that is not committed to any fixed expenses but that may be used in whatever fashion the owner desires. Just how that money gets spent provides an insight into the psychology of the individual since the money may go to compensate for feelings of inferiority in any area of life, to purchase friends, to make a good impression on others, or even to help others.

Because of their wishes to keep up with trends and their lack of caution in dealing with money, adolescents are particularly vulnerable to advertisers. Consequently, a great deal of advertising is beamed at them since they tend more than other age groups to accept it as truth and are less critical than they will be later on in life about claims made by manufacturers. They are also not very capable of separating things they really need from luxuries, and what happens is that they overspend and then run short of money, even when they are earning a fair amount.

Parents are often faced with the question of whether to allow their adolescents to have a credit card. It certainly is a convenience for both parents and children and prevents children from having to steal, or at least it should. It also lets the parents see an accounting of how their adolescents spend their money. The negative side is that it also gives the adolescents access to more money than they ever had before, the maximum allowed by the credit card company. Adults too may have trouble controlling their spending impulses when given what seems to be an unlimited amount of money (with payment in the future seeming very far away) but adolescents, as a group, are even more susceptible to the idea of being able to buy anything and everything they wish with no thoughts about future consequences.

Lucille was allowed a credit card on her parents' account on the occasion of her graduating high school. The idea was that she would learn how to use it while still under her parents' wings during the summer and then could take it with her to college out-of-town in the fall. Lucille used it only twice in the first two weeks that she had it and found it hard to believe that all she had to do was sign her name and she could have whatever she wanted. The tempo of her purchases on the card increased, and there was no problem until her parents received the August statement which contained everything Lucille had bought on credit. At first, they thought that someone had stolen the card and run up the charges but, after checking it with her, they realized the true state of affairs and imposed reality on her, threatening to put her on a very tight allowance with no credit freedom for the next four years. Lucille was quick to learn that, ultimately, you have to pay for what you buy, and that nothing comes to you just for signing your name.

It's a good idea for parents not to permit their adolescents to have their own credit cards; by no means should they allow them to have an extra card on the parents' account. If some sort of card is necessary, it's preferable to have a debit card which is valid only as long as there's money in the account to back it up. That sets a limit on how much an adolescent can spend and prevents him or her from running into serious overspending which can happen when a parent's credit card is being used. Alternatively, adolescents can be given credit cards of their own with built in smaller limits on the amount of credit they can build up. There are, of course, exceptions when an adolescent has proven serious and reliable about money affairs. Once the adolescent has gone beyond the age of expansive-ness and has demonstrated real understanding that whatever is charged on a credit card eventually has to be paid off, and the longer it takes, the more interest you pay. At that point he or she might be considered able to handle money and credit well and to have earned the right to a credit card of his or her own.

What are some of the other factors that contribute to adolescents being creditworthy? For one thing, they must understand that material objects have prices and they must know when the prices are appropriate and realistic. Second, they must understand that what you spend has to have some relationship to the amount of money you have, and that in turn is related to a certain amount of work and effort. Once they understand these fundamentals and that they may have to make choices, they can be considered for some sort of credit arrangement. Still, parents should opt for a card with definite limits to start out with, only increasing the limits when they are sure that the adolescent is acting responsibly.

Unfortunately, financial institutions which issue credit cards tend to encourage parents to provide their offspring with their own cards, even if these are still on the parents' accounts. These institutions know that, no matter how irresponsible the adolescent may be, there's a parent to pay for it when the account maxes out. They also know that, should the parents be reluctant to pay the debt right away, they are still responsible for it in order to maintain their own credit rating. Even when the adolescent is made accountable for the debt that has been run up, the financial institutions know that he or she has a long future ahead in which to pay off the debt, month by month, for years, in the meantime paying substantial rates of interest. If the young person should fail to pay, he or she might conceivably go into bankruptcy and lose a decent credit rating before getting started out in life.

So far, I've barely spoken of the physical changes that have been going on throughout adolescence. At the same time as all the other experiences that contribute to becoming mature in our society, adolescents have to contend with changing bodies, and a major new factor enters their lives: sexuality. Suddenly, they are no longer asexual beings whose sexual nature is revealed only by sports interests, clothing or job choices (even in this age of greater job opportunities for women, there is still a lot of type casting, and many girls choose distinctly "feminine" types of work just as boys tend to choose jobs that are considered "masculine"). Instead, they become aware of the opposite sex (or the same sex) in a different way than before, and they are concerned about how they stack up as potential sexual partners. Initially the emphasis is not so much on how they will perform, but on how they look. Anxieties about performance come later.

Some of this emphasis on appearance comes up in terms of the body itself. For a boy, this takes the form of such doubts and anxieties as whether he is tall enough, whether he has a good physique, whether he is handsome, whether his teeth are regular and white enough and whether his complexion is clear enough. If something is wrong, what should he do about it? For a girl, the worries take the form of whether she is pretty enough, whether she has good hair, whether she has a good figure which includes nicely shaped breasts and curves in the right places, and whether she smells okay, as well as the complexion and teeth worries that girls share with boys. Similarly, the question arises what to do about it if something is wrong. Trying to remedy what is seen as a bad situation often consumes a large percentage of the discretionary income available to adolescents (and, for that matter, adults).

A certain amount of wanting to look good seems to be built into our genes. Animal biologists who study the courting behavior of birds and mammals like to draw comparisons between what they see in the animals they study and in teenagers of our species. For example, peacocks, the male of the species, have flamboyant tails with spectacularly beautiful feather arrangements that serve no other purpose, as far as anyone knows, than to attract peahens, the female of the species and a rather drab bird. The males' beautifully colored feather tails indicate to the females that they are healthy and therefore the possessors of healthy genes which, if the females accept them as mates, means that they will have healthier offspring. In both sexes, handsomeness and beauty generally speak for a healthy constitution which contributes to making the individual a better parent, in the sense of having healthy children. Deformations and irregularities of appearance tend to speak against one's being healthy and having healthy genes, and make the bearer of such qualities less attractive to a potential mate.

Certainly, we see teenaged boys strutting their stuff to impress their girlfriends and potential sex partners that they have what it takes to generate healthy children, even when they have no awareness that this is the biological significance of their actions. A muscular male body is considered by anthropologists to be a desirable characteristic to the female of the species who will be able to rely on her man for support and protection in a dangerous society. He will also theoretically be a better food provider, able to go out there and kill game for his woman and children.

It's not just boys that strut their stuff. Except in certain religious subcultures in our society, girls spend their money on enhancing their attractiveness, showing off their sexuality and their ability to be good mothers. Not often appreciated is the fact that, when people admire a woman's breasts, the larger breasts suggest more plentiful food supplies for any future babies, and a curvaceous figure with sufficient supplies of fat means that she will be able to get through a pregnancy and the period of nursing without any worries about exhausting her supply of calories during that calorie-expensive period of life. So, girls who wear tight, low-necked blouses are proving their potential as mothers while boys who ripple their muscles are proving that they will be able to protect their spouses and their young.

There is a huge market that caters to sexual anxieties and promises solutions to all the worries that kids might have, some of these solutions being legitimate and some of them not so kosher. Many boys turn to gyms or adopt one sport or another to enhance their physical appearance and muscular prowess. Orthodontists are able to improve the way teeth appear and dermatologists do their share to control the ravages of acne. In the case of girls, there are beauty salons to fix their hair, curling it when it is not curly and straightening it when it is too curly for the adolescent's liking. There are also plastic surgeons who will expand or reduce breasts, and rearrange figures. When there are real problems, the work that all these practitioners do is enormously helpful for improving the adolescent's appearance and self-confidence.

However, there may be no real physical problems, just the standard difficulties that young people have in adjusting to the natural changes in their bodies during adolescence or neurotic anxieties about being acceptable human beings. The help offered may exploit these anxieties and serve as yet another drain on the finances of the adolescent and its parents. Many a money-strapped adolescent will dig deeply into his or her purse to buy a good appearance, even when judgment is lacking as to whether the original appearance is really bad and whether the proposed treatment is going to salvage it. And, of course, if the adolescent has more money, he or she is even more likely to spend it on improving appearances and supposedly increasing desirability. Seeing in what ways adolescents deal with their discretionary income provides a snapshot of what they really feel about themselves and where their anxieties lie.

Cheryl and Kelly demonstrate the uses and abuses of plastic surgery. Both are rather pretty young women who are now 25 years old. Cheryl grew up in a loving home and felt beautiful until she started high school when her very small, sloping chin made her an object of ridicule; she was called a chinless wonder and she had virtually no boyfriend. Her parents took her to a plastic surgeon who re-constructed her "weak" chin, making her face conform more to accepted standards of beauty. She confidently re- started her social life and soon had many boy friends; ten years later, she looks good and has no complexes about her appearance; she hardly even remembers that she had surgery and is busy leading a very active life.

Kelly grew up in a family where every physical feature and every action was a subject for discussion and criticism. Her large nose on her average size face created problems for her at home and also when she started high school where she was also ridiculed. She underwent surgery to obtain a "perfect" nose but that did nothing for her self-confidence and she remained highly self-critical. Ten years later, she has had several additional reconstructive procedures but still does not like the way she looks, even though men who meet her seem interested in her. She doubts their sincerity and thinks that their interest is yet another way of ridiculing her. Her outcome is poor, not because of her appearance but because of the psychological problems that her parents had created. These were compounded by the willingness of plastic surgeons to do yet more surgery on her although she has now reached a point where it is difficult to find a serious professional who is willing to perform an additional surgical procedure.

As a matter of fact, in the early days of plastic surgery, patients were required to undergo psychiatric evaluations to determine whether the goals expected from surgery were realistic and achievable. If the patient was considered to be unrealistic, either in evaluating current appearance or in expectations of a miraculous outcome, surgery was denied. That practice of psychiatric clearance for surgery has, however, gone by the wayside.

Money is used, as I pointed out in the cases of Cheryl and Kelly, to enhance external sexual characteristics. Sometimes, the enhancement is healthy as when a boy goes to a gym to build his muscles, establishing a pattern of regular exercise that will be good for his body the rest of his life. It's not so healthy when he feels the need to lengthen his penis through surgery because he feels basically inadequate sexually and has focused this feeling on the size of his penis. A desire for bulky muscles and a he-man look has also led to the indiscriminate use of steroids in teen-aged boy with so-far unknown long term negative consequences. Similarly, girls may go in for unnecessary breast enhancement which may indeed be appreciated by the opposite sex but carries with it the possibility of long-term complications.

On a somewhat smaller scale than surgery are other things that adolescents do to change their bodies in an effort to impress their friends and their potential sex partners. One that irritates parents enormously is body piercing. This started out with earrings for girls, went on to earrings for boys and then branched out to the piercing of almost any body part that you can think of, other parts of the ears in addition to the lobes, nose, eyebrows, lips, nipples, belly buttons and so forth. Another body "enhancement" is getting tattooed. Parents who grew up in an era when only sailors and Hell's Angels had tattoos try to prevent their kids from having this done, telling their children that they are maiming the perfectly good bodies that God gave them. This sort of preaching doesn't work and the kids compete with each other for the most original tattoos, the most colorful ones and sometimes just having more tattoos than anyone else in their crowd. They feel that they are expressing their individuality in their selection of tattoos and often go to great lengths to discover new and original ones. This is one area where parents and kids rarely see alike on the use of discretionary funds, but parents have to remember that these sorts of body changes are done to attract attention and to win over potential sex partners, a sort of carryover from what occurs in the animal kingdom.

That is a very unromantic view of adolescent sexuality but, nevertheless, the view of many scientists who study how adolescents go about perpetuating the species is essentially an unromantic one. Viewed from the perspective of money, it is all the more unromantic since money is being used in so many ways to enhance sexuality and attractiveness, sometimes realistically but all too often unrealistically and even harmfully.

Having said that, I want to point out that the amount of money spent from limited adolescent budgets on such items as make-up, hairdos, the latest fashion trends, perfumes and colognes and more other items than I can think of is absolutely enormous and keeps any number of manufacturers in business. All of these items are meant to enhance the attractiveness and apparent sexuality of the individuals, starting in adolescence and going on into the adult years. As I already pointed out, adolescents are particularly susceptible to advertising; this sensitivity is all the greater when it's a question of promoting their sexuality to others.

There are many more status items that adolescents get caught up in buying to enhance their attractiveness but, as we get to more expensive ones, we find that these are the same one that adults use for self-advertising, like cars, motorcycles, fancy vacations and so forth. In the same way, many of the money attitudes and habits of adolescence are transferred in part or in whole to adulthood where they may pose problems for individuals later in life.

One reason that adolescence is so hard to understand is that so many issues, sexual and psychological, are taking place simultaneously. This creates a very complicated picture which is often difficult for adults to comprehend, even though they've been through it themselves. A good approach to disentangling the mess is to try to see which factors are at play in any given situation, getting beneath the immediate superficial problem. Doing so makes the problem a lot easier to understand and deal with, that is for the parents. It is also more helpful for the youngsters since this is a stage of life in which they are struggling with so many issues and feel ashamed if they can't handle everything, even though they may make some horrible mistakes. Rarely are these mistakes fatal, but they should be regarded as inevitable parts of the learning process that underlies this phase of development.

In fact, the best advice that anyone can give a parent of an adolescent is not to get too upset about the way the youngster behaves, both in terms of money and in terms of other areas of life. It is important to keep track of their activities and be available to discuss problems as they arise with these discussions being held in a constructive fashion rather than in anger. Parents have to keep reminding themselves that adolescence is a period of learning and the best way to guide their offspring is to provide solid teaching, using every mistake the kids make as an opportunity to educate them.

# 3

# *Marriage*

Before I go into some of the psychological problems relating to money that arise so frequently in marriages, I would like to offer a definition of love since that is (or should be) the single most important factor in choosing a partner and in deciding to get married. It's impossible, though, to come up with a single universal definition since there are so many kinds of love between people, since there are different types of romantic love, and since people have so many different needs and emotions which declare themselves when they fall in love. For marriage to be considered, there has to be a degree of intensity and interest which appears likely to survive over the years in distinction to the love involved in more casual affairs or in short term romances, with or without sexual components. Often there is an important fantasy component involved in falling in love with the lover looking to the beloved to take him or her away from an unpleasant situation, familial or monetarily, and to make the future better than the past.

In my practice as well as in all my dealings with others, I have found it useful to think of the love that leads to marriage as beginning when two people meet and experience an interest in each other which makes them want to spend more time together and which also finds expression sexually. As they continue to see each other, these feelings increase in intensity, and there are more and more shared experiences which contribute to making them a unit. There may be disagreements between the two but the warmth of the overall relationship and the mutuality of interests far outbalance any negatives. After a period of time, the two realize that they have the makings of a permanent relationship, and this is cemented by marriage and by supposedly being happy ever after. In no definition that I have encountered and not in the definition I have just given is there any mention of monetary compatibility.

Nevertheless, marriage counselors, those psychotherapists who attempt to help people in troubled marriages, know that all sort of differences between the two that were not apparent when they fell in love may produce problems as the marriage progresses. There may be religious differences, there may be ethnic differences, there may be differences in social class and in education, as well as personality differences, all of which may not have seemed terribly important at the time they fell for each other and decided to get married, but which loom larger as the relationship progresses over the years and which put stress on the marital bond.

However, even many marriage counselors don't pay much attention to that fact that each member of the pair has his or her own attitudes towards money based on his or her family values and personal experiences of life. These monetary differences may take several forms; there may be differences in tastes, in setting priorities for spending money, and in styles of dealing with money. Such differences contribute to conflicts which may go one of several ways; they may be resolved amicably, may continue to be problems of a minor nature throughout the many years of a long and happy marriage, may be problems of a stormy nature which contribute to an ongoing, unhappy relationship, or may be the causes of eventual divorce when the two styles are totally incompatible.

Differences in taste are perhaps the easiest of the various types of money differences to overcome. For example, the wife might prefer to take vacations on Caribbean islands while the husband prefers to use the family vacation money to go skiing. There may be battles about where and when to go but they can easily resolve these conflicts by alternating where they go so that each partner is satisfied part of the time although it would be better if they each learned to enjoy what the other likes and didn't stand on ceremony about such divergences in taste.

Sometimes, the conflict may be resolved by each one going off in his or her own direction, but this is not such a great idea since it means that they will be spending their limited vacation time away from each other and will be meeting new people when the other one is not around. It is an entirely different matter when a long-married couple takes off in different directions for vacations than it is when the couple is newly wed.

This difference in tastes might also appear in how they choose to spend their weekends although a couple of days of separation if they go in different directions is hardly likely to cause major problems. However, when there is a limited amount of money, these differences in taste pretty much mean that one person gets what he or she wants at the expense of the other one's satisfaction, a seed of conflict for the future if it happens too often. Other differences in taste might be preferences in the type of furniture to buy or with whom to spend their social lives or whether to attend cultural events or sport activities, issues that are not usually money related.

More troublesome is the issue of how priorities get established for spending money, and these begin from early in the relationship, finding expression in events surrounding the engagement, the parties leading up to the wedding, the wedding itself and the honeymoon. They also find expression in the choice of where to live and in the way the new home is furnished. The wedding process entails the expenditure of large amounts of money and, if there are any incompatibilities in priorities, they show up during this period, not only between the bride and groom but between their families as well. While the enthusiasm for the relationship and for each other usually gloss over any differences at this phase of the relationship, disagreements often appear which continue to be irksome and which may have long term consequences. Let's look at some of the financial issues that arise, whether they are resolved or whether they are temporarily buried, and what some of these long term consequences may be.

From the moment the couple starts thinking of marriage, a number of money questions arise, one of which might be the bride's father wondering whether the groom can keep his daughter in the style to which she is accustomed. The future groom may be grilled as to his future prospects and may even undergo, whether he realizes it or not, a credit check. But the biggest single question is what kind of engagement ring should be bought, and the superficial answer for all parties is usually the bigger the better. The bride wants everyone to know that her intended is doing well financially and is a good catch, and her parents want that, as well, for their own reassurance and for the reassurance of other family members who are actively hovering in the background. Sometimes these hovering relatives make it look as if the marriage is a merger of two clans rather than an arrangement between two people. The groom also wants to give his fiancee the best he can and he may spend considerably more than he can afford to provide a respectable ring that she can show off to others. He may feel pressured by his own wishes and also by the bride's family but may not take much note of it; his parents and his family, however, are likely to be more critical of the amount he is spending and may argue against it right then and there or store it up as a grievance for future reference.

In addition to the cost of the ring being a possible bone of contention, the formal process of engagement may also be. Some couples as well as some parents want a large party to announce the event while others really don't care; however, a large party with both extended families attending as well as myriad friends does cost money, and there are no formal rules as to who pays for it except that the one who gives the party usually picks up the bill. That doesn't mean that they won't ask other close family members to help out with the expenses; everyone likes the idea of the party but is usually less than enthusiastic about paying for it or even being asked to make a contribution to the cost.

A short time before the actual wedding comes the bridal shower, another very nice party attended by all the women who are involved in the wedding or in the close family and friendship circle. This is usually an informal occasion, given at someone's home with all guests bringing along useful household gifts. While the expense of a party at someone's home is not that great, it can also lead to conflict over who pays for it. Some showers are given in a restaurant or in a hotel, and then the expense is much more considerable, again with discussions about who pays the bill. Sometimes, the cost is shared by all participants, sometimes by one individual who may be reluctant but who feels forced to pay for everything, contributing to future resentments. There are times when that future is not too long in coming since the fact that this person paid may be used in family fights to show how much that person did and whether or not it was appreciated. There is, also, usually a stag dinner given by the groom's friends but this causes less dissension since it is understood that they will all share the costs, and expensive gifts are not usually given at this event; it's more like a boys' night out.

The wedding itself may be a substantial affair, lasting for a weekend with a rehearsal dinner the first night, the wedding and the reception the second night and a brunch on the third day, especially if there is a large out-of-town contingent. The usual rule is that the bride's family pays for the wedding and the groom or his family pays for the rehearsal dinner and such items as flowers, but then the rules break down as the event becomes more complicated, and there may be unsettled questions about who pays for the liquor or for the photographer, all of which may contribute in the long run to problems between the bride and the groom, or between their families.

There used to be more formal rules about who paid for what, and there was little room for disagreement since proper etiquette was laid down by experts. In our more dynamic society with more and more variations on themes and breakdowns in traditions, the rule book is no longer consistently helpful and that allows room for disagreement, most of which falls back on who pays what. Although the cost for these parties is usually borne by their families, the couple does have a say in how the money gets spent.

These are just the first examples of establishing financial priorities in the couple's marital life, even when the money spent is not their own. When there is some limitation on the amount of money available, questions arise and choices have to be made. Should the emphasis be on a large engagement ring or a lavish wedding or on both? The same applies to the choice of where to go for the honeymoon. Since this is supposed to be a once in a lifetime event, should it be a no-holds-barred trip with expenses to be paid off some time in the future? Alternatively, should it be something that can be paid for up front? And, after returning home, where should the couple live? And how should they furnish their apartment?

Such questions are only the beginning of many choices that the couple will face during their marital life together and they might not always agree on what to choose or how to establish priorities, assuming that they are in the majority of the population who can't afford to pay everything up front right from the start. These are more than mere differences in taste and it may be more difficult to bridge the gap. Later on, suppose the husband wants to spend money in a way that impresses others, buying highly expensive, visible objects such as an SUV while the wife prefers to buy a car that's more modest. Or she may want to buy a large house while he may prefer a smaller one. Whichever one goes for the high-priced status symbols, the other one is bound to complain about the expense while the one who has done the buying feels that perfectly reasonable wishes to impress the rest of the world have been resented by an excessively cheap partner. Even when they can afford the high costs, the difference in priorities will create dissension and, should they have insufficient funds, the problem is likely to be more acute. What results is a continuing battle in which each attempts to pursue his or her own priorities. If these battles become too painful, a spouse may conceal purchases from a partner, introducing a certain amount of dishonesty in the relationship, and then experiences guilt about it. Others are more honest about spending the money and, in this way, avoid dishonesty, but at the cost of confrontations.

Even the gifts that the couple receives from friends and relatives on the occasion of the wedding can lead to discord. One partner may dislike and openly criticize as cheap and tasteless gifts given by members of the spouse's family; this dislike may be made clear to the givers and serves as a future source of strife with in-laws. Indeed, some are not pleased by gifts unless they are unquestionably lavish and, even in that case, the givers may feel they have done too much, and the thanks are too meager. There are may pitfalls, as you can see, in the finances applicable to weddings and it is rare that these problems don't arise.

Stan and Iris seemed to have been destined for each other and fell in love almost at first sight. Both came from financially comfortable families and both had good jobs in advertising with very promising futures. Stan was a couple of years older than Iris and had dated extensively before they met while her previous romantic contacts were fewer and less involved. They were so thrilled with their coming marriage that they were literally obsessed by it and wanted it to be the most stunning wedding that anyone in their family or among their friends had ever attended. As they went ahead with their planning, the projected expenses mounted to the point that Iris's mother who was a careful money manager became concerned and intervened to make some suggestions about cutting back here and there. Iris was agreeable but Stan became upset at what he felt was unwarranted interference, and he took the stand that Iris would have to choose between her mother and him. She, after much agonizing, agreed with him to go ahead with all the lavish plans they had made. Her mother took a back seat and withdrew all objections, and the wedding went ahead but at a cost to Iris' parents that they had trouble paying and at a cost to Stan and his family that put him and Iris seriously into debt. Things moved along well for a couple of years but ultimately Iris became upset with Stan's "flashiness" and began to drive home the point that her mother had been right all along and she was sorry she had sided with Stan in the dispute. Iris' mother, for her part, didn't miss an opportunity to criticize Stan's wastefulness and, ultimately, the marriage hit the skids.

Perhaps the greatest and most troublesome problem in managing money matters in a married couple is when they have different styles of dealing with money. This might show up in their different approaches to buying on credit, and this difference may appear as early as the engagement if the groom chooses to buy the ring on an installment plan. It arises again when he has to pay the cost of the honeymoon and it certainly comes up yet again in terms of whether they should buy or rent a home or apartment, and how they pay for the furniture. If someone was raised in a family where you never borrowed money and you only bought what you had enough cash on hand to purchase, you simply do not ever buy on credit. Owing money, which is what you do when you buy on credit, is anathema and is considered highly dubious in terms of financial stability and security. As much as you might want to look good in the eyes of your friends and business associates in terms of a great engagement ring, a fancy wedding, a fashionable resort for your honeymoon, a stylish address and expensive furniture, you simply don't do it if it means going into debt. Underlying this is a fear of losing everything if trouble arises and the debts cannot be paid, and a deep insecurity about financial matters.

Contrast this attitude with that of another family where buying on credit is considered normal, and the amount of credit you have is considered to be an extension of your salary; the more you earn, the better your credit and the more you can borrow. The difference in these two attitudes is so great that it's almost enough to start a war, yet how many young people entering marriage compare notes on their personal attitudes towards buying on credit, how they use credit cards and whether they allow the monthly balance to accumulate? The cautious non-credit oriented one will point out just how much money is going to the credit card company in interest charges while the more carefree one will emphasize how much fun they're getting out of using the purchases in the meantime and thank his or her lucky stars that all these things can be bought on credit.

What happens when these two attitudes meet in an otherwise good marriage. One person feels that the other is irresponsible and is putting the family in a dangerous position by creating debts which, in case of any cutback in income, can result in losing everything; this half of the marital couple feels that they don't really own these things which actually belong to the credit card company until the debt is completely paid off. The other party feels that the first is a fanatic who doesn't know how to live and to enjoy all the benefits of modern financing. It's not that these two conflicting 0attitudes must always result in permanent warfare but they must be aired honestly and openly when problems arise, and each party must understand where the other is coming from and make some compromises for the greater good of the relationship.

Ginger came from a lower middle class family which had seen its share of hard times and she was very careful about the way she spent money. When she first met Ed, one of the things she liked about him was his relaxed way with money; he seemed to enjoy every penny he had and didn't worry about tomorrow. He also had a very substantial job with a good income and excellent prospects for the future, so she felt comfortable in adopting his life style once they got married. However, two years later, his dot.com company went bankrupt and he had to take a lower paying job in another firm while she had to resume working. Money was in short supply and Ginger took over the finances, going back to the cautious habits she had learned as a child. Ed, however, couldn't seem to change his high-spending habits which drove Ginger crazy. They started to have frequent fights and their sex life fell apart because they were always angry with each other. Divorce was considered but Ginger felt that they should try to get some help before splitting forever. They consulted a therapist who was alert to the money issues and managed to get them to realize that their money styles were in conflict. With respect for each other and greater sensitivity to each other's feelings, they are in process of putting together again what had been a happy marriage.

An exception to the rule of not buying on credit is made by even the most cautious person when it comes to buying a house or apartment, in other words obtaining a mortgage. Here the amount involved is so great that it's unlikely that the couple will ever have the cash on hand to buy the residence outright, and they must turn to borrowing. One of the weird ways credit works, however, is that you should have borrowed previously, paid off your debts and shown that you are credit-worthy. If you haven't done this, the bank may give you a hard time even if you are a responsible individual with a good, well-paying job. So, in this way, the cautious user of credit who has no record of paying back debts promptly diminishes the possibility of getting credit when it's needed and may have trouble buying a house and sometimes even a car. Financial advisers often recommend that their clients take out small loans and pay them off, even when they don't need the money, just so they establish a good credit record.

Just as there are stylistic differences in regard to debt and credit, there are different styles in what one does with the money that comes in, and this shows up in how the couple budgets their expenses. One partner with a background of careful use of money is concerned that a certain percentage of income be put aside in savings of one sort or another. The other believes that the money is there to be used and that there's no sense in letting it sit in a bank account or a pension plan, even if it does earn interest. This is another one of those differences that it's very hard to bridge with one half the couple believing the other is a spendthrift and the other condemning the first for being too stingy.

Even when both partners agree that the money should be spent, one may be careful to search out bargains and be slow to spend anything until convinced that the best deal possible was found and utilized; anyone who does it any other way is seen as simply throwing money away. The other spouse feels that this is too miserly an attitude and that there's no sense in wasting all that time and effort to save a few pennies. Each one experiences distress at the other's attitudes and has occasion to wonder just who it really is that he or she married.

Giving or not giving gifts is another situation that can really stress a marriage. There are families that make a great deal of fuss about birthdays, anniversaries and Christmas with individual family members going to great length and expense to search out appropriate and costly gifts for each other while other families don't bother too much about the whole business, sometimes not giving anything, sometimes giving a small token and sometimes plain forgetting (although it's almost impossible to forget Christmas with all the hoopla attached to it). If the wife comes from a gift-giving family and the husband doesn't, she's bound to be disappointed and maybe even hurt and angry at his neglect while he thinks it's no big thing. He can learn over a period of years that he better not forget or else, but it still doesn't come naturally to him and he in his turn may feel anger at his being forced to do something that's not consistent with who he is. The question of forgetting to acknowledge special events has become subject matter for cartoonists but it is a real problem in some marriages, rarely a cause for a breakup, but still a persistent irritant. Of course, everybody's memory for events like Christmas and Mother's Day is constantly being prodded by massive ad campaigns on the part of manufacturers and stores but that doesn't help with more personal events like birthdays and anniversaries.

As I said, these differences in managing and handling money are seldom addressed by most therapists when they treat troubled marriages, and there is a preference for dealing with sexual incompatibilities. Yet, so many sexual problems start out as financial ones; it's very hard to feel romantic when you're with someone who you feel is endangering your financial future or with someone who is cramping your style, someone who doesn't seem to care how you feel or sympathize with the things that you worry about. There's an awful lot of self-deception about money issues with people denying that they're present or giving them less than full weight as marital problems. It's a lot easier to focus on sexual techniques and insensitivities but, in any case, the sexual may very well be the consequences of other problems rather than the primary difficulties, as we saw in the case of Ginger and Ed.

Many of the financial incompatibilities can be worked out and, if not fully resolved, can be made clear to both spouses so that each one understands the other even if they are not in full agreement. They can agree to disagree, recognizing that money issues will persist as sources of irritation but need not destroy all the other positives between them.

Prior to the marriage, each member of the couple was a financially independent concern, with his or her own checking and savings accounts, property ownership, stock portfolio, health insurance, credit cards, pension plans and so forth. At least, that is so if they are middle class wage earners who have finished their education and settled into a job. (Different situations prevail if they are poor, unemployed or very young although even here, they may have very different ideas about how money should be managed.)

Living together, even for an extended period of time before marriage, does not provide much of a clue to what will eventually happen should the relationship lead to marriage since it is pretty much understood that, during this kind of relationship, the two maintain their financial affairs separate from each other. There are usually informal agreements that the rent is divided with each partner paying his or her half. Phone and electric bills may be split in half, or each one takes care of one or the other of these bills. Sometimes, they engage in rather complicated calculations to figure out just who made how many long distance calls or who used more electricity on appliances; getting down to such nitty-gritty is generally not a good predictor of a successful marriage and suggests that not only is the current relationship a problem but all future relationships with others will be as well. Food is a little more difficult to work out since each one may buy some as the mood strikes them and not every bill is split in half. However, if one member of the pair feels that he or she is shouldering more than half the financial burden, unless there is gross disparity in incomes, there will be conflicts and this may even result in a rupture of the relationship. (By the way, a good way to destroy a friendship is to stay over at someone's home or apartment for a few days, eat the food from the refrigerator and never, never offer to pay some of the costs or to treat the host or hostess to dinner.)

Each member of the marriage, then, is a separate business entity and almost the first question to arise after the decision to marry is made is what to do about the two separate businesses that the couple represents. Should they continue to be maintained separately or should they be merged? Should some things be merged while other things remains individual? Part of the answer to these questions depends on the conviction they have about the long-term future of the relationship. If there's a degree of uncertainty, there is much more likelihood of there being a continuation of separate and distinct finances with agreements about how to split expenses, exactly the situation that prevails when two people live together without being married. If there's strong certainty about the relationship, there's much more likely to be a merger of finances, even if it occurs gradually. There are also some couple who just let matters drift, maintaining individual financial identities forever.

There are also problems when one member of the team is much wealthier than the other and brings to the marriage considerably greater resources. Even when he or she is not sufficiently alert to the possible financial complications if the marriage should result in a break-up, there is usually some family member in the background urging caution and advising against merging all finances. What often results is a pre-nuptial agreement in which the poorer member of the pair waives all rights to an equal split in the couple's resources should divorce (or death) eventuate, and agrees to make no financial claims on the partner in that case. Even though the various states have laws that relate to financial dispositions if there is a divorce (or a death), these laws can be set aside by a voluntary renunciation in advance, just so long as this pre-nuptial agreement is done legally. This does not seem like a romantic way to enter into a marriage but, in view of the very high divorce rate in this country, it becomes a very practical step.

When both members of the couple have their own independent finances and marry, what usually happens is that both retain their independent position for a while, but then gradually, as things go well, begin to merge their affairs. It is simply too cumbersome to divide expenses and to do all the calculations involved in such a state of affairs. Sometimes, this process starts by their establishing a joint account while maintaining their own independent ones, and shared expenses all come out of the joint account: the rent, the phone and electric bills along with food and transportation but with clothing and personal luxuries tending to come from their personal accounts. After a while, this arrangement is given up and there is a true and complete merger of finances. This also means that both are fairly optimistic about the marriage being a long-term success.

There may still be problems even in this total merger such as who handles the arithmetic of the checking account and the credit cards. Things were easier in the past (at least they seem so as one looks back) when the husband was the breadwinner and, for better or worse, did the bookkeeping. However, like all glances backwards which tend to sentimentalize the past, things were more complicated than they look to us today. It is true that the man was the bread-winner and handled most business affairs but it is also true that the wife had a great deal to say about where the money went and made her wishes known; the husband ignored his wife's ideas at his own peril which, in those days, may have consisted of nagging and "I told you so". While it was assumed that the husband could balance the books better, this was not invariably true, and he often messed things up so that his more efficient wife took over this aspect of the finances, even though she was not the bread-winner and supposedly not the boss of the family.

Over the last generation, there have been changes in earning power for women and it is often the case today that wives earn higher salaries than their husbands. This gives rise to the question of whether the one who makes more money should have the greater role in its management and in its spending. There has been many a battle between the two spouses over this issue with the husband trying to hold on to what he sees as his prerogative of being "the man of the house" and the wife insisting that she has the right because she earns more than he does.

When the couple decides to have children and the wife temporarily reduces her work load, the situation is generally restored to what it previously was with the husband making more. What happens to the balance of power between them, at least that part of it which depends on who makes more money and who contributes more to the family well-being? This issue may see-saw back and forth over the years with there being little permanent resolution and ongoing irritation and resentment, if not overt anger, as the babies come. How much of this a marriage can tolerate is truly a question, particularly when there may be little overt expression of the problem and the feelings it give rise to.

Another seldom addressed question, at least from the viewpoint of therapists, is the in-law factor which was seen as early as the engagement and the wedding. Each member of the couple comes from a family with complicated inter-relationships that began long before the new spouse appeared on the scene. In some ways, he or she is a temporary visitor to what is a life-long situation in a family, with loyalties and responsibilities laid out, both in terms of time and money.

For example, Bert, who came from a troubled home (an alcoholic father who physically abused Bert's mother and did not provide financial support), married Joanna whose family was troubled in a different way. Her mother didn't work but went from boyfriend to boyfriend, having four daughters along the way by four different fathers. Joanna's mother emphasized to her daughters that they all had to stick together and support each other, psychologically and financially. When Bert's bachelor brother died, he left Bert with a large amount of money and instructions to assist their mother financially since she had such limited means. Bert, however, responded to Joanna's pressure to help her family out and "lent" money to her mother and to a couple of the mother's more recent boyfriends while doing nothing to look after his own mother, even refusing to help her buy necessary medications and exploding in anger when she asked. The in-law factor was operational in this case, in addition to whatever was going on in Bert's head in relation to his own mother.

Even when stability has been established between the money management practices of the two members of the pair, that does not mean that it's going to stay that way forever. Once children arrive, a whole new set of priorities has to be set up to allow for the great expenses that taking proper care of children entails. But, even before children arrive, there has to be an agreement in priorities between the two about whether to have children at all and, if so, when. Many couples find themselves enjoying life and the spending of their combined incomes so much that they don't really think in terms of having any children since that would put a cramp in their life style. In fact, this situation is occurring all over western industrial societies with, as a result, falling birth rates and a lowering in population numbers, at least so far as native-born citizens of the country go.

In the majority of marriages, there is agreement about the idea of having children but there are often differences between the husband and the wife as to when this should occur. Traditionally, the wife is more eager to start in on raising a family since she faces the biological clock and will become infertile before the husband does. He is usually more reluctant and wants to spend the money and time on enjoyment with no rush to have any children. There are even times, as we all know, when the delay is so prolonged that the couple winds up not being able to reproduce at all.

Although there are those who claim that two can live as cheaply as one, implying that a marriage does not entail additional expenses over and above the cost of living singly, there is no disputing that three or four are more expensive and can stress a tight budget. Anyone who has had to buy cribs, strollers, car seats, play pens, toys and endless diapers is aware of these additional costs. Not only is a new baby expensive in terms of current expenses, but plans have to be made for its future and fairly fast if the mother wants to return to work soon. Nursery schools have to be checked out, plans made for schools later on and money saved for other educational expenses as they come along. This imposes new decisions concerning priorities on the couple since certain acquisitions and expenses have to be abandoned while money is put aside for the new needs. "Who gives up what?" can prove to be a troublesome question, particularly in a family where the husband and wife have maintained separate finances and, along with those, separate interests. The problem only compounds when there is more than one child.

You may remember that, at the beginning of this chapter, I pointed out that some people build into their definition of love a fantasy that their lovers will take them away from painful familial and financial situations, and provide them with a happier life. If this dream doesn't come true, as occurs when there are too many problems with money in the relationship, there is a tendency for that spouse to begin to look elsewhere for someone new who will make life better. Many of the infidelities that occur do so because an unhappy spouse is searching for a romantic figure who will make all of life's problems go away. If and when a candidate comes along who seems able to provide this sort of happiness, not only will there be infidelity but a divorce may very well ensue with marriage to the new person who seems to fulfill the dreams following rapidly after the divorce.

There are of course many causes of divorce but those that occur because someone is disappointed that a spouse has not solved everything will continue to look for a solution of all life's problems in the next relationship. Second marriages which depend on this kind of magical hoping that some one person can take care of everything are doomed because the same sort of conflicts that destroyed the first, at least from the viewpoint of money issues, will occur all over again. Eventually, the disappointed spouse becomes totally disillusioned with the institution of marriage. Far better to have a realistic awareness that money problems, along with others, occur frequently, and do something about remedying the problems rather than attempting to escape them.

In case you didn't already realize it, the United States is a mixture of subcultures and, while what I have described so far is applicable to most couples, there are subcultures which follow paths leading to marriage that are very much at odds with the practices of the larger society. For example, many marriages are arranged by parents, and financial arrangements are worked out with little participation by the bride and groom in any of these plans; at times, they don't even meet until the wedding. The larger society looks at these arrangements, cannot understand that the couple surrenders its rights of choice and wonders if the marriage can possibly work out. While these arrangements seem to be as successful as often as in those marriages where people freely choose their own spouses, finances can sometimes be a problem in spite of the best and most thorough arrangements made by both sets of parents. There may be differences in temperament and monetary styles between the pair, and there may be conflicts that are as stormy as those seen when individuals decide to marry on the basis of "love". However, in these so-called traditional subcultures, wives are often so subordinated to husbands that they may be forbidden to protest at all, and must accept their husbands' words as law.

No matter on what grounds a marriage is based, whether it be a wish to leave a disturbed family background, romantic love, or family arrangements, it inevitably involves two people by definition who may be different in any number of respects, no matter how much they have in common. One of the most important differences is in their approach to money in all the intricate ways it permeates society. It would be useful if these differences could be examined and dealt with before the marriage; it would certainly prevent a lot of the disharmony that occurs after the fact. However, it is too optimistic to believe that these problems can be done away with and it is a safe prediction that marriage counselors will have their work cut out for them forever.

# 4

# *Having too Little*

Rich people fascinate us because their life styles seem so desirable and because they are in a position to enjoy all the delightful material things that life has to offer, something we only wish could happen to us. They are able to do whatever they want whenever they want while the rest of us have to save and plan and too often are forced to get along without. We fantasize being like them and we have all kinds of ideas about what we would do with their money. On the other hand, we prefer not to think about poor people even though there are so many more of them, and they are never subjects of fascination and envy. A television program, "Life Styles of the Rich and Famous", was very popular, but it's hard to imagine a program called "Life Styles of the Poor and Unknown". Indeed, the only ones interested in the poor seem to be social workers whose job it is to help them, and sociologists and anthropologists who study them.

However, no book dealing with the subject of money and psychology can ignore poverty since its effects on people's personalities are so extensive. As I describe these effects, I enter a tricky area since some of these effects are negative, resulting in character traits that are considered to be unpleasant or unconstructive in society. Some cynics might even go so far as to say that there is really no shortage of books, movies, television programs and so forth dealing with the poor, and they would point to the large number of crime programs you can see almost any day of the week on television. What this proves instead is that there is a negative stereotyping surrounding this population, a stereotyping that I would very much like to avoid here. While it is true that there is a higher rate of what is known as social pathology in the poor, that's hardly the whole story. I will try to present a better rounded, more comprehensive picture since I am not trying to dump on an already sorely tried group of people by emphasizing their problems. I intend to talk about the positive effects of poverty, such as they are, although the negative psychological influences are, for the most part, more plentiful as well as being more painful.

Since poverty does have a large number of different psychological consequences on those who experience it, anyone who knows a large number of poor people knows that, as with the rich, there are complicated personality consequences with often contradictory traits in the same person and with traits that may vary from one person to another. And you also have to bear in mind that poverty is only one of many influences that play a part in personality development. It also matters whether someone is born poor or becomes poor (known as downward mobility), and whether one is surrounded exclusively by other poor people or whether one is exposed to wealthier people. Religion, cultural background, rural or urban settings, one's family, educational influences and role models are other contributing factors.

Although I'll get to the personality consequences of poverty, both positive and negative, a bit later on in this chapter, I'd like to start off by talking about factors which produce physical damage to the brain, especially before birth and in the early years of life; this kind of damage is not reversible in contrast to purely psychological damages. First of all, a lot depends upon a mother's age. If she is very young, and poor women do have children at younger ages than rich ones do, she may have just enough in good health and nutritional supplies to get through the pregnancy and yet not enough to produce a completely healthy child. And, young or old, if she has one child after another, there are likely to be shortages of nutrients that the baby needs which can produce, in addition to brain damage, defects and illnesses in other parts of the body as well.

When nutrition is seriously inadequate, there is defective brain development beginning even before birth while the child is still in the womb. Things are even worse if the mother drinks too much or takes drugs such as cocaine, heroin, barbiturates or virtually any one of a long list of mind-affecting agents, as well as standard medications. Too often, there is inadequate medical care during pregnancy with a resulting greater likelihood of a traumatic birth which can also have its effect on the infant's brain. After birth, there may be yet more inadequate nutrition for the infant with insufficient caloric intake and vitamin deficiencies, both of which have a negative influence on the developing brain. Anemia is also more common in the poor and contributes its share of damage. The child of poverty is more susceptible to infectious and other childhood diseases, and the inferior quality of medical care which is generally the lot of the poor predisposes to greater severity of illness and to more complications.

Lead in paint chips which infants taste and eat also plays its role in brain damage, the lead paint having been used more in older buildings which are now slums where poor people live; lead paint is much less frequently found in better neighborhoods with newer buildings. Also, many poor neighborhoods were originally built close to industrial plants with toxic by- products which, in the days before there was much attention to the question of pollution, were spewed out and saturated the soil. These chemicals persist for decades and cast their poisonous effect on those who live there, but most harmfully on pregnant women and infants.

The result of all these influences is to damage the brain and impair its functioning for the rest of one's life. This shows up as lower intelligence, greater tendency to seizures, hyperactivity, disruptive behavior, attention deficit disorders and various types of learning disabilities. Unfortunately, these consequences are built into the brain's structure, something psychiatrists call organicity and something that is pretty much irreversible, no matter what teachers, doctors or therapists do later in life to help the afflicted person. These limitations on brain function may prevent a person from ever getting a good education, even when exposed to it, and makes all the more unlikely the possibility of obtaining a better job and moving out of the poor category.

Fortunately, it's only a minority of poor children who suffer these injuries, and the majority go through their young years without being brain- damaged. There are some, though, who suffer lesser degrees of injury without this being clearly apparent to their parents, other family members or teachers; these injuries produce milder symptoms and make the child a slow learner or someone with adjustment problems in school. Only a specially trained professional can detect the real explanation for the handicapped performance.

The situation for poor children is compounded in terms of education by the fact that poorer neighborhoods generally have schools that are less effective in accomplishing their goals. In some areas, teachers and school administrators do make heroic efforts to upgrade the education that they offer, and provide enriched curricula to encourage students' interest. However, these are the exceptions that prove the rule since most of the schools in the slums, for a number of reasons, offer inadequate teaching and sometimes just provide a place for children to stay while parents are away from home during the day.

Very poor people also endure an increased rate of social problems. Such issues as unstable parental relationships, absent fathers, high rates of illegitimacy, maternal prostitution and substance abuse, child abuse, high crime and violence rates, parental imprisonments and so forth are more prevalent in poorer populations than in richer ones. These social problems seem to occur in poor populations the world over and have given rise to the term "culture of poverty" as an overall label. All of these impose extra stress on children born into such societies. Then, as if all this wasn't enough, there has recently been some evidence showing that poor people are more prone to Alzheimer's Disease. Of course, that shows up much later when they've gone through adulthood and are entering their older years. It's not clear whether this particular complication is due to stress alone or to inadequate nutrition, toxins, and infections, but that Alzheimer's Disease has an earlier onset in the poor seems clear enough.

These physical and social problems are far from being the whole story, only the negative side of things. Sociologists have repeatedly pointed out that, in the culture of poverty, there are also positive forces: a strong community spirit, helping others who are less fortunate financially, support of each other in times of trouble and the establishment of self-help groups. There is often increased family solidarity with more reliance on not-so- close relatives (the extended family) who pitch in to work together and care for children than there might be in the wealthier population where things are pretty much in the hands of the immediate relatives (the nuclear family), and whoever they hire to assist them in child-rearing. With a large extended family, children often pick out a preferred "mother" and "father" from a host of relatives (most often grandmothers are chosen as substitute mothers) to dilute the adverse effects of incompetent parents and reduce the damaging social effects of poverty.

That just about sums up the deleterious effects of adverse biological influences and the mixed effects of a bad social environment, but a child of poverty also has a lot going against him or her from a psychological viewpoint and this continues into adolescence and adulthood. From the earliest experiences out of the home, say in school, the child realizes that his or her life is different from that of more fortunate classmates, and usually ends up being singled out because of poor clothing or inadequate school supplies. There's a lovely and touching country music classic, "Dress of Many Colors", written by Dolly Parton, which is said to be autobiographical and which illustrates this. The singer describes how, when she was a little girl, her mother lovingly made her a special dress from a bundle of colorful rags; she was thrilled by the dress, and wore it to school with great pride only to be laughed at by the other children. She learned fast enough that what was good at home didn't always go over so well in school but she was also a tough little girl who could see the love and not be bothered too much by her classmates' reactions. On the contrary, she tried to explain to her classmates that there was love in every stitch, and she couldn't understand why they didn't see it. Nevertheless, it was probably not a happy experience for the young Dolly if the song indeed is about her life. This is a prime example of how, instead of feeling comfortable in a world which can offer so many good things, one can end up feeling different and sometimes hurting badly.

With a few more years under one's belt, comes the awareness of day-to- day economies such as having to watch every penny, constantly denying yourself, and worrying about where tomorrow's food is coming from, let alone tomorrow's rent. While, in our rich and prosperous society, hunger is not too common, the possibility of homelessness is, as anyone who watches the news realizes. These dangers hanging over one's head produce daily discomfort. But, more to the point, inevitably, constant worries about these matters slant one's view of life and shape how one turns out.

People who have grown up in the "school of hard knocks", a term used to describe difficult life experiences, often "graduate" with a sharpened sense of the toughness of life. They are more aware of the bitter realities underlying the often sugar-coated, sentimentalized presentation of everyday life we so often see on television and in the movies. Consequently, they manage their interpersonal and business affairs with more shrewdness and suspicion than do children of privilege who have not known the underside of existence. This often very practical approach has been labeled "street smarts", and is certainly more common in those who have grown up poor, seen the worst of the world first-hand and learned how to protect themselves.

These individuals often develop a conscious determination not to let such poverty continue in the new families they establish as they reach adulthood, and they may go to great lengths to prevent it, using their street smarts to get ahead, taking advantage of situations for personal enrichment that present themselves and not falling for con games. Others become compulsive workers, and avail themselves of every opportunity that comes along to make some money, often earning the label workaholic although this behavior appears in other groups and may have other causes as well. They may hold down several jobs, are always ready to work overtime, and never refuse to change shifts with a co-worker for the few extra dollars it might bring in. There is also, unfortunately, the converse, those who explore all sorts of dishonest enterprises to bring in money and prevent the poverty that they knew when they were younger. They use their street smarts to con others, to gain an edge over them and to turn this into money.

Often underappreciated is another consequence of poverty, the absence of privacy. In a middle-class home, it is assumed that every child will have his or her own bedroom. Not so with poor people where several children may have to share the same room and sometimes the situation goes so far that the kids share the room with their parents, learning to take for granted their parents' sexual activities. There is a tendency for all people as they grown into adulthood either to continue patterns of behavior learned in childhood virtually unchanged or to go to the opposite extreme. We can see this with the issue of privacy or with any number of other personal issues stemming from poverty. Some of this depends on whether these people remain poor and have to continue their lives in that state or whether they break out of it and can afford better things but, in either case, it's the childhood experience that shapes what happens. In the case of an adult who grew up sharing a bed room with five brothers and sisters and who can now afford a room of his or her own, he or she may miss the excitement and activity of the crowded companionship and actually feel lonely and empty when alone. Or he or she may relish privacy and resist any invasion of it although, if poverty continues, there may never be the luxury of a choice.

It's the same with the other characteristics they adopted early on in life to come to terms with their unenviable position. These characteristics demonstrate the deforming influence of poverty on personality since what stems from the poverty situation is not always suitable to the realities of the wider world. We psychiatrists call such inappropriate responses functional problems which means that they are not structurally built into the brain and are usually reversible, given appropriate treatment, in contrast to organic brain damage.

Poverty gives rise, first of all, to a feeling of inferiority, with shame and embarrassment coming right behind. There is a feeling of helplessness at one's lowly position in society and despair at ever making the successful leap out of that position. Fatalism about life and its inability to deliver on promises often appears, leading to a low level of aspiration for the future and loss of ambition. There is a sense of marginality, of not belonging and not counting for anything in the scheme of things. There may be little use for social institutions which seem to protect the more privileged but have little relevance for oneself. And at the same time as the loss of aspiration and the scepticism about whether society actually cares, there is a dependency on what society does provide to make up for that which one can't get on one's own, meaning going on welfare of one sort or another. (Some even become experts on knowing just how much to squeeze out of the system, and we hear stories of welfare "queens" who reap large benefits because of the tricks they play to capture benefits for all sorts of made-up individuals as well as for themselves). And let's not forget the jealousy that occurs when one realizes that others have and enjoy things that one can't even begin to dream of having.

These feelings may be experienced directly or may be experienced as the reverse, a kind of psychological defense against experiencing anything unpleasant. Or they may be shoved underground (repression is the psychiatric term for shoving a thought or feeling out of awareness) and find expression in a variety of other ways. People who, for example, feel inferior to others because of having grown up poor and having been made a target by classmates may extend that feeling of inferiority to other things about themselves, to personal appearance, to manners, to style of speech, to physical mannerisms, to matters of taste and to character traits, and they end up feeling like deficient human beings. They blame themselves and their imagined failings for having been poor, and may tend to feel guilty and blameworthy when things go wrong later in life. One way of managing these feelings is to try to make changes in all of the things they criticize, studying how wealthier and more socially accepted people behave and dress, and attempting to imitate it. Even when they've managed to handle their imitation well and grow into their new style of presenting themselves, a feeling of insecurity and a fear that they will be found out and their personal inferiority uncovered may well continue. These doubts and self- criticisms can last a lifetime. Shame and embarrassment are handled in very much the same ways as feelings of inferiority and remain sensitive issues throughout life.

Even when they accomplish substantial achievements, those who carry around with them these feelings of inferiority have trouble seeing these accomplishments as impressive. Rather, they continue to believe that they are not so good as others, and that virtually anyone could have accomplished the same things. They deny their talents and see themselves as not having done much of anything. In other words, they belittle everything they do and fail to recognize their own abilities. There's an old joke told about Groucho Marx in which he refused to join a highly select social club because he didn't want to belong to any club that would accept him as a member. Unfortunately, like many jokes, there's something real underlying it.

To combat even further their feelings of inferiority, they may resort to extremes to demonstrate that they do indeed belong. They overdo in their attempts to look good and often do things like denying their backgrounds and pretending to be carefree about money, behaving in ways that are sometimes foolish and wasteful, like wearing excessively costly, sometimes garish clothing and jewelry in contrast to the shabby garments they wore in childhood, buying overly elaborate furniture or expensive cars and other luxuries. In fact, they sometimes go into debt in order to buy things that might prove to the world that they have money to burn. Isn't this self-defeating since doing so can only get you back into the ranks of the poor? You bet it is but, at the moment, what's important to them is the denial of poverty, not the concern about whether or not they can pay off what they borrow or buy on credit. Here is yet another example of how people's feelings about money are illogical and how they hurt themselves because of it.

Books, as well as movies and television, often make fun of these "nouveaux riches" (French for newly rich) who lavish money tastelessly in order to deny their origins, unconsciously revealing the background which they are trying to deny. They may also incorrectly evaluate other people's status based on how they appear financially, not being able to be objective in this regard, and sometimes under-rating personal qualities as they do so.

Many employers take advantage of a poor person's sense of inferiority and often give out titles to employees instead of raising salaries. Someone who is looking for proof of worth is more likely to be taken in by this technique than someone who is more confident and looks for monetary advancement in addition to having a better job title. It's similar, with giving out such awards as "employee of the month" or medals for having worked many years for an organization. Such recognition is all very nice and certainly those who deserve it should be rewarded. Yet it doesn't really help the day-to-day situation of a poor person by upping his or her salary even though it does serve to build up self-esteem in someone who needs that kind of support.

Poor people who feel inferior about their monetary and social situations in life may turn to other qualities on which they can pride themselves in order to reduce their feelings of inferiority. There is a whole mythology that poor people have greater warmth in their interpersonal relationships, are more open and honest to others, and have greater sexual powers than richer people. I've worked with both rich and poor in large numbers over the years and I can honestly say that, in my experience, there's no difference, no matter what the myths say, not in personal relationships and not in sexuality. Furthermore, if you look at the issues impartially with no axe to grind, you can see that it's just not logical that poverty makes one sexier or more honest or more real as a person. Nevertheless, in spite of the realities, such myths persist because they definitely serve the purpose of making poor people feel better about themselves.

Another belief that poor people maintain to compensate for feelings of inferiority is that they are more ethical than rich people, and it is just those ethics that have stood in the way of their becoming rich. No doubt, in every group of people, there are some who are more ethical and some who are less so, and some poor people are more ethical than some rich people, as some rich people may be more ethical than some poor people. The trouble with this idea is that people adopt such beliefs in order to compensate themselves rather than because they've clearly examined the situation and come to an objective conclusion.

If people have a certain amount of personal confidence and do not share these feelings of inferiority, they do not need to use such defenses but feel comfortable with themselves. These are the ones, who when they make it out of poverty, can afford to be honest about themselves and not have to deny their early experiences (consider the Dolly Parton song) but integrate them into their lives, enjoying their new status and wealth. A case could be made that they are better off for having personally overcome hardscrabble origins since they know what life is like on both sides of the financial divide and can relate warmly and with understanding to old and new friends.

The case of Jose comes to mind in this regard. He grew up in a painfully poor home in Mexico where there was seldom sufficient food on the table. In early adulthood, he came to the United States illegally but received his green card during an amnesty and went on to become a citizen. From the moment he arrived in the States, he worked two jobs and eventually got into the restaurant business. Success followed him and eventually he owned a small chain of Mexican restaurants as well as a factory producing Mexican food. Jose took great delight in telling people how far he had come, an example of how America rewards hard work; newspaper and magazine articles have reported on him and his success. The fact that he had been born so poor and suffered so much in his early years only went to show how great his achievement was and justified his pride in his very singular accomplishments.

Many poor people are, on the other hand, stuck in their impoverished situation and are unlikely to be able to get out of it. They know that life for them will be a series of hardships and money crises. They may not put it into these terms, but they experience feeling of helplessness about making any change and devote their energies to survival. In terms of the larger society, they feel that they are meaningless cogs in the machinery and are marginal to the events going on in the world since, no matter what happens, they believe that it will have little effect on their lives. And this does become a self-fulfilling prophecy. For one thing, poor people in general are not particularly interested in census counts and they tend not to respond to questionnaires. As a result, they are under-counted which results in their districts appearing to have smaller populations and consequently getting less representation in government and, this is important, smaller amounts of money flowing from government into their districts. They also vote in smaller percentages than do wealthier people and politicians are more likely to ignore their needs.

Anomie is the name given by sociologists to this feeling, that one doesn't matter too much in the scheme of things and can't influence what happens to oneself, and it's not a very pleasant feeling. Most of us know that, no matter what, we can still build our lives the way we want and can make our own decisions on the major issues that affect our lives. Imagine that you suddenly are no longer permitted to decide for yourself, but have things forced on you; that's anomie, and it is usually accompanied by depression, not so surprising since any loss of control over our lives puts us into a kind of limbo. This is not the kind of depression that makes one commit suicide, at least not usually, but it is a grinding, always present feeling that continues on a lifelong basis. As a result, one of the most frequent diagnoses in any hospital or clinic treating poor people is depression, and any statistical survey confirms that the poor have higher rates of depression than do the wealthier classes.

I've mentioned sociologists who study the poor and social workers who are there to help them; this raises another point, the resentment of most poor people at being the objects of other people's interference and unwanted attention. For who wants to be examined and poked over, criticized and told what you're doing wrong? I have seen many instances of poor people, not only resenting such workers, but actually hating them for interfering in their personal affairs and invading their privacy. This is only aggravated when such a worker starts telling a poor person how to live life, how to handle himself or herself better and, worst of all, using oneself as an example of the good and proper way to act and do things. It is hard for the victim, already feeling inferior and experiencing anomie, to differentiate among constructive suggestions, personal attacks on oneself and on a psychological need on the part of the so-called professional to feel superior. It's no wonder that many poor people look askance at social workers and sociologists when asked to participate in studies, and often refuse if they have the option.

Claire was a social worker just out of school and was brimming over with enthusiasm about devoting her life and energies to helping others. One of her first clients was Rosie, a 25 year old woman with four children, one of whom had congenital malformations and was crippled. Rosie lived in a one- bedroom, fourth-floor walk-up, and tried to make do on her welfare payments but occasionally picked up some extra money by prostitution. She didn't drink or take drugs but had considered dealing drugs on the side for a little extra income. Naturally, her wardrobe was ragged and hardly flattering. Claire was determined to rescue Rosie, and set herself up as a model for Rosie to follow. She began to teach Rosie how to walk and talk, and made suggestions about how she should dress, in the meanwhile advising Rosie on which men to avoid and how to budget her limited income. Rosie at first welcomed the interest but gradually became angry to the point of fury at this intruder who always knew better than she herself did and who criticized her seemingly non-stop. Eventually, on one of Claire's visits, Rosie hauled off and slapped her and ordered her out. Fortunately, Claire was too "noble" to press charges, and was removed by her supervisor from the case. Unfortunately, it was Rosie who was seen as the difficult one and Claire as the unappreciated good Samaritan.

Many poor people, who feel fatalistic and helpless about their situation, know they cannot improve their lot in this world. They may interpret their poverty as something that God has willed, for whatever purposes of His own. Perhaps He is testing them out by making their lives more problematic here. It then becomes their responsibility to make the best of it so that afterwards in the next life, they can more successfully go on to heaven. Jesus is reported in the Gospels to have said that the possibility of a rich man going to heaven is less than the possibility of fitting a camel through the eye of a needle. What is meant by this saying is that rich people or people who become too enamored of money get into all kinds of mischief, and their virtue plummets. The converse of this is that poor people stay away from vice (either voluntarily or because they have no choice in the matter), and they do not get into trouble. Somehow, they're considered to be purer without money than if they had it, considered so by both themselves and by others. This belief is held on to pretty tightly in spite of all the evils implicit in the culture of poverty. Perhaps this belief became so widespread because of the idea that you've already paid for your sins here in this world, and then some. Anyone who says that being poor is good is denying reality and, when this is practiced or believed to an extreme, such an idea can pose problems for those who truly believe it, whether they are the poor themselves or people who work with the poor.

Nevertheless, the consideration of poverty as a virtue somehow continues to be a popular one. Let's look at one of the way this comes up. Our society, in spite of the above mentioned religious philosophy, still believes that rich is wonderful and having money to throw around really shows just how well off you are, how successful you are, and what a spectacular human being you are. The poor person who cannot do this reacts against this to emphasize the virtue of small things, of finding bargains, of paying less for things after a heavy duty search for the best prices. Throwing money around has nothing to do with just how great your personality is, and while it is nice to find bargains or to be economical about budgets, there is really no character building involved. It is wasteful that people have to devote hours to bargain hunting, going from store to store endlessly to save a dime when it shouldn't be necessary and to trumpeting about how successful they are in pinching every penny they have. Granted there are people who are so poor that they truly have to do this but there are legions of not-so-poor-anymore people who maintain this practice when it is no longer necessary.

Cynthia, like Rosie, had an almost impossible life situation while in her twenties but, as time, went on and her children left home, she was able to get a decent job and make an adequate living. She found a good apartment in a safe neighborhood and was even able to save some money every month. However, she couldn't give up the habits learned over a lifetime and still spent hours each week shopping for bargains. She knew every store in the city that had low prices and studied the newspapers (which she never bought but picked up in the subways or the street or out of trash cans) for sales. The amount of time she put in on saving pennies was absurd but this was a habit she couldn't give up; she justified it to herself and her children as being thrifty.

Jealousy felt by the poor of the rich may be felt as just that, jealousy. When you look at television and see people with beautiful homes, nice clothes, computers, great cars and the possibility of vacations all over the world, you realize all the more sharply what you're missing and can't help but resent the others, the haves of this world. I sometimes wonder whether being poor in a country that's completely poor is as painful as being poor in a rich society because people in poor parts of the world, while they may know there is a better life somewhere, don't have the contrast thrown in their faces all day every day.

One outcome of the jealousy felt by the poor for the rich is a desire to take away from others the things that they have and use them oneself, stealing. Sometimes, the stealing may be part of a violent act visited on the rich, punishing them for having more, making them suffer for it. In the mind of the criminal, he (more of the offenders are men than women) is justified in making others suffer as he has.

Channeling the angry feelings into constructive criticism of society sometimes occurs. The poor person who has known first hand where the larger society falls short and has suffered because of it is sometimes able to pull himself or herself out of the angry mode, see what is wrong and where things might be improved, and contribute to a resolution of some specific social problem. Of course, sometimes the solutions that are propounded are not too objective or easily accomplished, but sometimes they lead to reform and an easing of the burden.

Others are not able to control their anger and see a need for radical change in society. This gets translated into a movement towards revolution. History is full of examples of poor people who tried to overthrow the establishment and who had visions of a utopian world replacing the old regime. Unfortunately, most revolutions lead to bloodletting with only transient improvement in circumstances before the bad situation again returns. Nevertheless, even if revolution is not the answer to serious social problems, it does indicate one response to a persisting unpleasant life situation.

Let me emphasize that the vast majority of poor people do not turn to lives of crime or violence; they make adjustments to poverty and the feelings it gives rise to in other more peaceful, ways. Indeed, some are very consciously against violence and the use of it to force change. They recognize that, in the long run, they will suffer because of it and they attempt to lead their lives quietly, enjoying what they have and hoping for more, some day.

Poverty may also warp one's sense of what to do with money when one has it. What happens when a poor person suddenly acquires a sum of money, as when one receives a large check for accumulated back Social Security payments or receives a small inheritance or wins a state lottery, for example? Let's start with the big Social Security check since it's a somewhat more frequent occurrence. Someone who has become accustomed to sweating matters out may feel, at first, a great sense of relief because, for a change, the pressure is off. Now is the time to treat oneself, to return favors, to spend fast before the spate of good luck is over. Sometimes the expenditures are foolish and it appears that there is little understanding that, once the money is gone, there's no more and it will be back to the same grinding routine. For someone who has become accustomed to the grind of poverty, returning to it is less of a problem than it would be for middle-class types, something that most of us would see as exceedingly painful. However, for many poor people, the idea is to enjoy it while you have it because you won't have it for any length of time. Saving it for a rainy day or budgeting it to improve matters over a period of time is just not part of their slant on things. Those who have not been used to poverty condemn this spending as pure waste without realizing how life experience has taught a poor person differently than a rich one and how the two don't think and act along the same lines.

Ordinarily, we don't think of poor people as inheriting money yet poor people may have rich relatives. Also, even poor people do accumulate assets and, when they pass on, leave them to their families. So, inheritances may be large or, more often, fairly small. Nevertheless, the money comes as a break in the unrelieved poverty of their lives and the way they handle it is indicative of their attitudes. Too often, it is seen as a one shot event which should be enjoyed to the maximum while it's there and then it's back to the situation as usual. It may be difficult in any case to hold onto it since welfare payments stop and in some situations one has to pay back past welfare benefits. So it does make sense to use it up for fun and not think about putting any away for future needs.

On an even larger scale is what happens when a poor person wins a state or multi-state lotto, and millions pour in. This time, there really is a lot of money, yet the newspaper accounts of how big-time lotto winners end up becoming poor again are plentiful. Some of the same attitudes that we saw in handling accumulated social security funds are present here, too, but of course involving much greater amounts. There may be a making up for lost time with a frantic rate of spending, treating others to gifts, making foolish and impractical investments, giving it away to friends and relatives, so much so that the money seems to evaporate and one is back where one started from, sometimes in a worse position because taxes were not paid on the winnings; really poor people don't think in terms of taxes. In fact, as you can see, there are many fundamental differences in understanding and managing money in the different groups of haves and have-nots.

You may have noticed that I mentioned treating friends and giving the money away to relatives. Although these may be unwise moves if you want to remain rich, they also indicate a certain kind of generosity that may be lacking in people who have had much more money throughout their lives. This is also reflected in giving to charity where studies have repeatedly shown that poor people tend to give away a larger proportion of their incomes than do other, richer segments of the populations; just see who it is who gives to the beggars in the street or in the subways. It is rarely the executives but more frequently, the lower echelon workers, to judge by their clothing, blue collar rather than white collar.

When we hear that a billionaire gave a hundred million or so to a charity, we find it most praiseworthy, but that is less percentage-wise than many poor people give even though the amount is so much larger. What motivates such generosity? Is it that poor people know need and are more prone to try to relieve it in others? Or is it that they are less practical about money matters and give on impulse? Or is it a reflection of greater involvement in religious activities? Or is it all of the above? In any case, it's part of the generosity that makes the world a better place.

Winning a lot of money in a state lotto gets us into the subject of gambling. Reformers often protest that poor people, those who can least afford to lose the money, are the ones who indulge in this activity in greater numbers and in greater percentages than do rich people. These reformers forget that it is just such gambling, no matter what the actual game, that has tremendous importance psychologically to people who don't have much to start with (not that gambling is by any means restricted to the poor). For poor people, it represents a dream that they can change their luck, and move from the have-nots to the haves. The fact that the odds are against this happening is not so important as the dream itself.

Fortunately, most of the time, the amount lost is not too much of a challenge to the weekly budget and doesn't create a crisis. However, the amounts gambled and the losses sometimes do throw one over the line. Advertising for state lotteries, the most accessible and widespread form of gambling, emphasizes the dream and encourages the fantasy component, while not being realistic about the odds against winning.

Another way of escaping the grim facts of poverty, even if only very momentarily, is to take drugs or to drink too much. It is a gross simplification to say that substance abuse is entered into only to overcome economic distress, particularly since the substances are not always cheap, but poverty and the wish to escape it may contribute to substance abuse in its early stages. Again, it is not only the poor who indulge these vices, but the percentage of abusers among the poor is higher.

With all the emphasis on the problems of poverty, it should be said that not all the problems ascribed to it are indeed so. In Vincent's case, this was particularly true. He was a 27 year old man who had been picked up by the police on three occasions for sexually exposing himself.

The judge referred him for psychiatric treatment but Vincent was a reluctant patient. The way he saw things, and he genuinely meant this, was that he was poor and couldn't afford to either get married or to go to prostitutes. Therefore, the only way he could have sex was to expose himself to women in quiet locations and get his stimulation that way. He honestly believed that, if he had money, there would be no need for the exhibitionism. Exhibitionism is one of those conditions that have eluded complete clarification and perhaps its presence in Vincent did really have something to do with his childhood experiences which were typical of those seen in very poor people but too much else contributes to such sexual behavior to dismiss it simply as a result of poverty.

A word has to be said about the very special problems of those who were born to better circumstances but who can't make a go of it, usually for psychological reasons, but occasionally because of bad luck. They have to adjust to poverty at a later age. One such group consists of chronically ill mental patients who can't hold down jobs, maintain apartments or handle the limited financial assistance to which they may be entitled. Such unfortunates are truly in a situation that is over their heads. They are sometimes so mentally ill as to be unaware of just how far they've fallen and just accept the new situation as they accept all of life's indignities. It's somewhat different for those who have their wits about them and who suffer because they really can't make the adjustment to poverty required of them. They are unable to adopt personality traits that might make life more bearable.

Both situations are called downward drift, emphasizing that these individuals move slowly down the social ladder, the opposite of those who strive mightily to climb it.

You can see how the problem of poverty affects people in so many different ways. It is impossible to make generalizations that "all poor people are this" or "all poor people are that", but it is not impossible to demonstrate how their whole lives are affected in so many ways by the poverty they experienced so early on in their lives; what happened to them at an early age has formed personality traits which stay with them virtually forever.

# 5

# *Taking Other People's Money*

You might raise your eyebrows at my putting a chapter on stealing in this book. Here I was talking about the many ways that money and psychology are related and suddenly I'm going to talk about criminal behavior. No doubt you've had enough of psychiatrists and psychologists trying to explain away crime by saying that it's the result of cruel or inadequate parents or a bad social environment, and that the perpetrators are more to be pitied than punished. That's not the way I see it, a crime is a crime, and the last time I looked, it was still against the law to take something away from another person just because someone decides he or she wants to have it. And that's the essence of stealing, no matter what form it takes and no matter how you try to understand it. People steal in many ways and I'll try to explain where I can what all these forms of stealing mean to the people who do it but nothing I say should be interpreted as meaning that I in any way approve of it. However, what society does to people who have stolen should have some relationship to the whys and wherefores involved in each specific case. Sometimes, the thief can be "cured" and sometimes not, and methods of cure, if cure is possible, should be provided. But two things to bear in mind are that an explanation of a crime is not an excuse, and to understand why someone does something is not to condone it or to let that person get away with it.

While money is probably the thing that people steal the most, the fact is that almost anything that can be stolen will be, whether it be jewelry, real estate, grocery or other merchandise, or credit card and social security numbers; these are the things that a lot of people call money equivalents since they represent money or can be turned into it. Also the stolen items might not even be things a person needs or can possibly use; this is one of the things that makes stealing such a complicated and interesting subject.

What are some types of stealing? There certainly are a lot of words available in the English language to label different kinds of theft, some of them being robbery, thievery, burglary, larceny, pilfering, kleptomania and shoplifting. While I'm not sure that any police department or district attorney would back up the way I break stealing down in to the categories I do, there is clearly a range in seriousness from fairly minor to very major. To begin with, one has to separate stealing without physical damage or injury to people and property (theft) from stealing that physically hurts people, inflicts violence and destroys property. Some not so serious instances of stealing are breaking into pay telephones, jumping turnstiles (known as theft of services) and pilfering from work. Then there's serious and dangerous crimes such as armed robbery, breaking and entering people's homes (burglary), robbing banks and so forth. Somewhere in between are picking pockets which could become violent and kleptomania which might involve large items and get otherwise law-abiding people into big trouble. Then there are frequent small-time instances of stealing in day-to-day life such as selling damaged goods, adding up bills incorrectly, giving incorrect change and kids slipping money out of parents' wallets. There are many ways to steal in the financial world (larceny) such as forging documents, getting someone to buy stocks in non-existent companies and other stock market manipulations. The world of gambling includes opportunities for stealing such as rigging games of chance and card-sharping of one sort or another. There is also misappropriation of funds entrusted to them by supposedly honorable people such as lawyers and accountants, and influencing the writing of wills in one's favor.

Let's start with the easiest kinds of stealing to explain. The first is when you're starving and you take food simply to survive. We all know the story of Jean Val-jean, the hero of Victor Hugo's novel "Les Miserables" (made into the popular and long playing Broadway musical "Les Miz").

Poor Jean stole a loaf of broad to feed his family and the consequences haunted him the rest of his life, constituting the story of the novel and the musical.

Another easily understood category of stealing revolves around the fact that you don't have something, you see it and realize that it can be yours for the taking providing no one is looking. So you take it. You now have it and can use it to your heart's content. There's no complicated psychology involved in the matter, just satisfaction of your wants and a lack of consideration of the original owner's needs, wants and property rights. These two considerations, putting your wants and needs first and not caring about someone else's are probably present in all degrees of stealing even while other motivations as well as other circumstances contribute their share in determining the type of stealing that occurs.

Psychiatrists have had a lot of trouble understanding the kind of individual who seems to lack a moral conscience and takes what he (this is more frequent in men) wishes with no consideration for others. Over the years, as these case have been studied looking backward from the present crime over the criminal's whole life, it's been shown that many such people have had severely disturbed childhoods with problem parents (that means criminals, prostitutes, alcoholics, drug addicts, child abusers and absentees). Somehow, they've grown up with no regard for the property or feelings of others and no sense that, in a civilized society, one must accept rules and live in concord with the rest of the world. They've been called by different diagnostic names like moral idiocy, sociopathic personality, psychopathic personality and antisocial personality disorder, (the current name) but none of these labels has clarified how to treat them, how to get a moral sense into their heads. It's been said of them that a dumb psychopath is so conspicuous that he ends up in prison while a smart one becomes an expert at manipulating the system for money, sex or political power. Fortunately for society, the majority of such people are, at any given time in prison where they are temporarily unable to steal (although they may act up in other ways) but, unfortunately for society, they relapse after they are released and return to their lives of crime until, with age, they kind of burn out, succumb to drugs or get themselves killed.

Another very common motive in many types of stealing is the feeling that one has the power to put something over on somebody else and get away with it. This brings with it a feeling of superiority, that the thief is better than the next guy. People in this category, when they steal, get a real charge out of it and there are times when they steal just for the sheer pleasure of feeling better than others; it proves to them that they have real savvy about how the world operates and how to run circles around others. There may even be something addictive about this motivation since, any time they feel down or oppressed by the world, a little stealing (and getting away with it) improves their self-esteem and boosts their egos. Of course, if the perpetrator gets caught, that puts an end to any pleasure in committing the deed.

Not only do some people get a charge out of besting others but there are some who get real pleasure out of breaking society's rules, challenging authority and coming out ahead. These folk usually have a real dislike for society and the way it operates. Sometimes, they are just against everything and sometimes the dislike is directed towards specific people. As our society becomes more and more structured with almost everything we do being recorded by computers into our very own personal files, there certainly is room for irritation at the regimentation and lack of freedom that occur. The wish may arise to break away from this, declare one's individual identity and do something that violates society's regulations. It's a private declaration of independence, an assertion of selfhood, even though this is hardly the best way to declare who one is.

Feelings of entitlement also play their part in stealing. The word entitlement means just what it says, the thief feels entitled to something he or she doesn't have and so "corrects" the situation by stealing it. In such circumstances, the perpetrator doesn't believe that he or she is stealing at all even while being aware that society might see it as a crime. Rather, there is the belief that one has been used unfairly by the world and that taking the money or the thing is perfectly appropriate, something that will even out the score. This feeling of entitlement may be present in both small-time stealing and in the taking of goods worth millions. One example of this phenomenon is when there's an electrical outage in a poor neighborhood and the people who are affected go on a looting rampage. They, the have-nots, smash store windows and take appliances, food, clothing and so forth from the storekeepers, the people who have. Again, it's not certain whether these looters see what they're doing as criminal or just a simple re-balancing of the economic scales.

Some of the same motives are present in such entities as turnstile jumping, which is fairly common in New York City as well as in other cities, both in the United States and abroad. Here, the perpetrator waits for a train to enter the station, then instead of paying a fare and going through the turnstile, leaps over the gate and gets on the train, being whisked off before anybody at the station can do anything about it. Only rarely does it happen that he leaps right into the arms of the law and get arrested. Even when these cases come to court, judges regard such stealing as so minor that they rarely impose punishment unless the offense appears repeatedly on the thief's rap sheet. The amount of money to enter the subway is, in New York, only $1.50 but even with very poor people, saving the money is rarely the reason the turnstile jumping is done. The motivation is rather to thumb one's nose at society and to state that one is entitled to a free ride because one is poor and underprivileged. This is a theft committed mostly by men and rarely, if ever, by wealthy people.

Feelings of entitlement also prevail among those who break into pay telephones to empty out the coin contents. (With the rise of cellular phones and a reduced need for pay telephones, this may soon be a crime of the past.) The thief wants the money, feels that society has dealt him a bad hand and wants to laugh at it and its rules by taking advantage of the telephone's easy accessibility, particularly at night. Sometimes, youngster break into phones, however, just for the money and with no particular psychological motivation on top of that.

Believe it or not, boredom is another reason people steal. They find their lives unsatisfying and search for something exciting to give it some spark (Why they find life so boring is another question.) Planning to steal something, working out preliminary arrangements, figuring out how to take the goods and plotting the escape are all challenging, as are the questions of whether one will be caught and what would happen then. The crime becomes an entertainment for the thief in its own right. Incidentally, elegant and original heists are a subject of great interest to the population at large, to judge from the number of films produced about the subject.

Also a source of excitement is the question of just how much one can get away with. A crime, once committed, is over and done with, and the satisfaction soon wanes. The criminal develops the urge to do it again and this time wants to go on to something a bit more complicated, a bit more challenging, a bit more daring. When this has been accomplished and its satisfaction has waned in its turn, yet another crime, more exciting in nature is planned. Eventually, the thief exceeds his luck and his abilities, and gets caught.

One unusual example of a telephone thief who combined several of these motivations was Timothy, a 40 year old man with a long, complicated psychiatric history. He came from a wealthy professional family and started having academic and interpersonal problems during his high school years. He attended several colleges, dropping out of one after the other without accumulating any credits, then went traveling around the world in order to "find himself". Instead, he began to believe that the FBI was following him and spying on him constantly. He returned home and, because of his suspicions, killed a close relative who he thought was an FBI plant. The fact that he was psychotic was apparent to everyone who dealt with him, and what followed were years of placement in a number of psychiatric and criminal facilities with virtually no improvement in his condition; in fact, he believed that all staff, no matter what institution he was in, were really FBI agents in disguise. Timothy felt himself to be hopeless, not because of illness but because of FBI persecution, and doomed to a life in custody. He was bored and lacked the concentration to read or even pay attention to television. It was noticed by the staff that he spent a lot of time on the telephone, however, and when he was asked about this, he stated that he had friends all over the world who kept in touch with him. However, after two or three months of his being constantly on the phone, the hospital received notification from the telephone company of huge bills that he had run up. He had used his very considerable intelligence to perfect a scam in which he obtained telephone credit cards in the names of very wealthy, well known individuals, people who were not likely to review their phone bills too carefully. One or two did, however, and the calls were traced to the patients' telephone on the ward and eventually to Timothy. When this matter was discussed with him, it was apparent that he was treating his boredom with these calls and felt entitled to run up the bills because the world had treated him so "unfairly". He took great pleasure in the inconveniences he had caused to the staff, the phone company and to the wealthy individuals who were billed for his calls. He also claimed that the only people whose telephones he fooled around with were people who had committed crimes against society and deserved to be punished; Timothy was the avenging angel. One of the people he abused in this way was a former ambassador who eventually called in the FBI to investigate the case, finally making Timothy's delusions about persecution approach the truth.

Taking items from one's job is another common form of stealing that is engaged in very frequently. Usually, what is stolen is small and almost meaningless, for example, soaps or linens taken from hotels by some of the housekeeping staff or stationery and office supplies taken from offices by personnel. Such theft is a source of great irritation to corporations because, while the cost of each pilfered item is relatively small, the total amount in a year may be considerable, although rarely enough to make much difference in whether an organization stays afloat or goes under. It would be a mistake, though, to think of pilfering as something done only by lower level workers. What about executives with corporate credit cards who charge dinners with families and friends as business expenses and have their companies pay for them? And what about others who manipulate all sorts of other benefits from their employers along with their salaries? The fact that they get away with it does not alter the basic dishonesty involved in this kind of stealing. In any event, there may be a method to the practice from the employers' viewpoint since some studies have shown that staff morale is better when pilfering goes on. It helps individuals to balance out any anger they may have toward the employer, and allows them to feel that, even when they are mistreated and underpaid, they still have a way of paying the organization back and evening out the score. But, since officially it still is stealing, the perpetrator is likely to lose his or her job if caught or if the matter comes to public attention.

Parents often experience concerns when they come across stealing in their young children. There is less concern in infancy when the tots seem to have no sense of property but take anything that interests them.

If the object happens to interest another tot who also wants it, a bout of screaming and crying will ensue. There's no sense of something being "my property or your property", just a wish to have the thing, at least for awhile until the child's focus of interest moves on to something else. The action can't even be considered stealing in the adult sense since the idea of ownership is lacking although a couple of years later in childhood, the child knows well enough what belongs to it and resents another child's taking that away, even temporarily; we see that the idea of property is already developed at a relatively early age.

A situation analogous to that "stealing" in early childhood is often present in less developed societies around the world. Often, in these societies, there's no such thing as individual property; instead, whatever is available belongs equally to all, and one takes what one needs as the occasion arises with no complaints from others. You can well imagine what happens when such a society comes into contact with a more developed society where individual property rules prevail. The "primitive" takes an object from a person in the more developed society who interprets this as stealing and tries to teach the ideas of crime and punishment to the "thief" and to the less developed society, often with bloody consequences. This conflict of cultures has been repeated time and time again through history as Western European countries explored other parts of the world and came into contact with peoples who had different ideas about property. It certainly prevailed in this country as European settlers encountered Indian tribes as they marched westward. One has only to recall the experiences of Lewis and Clarke as they explored up the Missouri River and across the continental divide to the Pacific and encountered different Indian tribes; this problematic situation has been described in Stephen Ambrose's book recounting their trip, "Undaunted Courage".

Of greater concern to parents, however, is that frequently their children steal from them. The parents find money missing from their wallets or from whatever place they keep their cash, and they try to figure out at first whether they made some error in bookkeeping. After a while, they realize that it's an inside job and that their child is stealing money from them. A huge confrontation follows in which the child is accused of being a thief and of biting the hand that feeds it, and the parents go through a period of self-questioning: what did they do wrong in their rearing practices to have produced a criminal? In most cases, the amount of money stolen is rather small and represents the child's need for a little something extra which it did not feel it could openly request from the parents. The phase of "stealing" is usually fairly short in duration and has no long term consequences. When such an event occurs, the parents would do well to sit down and discuss it with the child in an attempt to find out what the child did with the money and what needs it had that weren't being met. Often, a small increase in allowance is all that is needed or a frank talk about monetary management. As

I've said, this behavior is usually short lived, and the child moves on to get a parttime job to pick up any slack in money that the parents can provide as an allowance. In other words, parents should not assume that they're raising a thief and should not overly condemn the child.

Kleptomania and shoplifting are the next types of stealing that I'd like to look at. The "klept" part of the word kleptomania comes from the Greek word meaning to steal. It's the "mania" part of the word that suggests something more psychological since it conjures up an emotional problem and not just a crime. Kleptomania involves taking things that you can basically afford to buy and also suggests that you are driven to do so by some internal need or pressure. The question arises as to how kleptomania differs from shoplifting. Shoplifting represents more of a systematic way of life in which the thief steals very consciously and purposefully, and is not under the influence of some strong psychological drive. For many shoplifters, this is their life's work, the way they gain their livelihood and put food on the table. They have refined tricks for getting merchandise out of stores and for getting around the store's security forces in their efforts to police what comes and goes. It's a specialized variety of stealing done for criminal purposes. Kleptomania, on the other hand, even when planned in advance, is the result of psychological forces which compel a person to lose control. It may be the result of a feeling of entitlement or a need to get around others or to obtain some object to enhance oneself and to combat some feeling of inadequacy. While shoplifters are both men and women, kleptomaniacs are usually women.

Bettina was a kleptomaniac although she had many other psychological problems. She did not come in for psychiatric treatment for stealing but because of a severe eating disorder. At the time she started treatment, she was 22 and a college graduate who was attending journalism school. She had developed the habit of gorging food during her college days but originally did so only on those Saturday nights when she had no date. After a while, she began eating enormous amounts of food (a box of a dozen donuts, a quart of ice cream, a whole cake) on an almost daily basis. She attempted to control herself by vowing each day not to do it any more but eventually, later in the day, would give up and repeat the pattern. In no time, her weight ballooned, and she then began to force herself to vomit in order not to gain weight. This was the situation when she started her psychiatric treatment. On her first visit, she was seen to be a strikingly pretty young woman who obviously paid attention to her wardrobe and to her makeup. She was pleasant and discussed her eating situation reluctantly but honestly, denying however any emotional problems at all. As her psychotherapy progressed, it was apparent that her self-image was bad and had been for years, long before any eating disorder arose. She just could not see herself as the pretty, intelligent person she really was. One day, I received a panic- stricken call from Bettina who had been arrested for shoplifting (the law does not differentiate between amateurs and professionals) and who was frantic about her parents and friends finding out, let alone whether she would have a permanent police record and might even have to go to prison. It turned out that this behavior had been going on for years; she would enter a store to do some shopping and get an irresistible urge to steal some small item of cosmetics: a lipstick, a bottle of nail polish, eye shadow or face cream. These were all things that she could well afford to pay for. Surprisingly, though, she never took anything that was food related as one might have expected, only things that were used to emphasize the femininity she felt was so lacking. The judge who tried her case did not impose a penalty on her but recognized that psychological problems were involved and was willing to accept the fact that she was in treatment and was trying to do something about them. Fortunately for Bettina, it was possible to help her stop stealing and also to stop her gorging behavior.

Of course, not all bulimics (food gorgers) and anorexics (self-starvers) are kleptomaniacs, just as not all kleptomaniacs are bulimics or anorexics. People steal many different things when they get the sudden, uncontrollable urge and, as amateurs, are more likely to get caught than the professional shoplifters. To understand what propels the kleptomaniac, it is important to know the psychological state that precedes the actions and to see what is stolen under the influence of the urge. With this information, it is often possible to see the connection and then to help the individual overcome this bit of disturbed behavior.

Picking pockets is another form of a systematic approach to stealing, like shoplifting. It involves special training and is often part of a complex act involving one or two associates who assist in distracting the victim as his or her pocket or purse gets picked. Charles Dickens, in "Oliver Twist", described Fagan's rather sophisticated academy for pickpockets in which young boys were educated in the refinements of the trade.

Up to now, I've not talked about the subject of greed, the wanting more than one has no matter what. In the case of greed, the thief already has enough to take care of himself (again, this is mostly men) and his family, and is far from being in need. Nevertheless, he feels that what he has is not enough and attempts to get more and yet more. This of course raises the philosophical question of just how much one needs: how many cars, how much money in the bank, how large a house, how many expensive vacations, how much jewelry and so forth. Even if one has a great deal, what kind of reassurance does it give to own more? Sure, there's some question of outdoing the neighbors for those who want to make a social splash but even then why bother and why get the money through criminal means?

Since these are people who usually are already in good financial states and usually work in offices on a regular basis, this kind of stealing has been called white collar crime. There is no violence involved and rarely other accompanying motivations except for the feeling of being smarter than others and able to get away with misdeeds. There seems to be an infinite variety of white collar crimes, of which I will touch on only a few of the ones that are encountered more frequently. One of the favorites is misappropriation of funds from an organization by the treasurer or by the book-keeper. Cooking the books in such a way as to conceal the embezzlement, they can go on for years until a more searching and sophisticated accountant picks up the discrepancy.

Often involved in this sort of stealing is forging signatures although this can be done in virtually any situations where transactions are recorded on paper. One example might be that of a lawyer who re-writes a will in his or her favor and then signs the name of the person whose last will and testament this is supposed to be. Likewise, signatures can be forged on checks or on stock market transfers.

There is a lot of room for white collar crimes in the stock market with buying and selling going on in a turbulent atmosphere all day long. Huge sums of money get transferred and even the broker's charges, a small percentage of the cost of the stock, are huge and all of this can be played with. At times, it's difficult to clarify the dividing line between stealing and manipulation for one's own profit. It was, until recently, the practice of many brokerage firms, when they bought stocks for their clients, to charge them the high price of the day instead of the price at the time of purchase. When they sold for the client, they gave him or her the low price for the day instead of the price at the time of selling. This practice was essentially legal although offensive and of questionable honesty. There's much more room for profit, still legal, by urging the client to buy poor quality stocks at inflated prices. In some cases, fly by night firms have sold non-existent stocks, a flagrant example of stealing. In spite of governmental efforts to control stock market excesses, borderline dishonesty and overt stealing continue.

There are many examples of mail order fraud which the post office attempts to control. As people turn to the Internet, thieves develop new scams in order to obtain credit card numbers or to sell non-existent merchandise. There is also a lack of clarity concerning certain Internet transactions such as downloading music which have not yet been determined to be legal or illegal. It seems that every new advance in human knowledge or technology brings with it new techniques of white collar crime.

Another form of white collar crime is the stealing of ideas or words (plagiarism) from some one else, also for profit. Periodically, we learn that an author has lifted entire paragraphs or pages from another author's work without permission and without due credit. Story lines for movies are also argued over in terms of whether one person stole another's ideas. This also occurs in the music world where a theme by one composer may suddenly appear in another composer's works; it takes the efforts of a skilled judge to determine whether actual stealing has occurred or whether the idea coincidentally arose in both people simultaneously.

A very skilled kind of stealing has appeared quite recently, and that is the stealing of identity. In this case, the criminal is motivated by greed to obtain all the important documents relating to another's life: birth certificate, driver's license and credit cards. The criminal assumes the victim's identity and runs up debts which the victim often cannot pay, although at times, there are protections for the victims and they don't have to pay. Attempts to clarify matters cost hundreds of hours of time and are not always completely successful. Indeed, a secondary industry has developed in which certain organizations, for a fee, guarantee to keep you posted about your credit ratings on an ongoing basis so that you can know what is going on an almost minute-to-minute basis.

Blackmail is another white collar crime with the primary motivation being greed with some admixture of an attack on another person's credibility and reputation. The blackmailer rarely uses force or violence but uses confidential information that may have been obtained legally or illegally to embarrass another person into paying up to prevent public disclosure of the information.

Stealing often occurs in the world of gambling but here, too, there's a fine line between exploiting the circumstances and actually committing a crime. In any casino, the odds are always in favor of the house when the game is played honestly and, over the long haul, the house wins (and you lose). It becomes tempting for some casino managers to increase the odds in their favor by tilting tables every so slightly or by using magnets which are essentially undetectable by the players. In other forms of gambling, cards may be marked so the professional card player can know exactly what your hand is. These forms of theft are motivated by greed, but sometimes serve as an individual's primary employment and represent the only "salary" he or she receives.

Car theft is another crime that is extremely frequent, and virtually all such thefts are done for greed rather than to compensate for feelings of personal injury. It makes sense from a criminal's viewpoint to take your $30,000 car from a parking lot or a city street, and sell it very rapidly either for parts or for export out of the country. Again, a secondary industry of car security including alarms and special locks has arisen to prevent this from happening but the criminal is often ahead of the technology, and can usually be off with the car in a minute or so. Most people who see the theft as it's taking place are afraid to intercede for fear of injury.

I've mentioned the use of violence as something that is present in extreme examples of stealing such as armed robbery which would include breaking and entering, burglary and bank robbery, and also in kidnaping. In these instances, violence may not be the prime motivation; rather the prime motivation is the one we see so often, greed. What distinguishes these crimes from lesser stealing is that the crime is usually performed by direct confrontation, and the victim is absolutely not willing to go along but is forced by threat to comply. In these crimes, the perpetrator is always supplied in advance with a life threatening weapon, usually a gun but sometimes a knife. What these criminals usually want is to obtain the goods and get away quickly without inflicting injury on others and without being recognized. However, they are obviously ready to use violence and kill or injure to accomplish their aims. So, even when the weapon is not used, the very fact that it is present indicates that the perpetrator has thought about using it and is willing to do so to obtain his ends, making all such crimes fit into the category of violent ones.

In a small percentage of cases, the criminal does indeed wish to injure the victim and, even though the monetary goals are rapidly attained, stops to beat, rape or kill the victim, often with torture involved. Unless the stealing has this violent component so necessary to satisfy the criminal, the crime is not a success in his eyes. What makes people so sadistic is beyond the scope of this book but its presence in some instances of stealing must be mentioned and we can only speculate whether these people want to punish society, get back at certain individuals or types of individuals, or feel a sense of superiority over others whose lives are in their hands.

A famous bank robber of the 1930's, Willie Sutton, was once asked why he robbed banks; he responded by saying that that is where the money is. It's also in stores, gas stations, coffee shops and malls, and we see similar tactics used in holding up all of these businesses.

There is the category of stealing called Robin Hood crimes. This name is used when someone steals from the rich to give to the poor and it supposedly represents a totally selfless form of stealing since, theoretically, one takes nothing for one's own personal use. The whole purpose is to help others and to make up for the imbalance of property between the rich and the poor. However, most of the time, people who claim to be Robin Hoods manage to hold back at least some percentage of what they have taken and, again the motivation of greed can be seen.

One remarkable case of bank robbery that might have been considered a Robin Hood crime but expanded far beyond it in severity, including the taking of hostages and the death of one of the robbers, was eventually made into a movie, "Dog Day Afternoon", starring Al Pacino in the role of John S. Wojtowicz, the bank robber. The case, which the film follows fairly closely, grabbed the attention of the nation one August afternoon about thirty years ago when a small group of robbers took over a bank branch in Brooklyn and held the staff as hostages for two days. The leader of the robbers was Wojtowicz, who was in his early 20s at the time. He had grown up in Brooklyn, served as a soldier in Vietnam and was married with two children. He himself had worked as a bank teller and knew the workings of banks from the inside. About a year before the crime, he fell in love with a male trans-sexual who was strongly desirous of having surgery to become more female. These operations were rare at the time and quite costly, and neither Wojtowicz nor his lover had the money. The lover made a very serious suicide attempt and hovered for a while between life and death. At this time, Wojtowicz decided that he would have to provide the money for the surgery as a life-saving measure and the only way he could think of to obtain it was from a bank. He enlisted the help of two companions and they provided themselves with weapons and worked out a loose plan of bank robbery which they attempted to carry out. As things turned out, it was not a quick in-and-out operation and the New York City Police Department called in the FBI to help. The situation dragged out for a couple of days and finally Wojtowicz and the two other bank robbers were able to leave the bank along with some hostages to head for the airport and a plane waiting to take them out of the country. At the airport, arrangements fell apart and one of the robbers was killed, Wojtowicz was captured and the remaining hostages were freed. Wojtowicz did time in Federal prisons and was eventually released. The lover managed through other means to have the surgery, lived somewhat more contentedly for several years and then succumbed to AIDS.

This particular instance of bank robbery shows that while taking money was the principal purpose of the crime, it was for a very special cause. It seems clear that the other robbers were in it for the money, and one can speculate that Woj-towicz was also, making him a Robin Hood plus in terms of motivation. It also seems, as one reviews the case, that little thought had been given to complications that might ensue such as the lengthy hostage holding situation and the manner of escape. Many crimes occur because the taking of what one wants seems so easy and there's little comprehension of the complexity of the situation and all the implications of the crime.

Stealing is pretty clearly a very complicated behavior in which many motivations play their part. The message for law-enforcement authorities is that any instance of stealing should be examined in terms of what was actually going on to produce the crime and what the motives were. In some cases, the reasons for the stealing are one-shot events or are possible to reverse, and the perpetrator may never do it again, given proper treatment. In other cases, the reasons are pretty permanent and no amount of treatment or help is likely to do much good. Sentences to prison or to other forms of punishment should take these factors into consideration for the penal system to be effective (it's there to rehabilitate as well as to punish).

Similarly, for the justice system to respond constructively and appropriately to the crime, there should be some understanding of what the whole thing is about.

# 6

# *Having too Much*

There's hardly anyone who doesn't dream of being wealthy. What a delightful prospect, to be able to go where you want when you want and to buy anything that catches your eye! You can choose the most elegant surroundings to live in, drive the best cars in the world, wear the most luxurious and fashionable clothing, and eat in the finest restaurants. Your every wish is fulfilled almost before you express it, even before you experience it. Best of all is not having to worry about where your next dollar is coming from and not having to trudge to work day after day to earn your living. Nevertheless, being rich is not all fun; in fact it brings with it many internal psychological problems and many interpersonal ones as well.

However, not all wealthy people are alike. Even in a group of wealthy people, while some of their personality traits and the issues they face may be comparable, there are major differences between one person and another in terms of what they feel and do, and their psychological adjustments to money. Also, the experience of those who were born wealthy and those who became wealthy later on in life (either through inheritance, through marriage, through their own efforts or even through winning some kind of lottery or television game show), may be quite different. A lot also depends on the way your family and friends all related to each other as you grew up, in other words how you became the person you are today with your own unique personality.

Viewed from the perspective of the common man, rich is rich, but the truth is that one person's view of what it takes to be considered very wealthy is different from another's. What may seem like wealth to a poor person may just be a moderately good standard of living to a middle class person, and what seems rich to a middle class person might in reality be merely a slightly greater degree of comfort than he or she has. There are of course the really wealthy, people with enormous amounts of money. One of the classic comments that illustrates how people in different situations look at what amount makes a person rich is John D. Rockefeller's statement about J.P. Morgan, the nation's major banker at the end of the nineteenth century and the beginning of the twentieth. Morgan left behind him an estate valued at about eighty million dollars (probably several billions or so in today's dollars) and had given away huge amounts of money and art during his lifetime. Rockefeller remarked that, prior to hearing Morgan's monetary worth at the time of his death, he had been under the impression that Morgan was a wealthy man, indicating that he now felt otherwise. Perspectives change depending upon what rung on the financial ladder you are standing.

Not every person in every part of the world tends to regard money and the rich in the way we in the United States do. In this country, we tend to admire rich people, are fascinated with the details of their lives and want to know more about them, how they live and how they spend their money; however, not every society throughout history has regarded wealth as a great advantage or even as something special. In some societies, the value of having a lot is that you gain status by giving it away, lavishing it on presents for others and providing great feasts for the clan. In other societies, having lots of money is seen as a threat to one's spiritual welfare and, in yet other societies, there's no such thing as money; you do just enough to take care of yourself and your family. But in our society, the case is that money talks and the wealthy are usually looked up to and, whenever possible, imitated. By and large, most of us want to be like them.

I will be talking about the very wealthy and, in contrast to Rockefeller, I would consider Morgan to be in that category. It's impossible to set a dollar amount these days on what constitutes great wealth but I will be discussing the problems I've run into in people who have many millions of dollars, enough to live off their holdings without working and enough to do pretty much as they wish without having to feel any restrictions due to not having enough money. In spite of the fact that I concentrate here on the problems that go with great wealth (this is what psychiatrists are all about, helping people with problems; we're not usually involved when they're happy), there are rich people who enjoy their money and are not influenced by it in any negative way.

Admiration by others is just one of the emotions that wealthy people become accustomed to dealing with as they go through their lives and, as I already mentioned, there are differences between those who had lots of money from the time they were born and those who obtained their wealth by their own efforts later on in life. Let's begin by examining the situation of those who were born rich, those with the proverbial silver spoons in their mouths. The very expression silver spoon tells us that they must have had plenty of good food which served as an introduction to a life of plenty in other spheres as well. Their parents never ran short of money and there was never a moment's anxiety about where the next meal was coming from, whether the rent would be paid or whether there would be enough to buy a new pair of shoes. In fact, it might be hard for children who grow up in such an environment to comprehend how much of a problem these simple expenses create for those who are born with less. To some extent, this results in a lack of empathy with those who are poorer since it requires such an enormous stretch of the imagination to realize that life can be so difficult for someone else, viewed from the material as well as the emotional perspective.

This lack of empathy often arises as an issue in politics where a rich candidate (and it seems that to be a candidate, one must have money) is criticized for not understanding the common man while someone who had a more difficult life situation is felt to be more sympathetic to poor people and more willing to go to bat for them. When rich people have this lack of understanding of the financial situation in which others, the majority of the population, find themselves, they are at some disadvantage in dealing with mere mortals. Not only don't they understand what is happening, but they may have a feeling of entitlement, that being rich is their right because they are special or their families are special. Life showers good things on them because of their special qualities, and those who are in need must have done something wrong, are certainly not special and are not entitled to the same rights and privileges. Sometimes, this is accompanied by feelings of dislike and disrespect for others who are not in the same fortunate boat, and sometimes this is aggravated by a fear that these good things will be taken away.

But let's get back to the wealthy child's entry into the world, something that is quite different from the experience of a really poor child. For one thing, the child's mother is usually well fed and in good health, receiving the best medical care that money can buy. For another, the delivery occurs in a good hospital with the most up-to-date equipment, reducing the risk of illnesses and complications at this crucial time. Then, afterwards, at home, there is usually excellent care with all of the infant's needs being taken care of. An infant doesn't really know much of what's happening just so long as it gets fed and cleaned, and is treated with love. As the child begins to gain some awareness of the world around it, it also becomes aware of whether or not it's comfortably dressed and whether or not it has enough toys and amusements. Obviously, when the parents are wealthy, there's plenty of stimulation and plenty of fun with minimal discomfort, and needs are taken care of very promptly.

Of this care, in the very wealthy, is delivered by hired workers who relieve the mother and father of the daily chores relating to the rearing of their children. Many of these parents use the resulting free time to do things outside the home and, since caretakers are present while they're gone, they are able to pursue their own interests without concern for their children. Indeed, the fact that they have so much money gives them an enormous choice of things to do, and that might include some heavy-duty consumerism. They are in a position to take long vacations, to take up sports, to shop, to work out, to party, all on their own without having to worry about their offspring. Nursemaids, nannies and governesses take over the job of raising the children and sometimes become more important to them than their own parents. Needless to say, the best caretakers for all children are their own mothers and fathers although having them around all the time is certainly something that cannot be guaranteed, not even in less wealthy families.

In today's world, both parents may have to work to keep up with expenses; indeed, this is rapidly becoming the norm and it is sometimes difficult for working parents to spend time with their children. Even when they have to be away for significant parts of the day, they usually manage to spend some time every day with their children. However, in very rich families where nannies and governesses are involved, the real parents often bow out and leave the child-rearing to these hired employees who, no matter how good they may be, still have their own lives to pursue and may be only secondarily involved with the children they are looking after. In fact, many are transient workers and move on to other jobs or to families of their own. What eventuates is a series of caretakers with little or no stability in any one relationship; the mother and father are of course stable figures but are not always available. The rich child is, in this way, required to make frequent re-adjustments to new mother figures and to get accustomed to having a father who is not around, and this may set the stage for later difficulty in forming fixed relationships, with family, with friends and, when the time comes, with romantic figures. It is a real question who is the primary mother figure in such families, the biological mother or the hired mother; maybe there is really no one who fills this role to an optimal degree. Rarely does the child feel that it is receiving the emotional involvement that every child deserves and needs.

Throughout their early years, wealthy children tend to get what they want since there is no financial need to delay buying anything. Their tastes for toys and objects are shaped by what they see on television and in toy stores, even in clothing stores. You wouldn't think that fashionable clothing is something that children would think much about but that too becomes important, and they demand and get the best. Initially, having these things is seen as something that's pleasurable in its own right but, after a time, as the child begins to get out into the world a bit, it becomes something that confers social advantage and prestige, having something that others don't have and might want, and that feels good.

Children who get everything they want are often called spoiled which generally means that they are being taught that their wishes come first and others' situations are not important. They are also not learning that life can often frustrate and that one doesn't always get everything that they want. People who are concerned about spoiling their children often want to build in a little frustration to their growth experience but this is an controversial idea and a somewhat artificial one. How can one plan just the right amount of frustration to be educational and not to be traumatic? In any case, the children of the rich are considered spoiled by many people who have less and can't afford to do the same things for their own children.

At times, children of wealth become aware that others may dislike them for having possessions that the others want and don't have, and they learn that there is such a thing as jealousy. This negative response is something that comes upon these children as a surprise and they may not recognize it at first. However, they can't stay ignorant of jealousy and its consequences for very long since people who don't have things that you have, may tell you in all kinds of ways that they don't like the situation and then can make life miserable for you and even take these possessions away from you. Imagine a rich child growing up in a small community going to the local school. He or she may have a new bike or the latest styles in clothing which may result in verbal criticism and snide comments or in being picked on by others. This may lead to an escalating situation where, in response to harassment and bullying, there may be greater recourse to flaunting what one has. This in turn this can generate further resentment and anger and may go so far as to result in the other children physically ganging up on the rich child, beating him or her up or even leading up to having these things stolen. Parents who are aware of such things can protest to community and school authorities, asking them to rectify the situation but it is a far cry from what the authorities tell children to do and what the children actually do, and this is one way that the blessing of having too much may turn into a curse. Certainly the rich child does not always have a picnic and learns early on that he or she is different from the others.

The converse is also in operation. A rich child may, just because he or she has so many possessions, prove attractive to other children who try to get as close as possible. If they can become friends of the rich kid, they think, they can play with his or her toys, and maybe even have some of the good things rub off on them. They may sometimes get gifts of these goodies but it usually doesn't happen that way in spite of their fantasies. At some point, rich children realize that part of the reason that others like them is that they are in a position to do something for them, and not because they have wonderful personalities. The first time this happens, there is disappointment and hurt but it is a theme that occurs again and again in the relationships established between the rich and their poorer friends, and may contribute to lifelong suspicions concerning others' motivations in establishing friendships.

One solution to the problem of the rich child relating to poorer ones with these destructive personality consequences is to remove the child from its poorer fellow students and friends, and enrol him or her in a school which caters to the wealthy. This leads to surrounding him or her with children of similar backgrounds but also reduces contacts with diverse classes of society and isolates the child even further from the realities of everyday life, leading to the lack of empathy I previously mentioned. There may also be exposure to competition with the other rich children over who has how much, whose parents have better cars, bigger homes, make more money and go to fancier or more expensive resorts.

The expression "poor little rich girl" has entered the language to denote some such person, someone who has scads of money and should be happy, according to the expectations of the rest of the world, but who always remains forlorn and unhappy. While it's possible to dispute how one gets this way, I have mentioned some of the factors that contribute to producing such a person, one of the earliest being the absence of an ever-present, loving mother who can provide the stability and regularity in which the child grows up to best advantage. Rich kids also may have inconstant and frequently changing parental figures with only distant relationships with their real parents. As the rich child gets older, the attitudes that he or she was exposed to at an early age become more firmly embedded. These children may have difficulty relating to poorer children their own age and be ferociously competitive with other wealthy children. They have learned at an early age that having lots of money can be a problem, even when they don't come right out and say it this way, and they may not even be fully aware of how they feel about the matter.

As they enter later childhood, school issues become more important in their lives as they do for all children. All kids want to learn new things and usually enjoy finding out how the world operates. Also, for most children, school is something that leads to an eventual career. They know because their parents tell them so that they will have to earn a living some day, and the harder they study and the better they do, the more money they will eventually make and the more comfortable their lives will be. The urgency to do well in order to make a better living is simply not a consideration for rich children since they have enough money and know they will always have enough. While they are certainly as bright as any of the other kids in school and maybe even brighter (since someone in the family had to be real smart to amass all that money and the smart genes have to have been passed on), they lack this particular incentive that poor and middle class kids have. Not infrequently, school performance drops as they go along through the educational process and they are likely to focus more on the fun things in school and less on its educational objectives. Ultimately, when their education, such as it is, is completed, they will automatically be offered good jobs through their family connections and they certainly don't have to worry about salaries. In fact, they may be offered a whole series of jobs if they don't like the first or second ones they have taken. They simply don't have to prove themselves on the job, and can look on it as an activity rather than as a career.

Even when serious about their work, both during school days and in the larger world later on, they face another problem which is their reaction to criticism and approval. The pattern was set earlier in their lives when they saw how some people automatically disliked them while others tried to butter them up for personal advantage. As part of the educational process, teachers have to correct the work done by their students and, in doing so, there is inevitably criticism of errors and approval of whatever is well done. What happens if the recipients don't feel sure of what is intended when criticism and approval are given and wonder whether the teacher wants something from them in return for good words or is punishing them for having greater advantages financially? There may be great difficulty accepting these comments and uncertainty about how to incorporate them and improve what one does. Based on their life experiences, they may have trouble separating genuine positive and negative reactions from those that mask an ulterior motive.

Not being able to distinguish constructive from destructive comments and criticism often makes rich people difficult patients in psychiatric treatment. They are often reluctant to accept their psychiatrists' comments as objective and often lack trust in the very person whose help they need to understand themselves and to overcome their problems. Additionally, when they feel angry at their therapists, they are in a unique position to one-up them based on the therapists' usually lower financial value. It's easy enough for them to win a competition with the therapist on these terms which they have set up to protect themselves and easy enough for them to devalue the therapist.

The same sort of confusion and distrust about other people's motives extends strongly into the romantic arena. They may be charming and lovable individuals but they have learned to look at admiration and other positive responses with a certain amount of skepticism. They know without being told that there are gold-diggers and fortune hunters surrounding them, and they're not sure who's for real and who's not. Even when there is genuine love in the relationship, the rich partner has a tendency to keep testing out the sincerity of the partner's feelings. After going through a whole series of tests, the partner may become disgusted and want out since there's only so much proving that one can do before weariness and irritability about repeated testing and uncertainty about the future of the relationship take over.

One can also see the continuing testing of others occurring in friendships. Rich people may share experiences with others that would ordinarily cement a friendship between two people. Yet, they are never sure that the other person really means it, and they devise situations in which the other person's loyalty is put to the test. After passing many such tests, one of these "friends" may come to be regarded as a true friend, someone who can be trusted and relied on, and someone who will extend himself or herself. In spite of this, there is a persistent nervous quality to the friendship, and any possible disagreement or pursuit of other goals or people on the part of the other one may put the whole relationship into question. In other words, rich people make demanding friends, and it is sometimes hard for an ordinary mortal to provide them with the ongoing blind loyalty they seem to be demanding.

Some very wealthy people acquire the reputation of being skinflints because, for one example, they seem unwilling to not only pick up the tab but to pay their own way in a restaurant. People even joke that that is the way they made so much money, by not paying their way and by letting others pay for them but there's really another reason they are so reluctant to pay for someone else; it's one of the tests they use to see whether they're being used as a deep pocket or whether someone else is willing to pay for them, another little proof that they mean something to that person.

Another way in which wealthy people look like misers is the extraordinary reaction some of them show if they lose small amounts of money, either by misplacing it, having it stolen or suffering a business loss. Of course, no one likes to lose money, no matter in what way it happens but most of us shrug the loss off and go on about our business, vowing to be more careful in the future. This was certainly not what Francine did. She was a middle aged woman who had been born into a family of substantial means; she married a wealthy man and also had an extremely well paying job; in other words, she had nothing to worry about. You wouldn't know that when one of her stocks took a plunge. Her actual loss was quite small and, in no way, did it significantly reduce her purchasing power. However, her reaction was marked and she decided she would have to cut back on many expenses in order to make ends meet. She began to bring her lunch to work instead of sending out for it, and she decided that she could no longer afford to take taxis, instead either walking or using public transportation, something she hated to do. The amount of money she saved on these economies was trifling to a woman in her financial position but she had a real fear of becoming destitute in spite of the reality of her continuing to be enormously wealthy. Perhaps she was so unsure of herself that any loss could threaten the security that her money gave her.

Back to romantic matters; wealthy people often feel safer relating to someone in their own category instead of someone outside it because, with their peers, no matter what else goes on in the relationship, they know that they're not being loved for their money. Sometimes, they're not even being loved for themselves since the partner may have the same problems, and what results is a marriage of convenience rather than a love match. Even when they are truly in love, there is a tendency to test out the sincerity of the partner's feelings, as we have seen with friendships.

Sex may also become a problem, even in its more casual expressions, since it usually represents (that is, for most people) a spontaneous physical need, and the urge may be felt towards any number of partners based on looks or style rather than on any thought-out reasoning process. Rich people are considered sexy by a whole lot of other people based not on physical attributes or personal qualities but simply on the basis of money, and there are those who attempt to captivate the rich person through wild and enthusiastic sexual expression, some of it faked. In this sense, sex may change from being a pleasant experience between two people into a trap which one has to be wary of. With the resources at their command, it often becomes easier to purchase a sexual partner for a short episode with the understanding that this is a financial transaction with no other aspects.

By the time they reach late adolescence, some of these very wealthy people may have clearly defined psychological problems with trusting others, in friendships and in romance. They may have trouble committing themselves to a course of study or a job, and may feel disconnected from the rest of the world. On the other hand, they have the financial resources to buy themselves all kinds of pleasures, and there is a tendency to do so to fill in the empty spaces in their lives. One way is to buy fast cars which are not always handled in the safest way possible, and there may be a tendency to fall back on drugs for pleasure and stimulation. Certainly, the cost of the drugs is a pittance for such people whether it be something as legal as alcohol or as illegal (and dangerous) as cocaine. In contrast to poor people who buy cheap crack cocaine which is more addicting and more psychosis- inducing, the wealthy can buy cocaine in its pure form which is perhaps a bit safer.

Along with drugs and fast cars is a willingness to engage in more challenging behavior and sports, things to set the blood racing and provide excitement, contact and stimulation. The need to face challenges may take a constructive turn and they may undertake daring explorations, of the sea or of caves or of previously unknown geographic regions. They may also get involved in the newly-named extreme sports in which they literally challenge death each time they participate. All of these activities require that one have a full wallet and all, if successful, guarantee significant approval ratings.

Getting approval is important to these people since they are so often uncertain of their value as human beings. They have grown accustomed to being respected for their money, and they welcome any statement that they have merit as individuals over and above their finances. Unfortunately, too often, they imbibe the values of society which so respects wealth and they tend to not respect others who are not similarly wealthy. In other words, they may judge others by external signs of material wealth. In the meantime, they expect and demand respect from others, for their wealth and standing, even in the absence of accomplishments.

Rich young people are exposed to experiences and people that other young people are not, and this often shows up as a sort of false maturity. Since they have access to all the goods of society and have been everywhere and done everything, they look and act older than their years. However, at the same time, they are still young people who have had a limited amount of life experience, and what they have had has been of a very special kind, unique to rich people in a protected environment. They lack an understanding of others and have little awareness of the problems others face in life. Underneath the pseudo-sophistication, there may be a profound lack of judgment and inability to assess others and their real personalities.

Becky was a good example of this sort of apparent maturity covering up a naivete which was severe enough to get her into serious trouble. She was the daughter of a wealthy man who had become well respected as a creative artist and, in the course of her growing up, she had met many celebrities at her parents' frequent parties. She could chat easily on all sorts of artistic and political subjects, and everyone felt that she was wise beyond her years. She became enamored of a much older man, a well-known film star, and they soon had a wild sexual affair going, a May-December thing, she being 20 and he being more than three times her age. Not knowing much about contraception, she became pregnant. The actor had already lost interest in her and left her to handle the matter on her own. She was too embarrassed to discuss her pregnancy with her parents and went ahead to arrange an abortion on her own. It was done sloppily and, after a rocky period of infection and hospitalization, she became permanently sterile. Everyone in her circle was surprised that she didn't know more about how to take care of herself but they were fooled by her external appearance of wisdom and had no idea of her lack of real knowledge of the world.

Most of us do not realize that we constantly learn from the jobs we have; we learn the substance of the job and we learn how to get along with people and with the systems in which they operate. Every defeat we experience leads to some growth, what to do or what not to do the next time around. If we were able to just pick up and go, to walk away from the problems, we would have no need to figure things out. But, since we need the job for our survival and for maintaining our families, we stick around and we sweat the problem through. By the time we're ready to move on to another job, we have grown and matured. Needing to stay on a job and work things through does not apply to wealthy people. On the contrary, they can change careers when the going gets rough and they have no need to stay on any one job. This may lead to a life of multiple careers, one after the other.

Let's look at the case of Andrea, a 35 year old woman from an extremely wealthy background. As she entered college, she became interested in music, a philanthropic interest of her family. She was not creatively gifted and didn't wish to study it on any sort of professional basis, though. She became acquainted, however, through her family, with many musicians. After college, she established a open house for music students and for people just starting out, seeing her home as a salon where they could discuss and develop their work. After a while, she began to advance loans to some of the struggling young artists, got more and more involved in their lives and went on to advise them what music to play and how to play it, suggestions that were far beyond her real knowledge. The musicians universally rejected her advice and most gave her back her money. She was very disappointed with the whole field of music after this experience, and went from it into the world of painting; essentially the same thing happened all over again. From there, she began to "work" with writers, and the same difficulties arose yet again. She took off a few years to find herself and to consider her next moves but really couldn't get into anything else, and retreated into an isolated social position. Not only did Andrea lack any real life goals which would force her to work through problems the way most of us have to do, and learn from this process how to do things better the next time around, but she also interpreted the fact that she had a lot of money as the right to dictate to the various artists she helped, as if money gave her knowledge and judgment superior to theirs. Unfortunately for her, after all her moving around, she ended up in the same spot. She never had to suffer the worst that a job can do in terms of harassment, absence of recognition, or competition with peers, and she never learned to handle problematic situations when they arose. Andrea, as happens with many rich people, walked away from the whole scene only to have the same experience over and over again without benefitting and without learning anything.

Andrea also, through her great wealth, had a feeling of power over others. She believed down deep that she could command people to do her bidding by buying them and, sometimes, by merely promising to give them things or help them along with their careers. Ultimately, she ran up against the fact that people cherish their independence and resist the idea that they can be bought. This problem of buying people can be expressed in another way. Andrea believed in what's called quid pro quo, meaning that you give something to get something, and she organized her work and her personal life on this sort of transaction basis, kind of a business arrangement. While there are people who are eminently buyable, Andrea picked the wrong group, a bunch of independent-minded artists who prided themselves on their skills.

Since Andrea, like many wealthy people, had problems in her personal relationships and in her relationship to productive employment, one might well ask what made her tick, what gave her pleasure, what values she adhered to. The answer is that she believed in her money but that turned out to be hollow in terms of what it gave back to her. Ultimately, she was very unhappy even though she had lots of money to spend and could buy almost anything if not anybody. Very little gave her satisfaction in spite of her great wealth and, to dull the pain, she turned to drugs, even if in a mild way, never going beyond marijuana. In fact, she grew her own marijuana on her estate outside New York City until the county police discovered that fact, and advised her to stop before they arrested her.

What makes Andrea's story particularly sad is that she started out really wanting to help the musicians she gave money to and she really wanted to make some dent in the music world. Her attitudes subverted her wishes and prevented her from accomplishing anything. She would have been better off establishing a fund or participating in some already existing endowment but she attempted to use her money for her own personal enhancement, coercing people and that's a lot different from the philanthropy that many wealthy people get involved in. By pushing her own needs, she wound up defeating herself.

Many wealthy people, like Andrea, end up this way with their with their needs not being met and feeling isolated and bored. Their money allows them to be idle which, if carried to any great extreme, leads to depression and a falling off of interest in things. They often seem jaded, as if life has nothing more to offer them.

I mentioned that rich people are sought after as marriage partners and learn a certain amount of distrust of others who are poorer, often preferring a less romantic relationship with a person who is as wealthy as they are. There are other rich people who like the idea that they are pursued by so many possible partners and choose to marry someone poorer so that they can dominate the relationship, making the spouse a veritable servant. This was what happened to Cal who was born to a comfortable middle class background but who hungered after wealth. He was an unusually handsome young man and an outstanding student with great personal charm; he felt that he was valuable merchandise in the marriage market, and he only dated rich girls. When he met Stella whose family's wealth approached the billion dollar mark, he "fell in love". She liked him well enough but her parents kept telling her he loved her for her money. In spite of this discouragement, the two married and Cal got a job in his father-in-law's business, drawing a large salary for not too much work. It sounds as if he made a good bargain but the fact is that he quickly became the family retainer, being expected to do all the jobs and handle all the responsibilities that no one else wanted to do. He had little say in family decisions and was treated contemptuously by all, eventually including Stella who used him as a sexual toy. When children came along, he was pushed into a corner, having served his function as his in-laws saw it. Eventually, the marriage broke up because he couldn't take it any more and, once the divorce was over, he barely retained the right to see his children. Marrying for money in Cal's case entailed a very high price indeed.

Okay, as the expression goes, "don't marry for money but go where money is", but it all boils down to the same thing. If you are willing to sell yourself, you will become some kind of servant, even if a high-level one, and life will not be easy for you.

At the outset, I said that there are differences between people who grew up wealthy and people who created their own wealth. Those who worked for it usually grew up in homes where things were reasonably comfortable financially although some of them may well have known poverty. They learned in their childhoods that money was important but never had the feeling that people related to them pro or con on an exclusively money basis. They had to make their way in school, at home and with friends on their own and were accepted or rejected by others based on who they were and not on how much money they had. As a result, they tend to be more self aware and confident as a group, and are capable of friendships and romantic relationships without all the emotional baggage that those who are born wealthy carry around with them.

They do have one thing in common, though, with the people who inherited their money, and that is an awareness that people at this point in time see them through money colored lenses and try to become their friends in order to get something out of them. This distrust of others may be learned later in life as well as early on, but the ones who learn later tend to be less hung up about it and more realistic about their relationships.

Since they come to money later on, they also do not have the established social positions that those with inherited fortunes have, and they have to work hard at making a place for themselves socially. They do this usually through philanthropic channels; some of the greatest donors in the country are people who have made their own fortunes, and they often have buildings, schools, libraries and so forth named after themselves. Once they have done so, you start seeing their names in the newspaper gossip columns, and they become fully fledged members of the jet set.

Curiously enough, one of the situations that occurs regularly with men who have created their own wealth is divorcing the wife who was with them all these years (she always takes away with her an enormous settlement) and marrying a much younger woman. There is often a 30 year difference in the ages of the husband and the second wife, usually an outstanding beauty, often called a trophy wife. Obviously, this shows the world that the husband is rich enough and attractive enough (for whatever reasons) to capture the heart of a much younger woman. Outsiders looking at the situation assume that older men are just naturally attracted to beautiful younger women but fail to realize that, in the separation from the wife of many years and in the second marriage, there is an attempt to deny one's not so wealthy roots and a wish to join the world of glamour and hip as if one is a charter member from birth onwards. What makes these younger women so enamored of these older men I'll leave to your imagination, although it is not always greed. At times, the younger women finds herself fascinated by a man who has managed to accomplish so much in life; she likes his style and she feels she can learn something from him. She may also enjoy the social advantages he can provide for her; she will now be traveling in the highest social and political circles, and will have access to all sorts of interesting and well-known people.

Let's not forget that there is also a possibility that she feels genuine affection for the man maybe even to the point of loving him.

Sometimes, the newly rich individual is not a man but a woman, particularly in these days of greater opportunity for women and the gradual breaking of the glass ceiling that previously limited their advancement. These women who strike it rich also may wish to unload their long term spouses and try for something newer and younger in the marriage market. We see women in this category trailing around their new "boy-toys" as they hit the society news and establish positions for themselves in the social hierarchy. While they and their younger boy friends probably have the same motivations as what we see in their rich male-trophy wife counterparts, so far, there are relatively few of them and I've had little contact with those few, too little to explore their motivations and to understand where they're coming from.

I have presented a whole set of psychological problems that plague rich people but I'm glad to report that not all rich people suffer these problems. As I started out by saying, many are just like others in the sense that they have good relationships and enjoy their work, becoming happy in the process. These are the fortunate ones, the ones who use their money wisely and enjoy spending it without getting into terrible tangles with other people and without having recourse to false values or to power struggles. They are not susceptible to being conned by others eager for a handout, and they don't have to build walls to protect themselves. Sadly, the truth is that too many rich people are in the other camp where their wealth is a burden to them and impairs all their ventures. Still, you'll find very few of them willing to give up their accumulated wealth and try to get along without it.

# 7

# *Hoarding and Collecting*

Every December, as Christmas approaches, there is bound to be at least one television broadcast of Charles Dickens' "A Christmas Carol". As almost everyone knows, this is the story of Ebenezer Scrooge, a wealthy miser in Victorian England, a man who counts his gold, exploits his workers and seems immune to human relationships. Through a series of events, Scrooge (his name has entered the dictionary as a synonym for miser) thaws out and becomes a genial old man. Scrooge is only one of a number of misers who populated Dickens's work demonstrating the great writer's fascination with people for whom money has replaced ordinary human emotions. Most of us find such people fascinating and wonder what makes them tick. However, it is not only money that can become a collecting obsession but an extensive variety of objects, some of which have monetary value and some of which have no external worth whatsoever. People collect almost any thing that you can think of and for any number of reasons, some of which raise more questions than can be easily answered.

For example, every so often, we hear that, when some elderly recluse died, his or her house or apartment was found to be impenetrable owing to the collection of years of trash, garbage and newspapers. The classic instance of this was the Collyer Brothers, Homer and Langley, who died within a few days of each other in their sixties in 1947. Their name has become synonymous with both the accumulation of worthless objects and the inability to throw anything away. Their hoarding was so extraordinary that no discussion of the subject is complete without a retelling of their story.

They were born in New York City, sons of a physician father and a musician mother who were first cousins. Their ancestors had come over from England on the Speedwell, one of the first ships to follow the Mayflower. They were related to the Livingstons, one of the most eminent old New York families, and their grandfather owned what was reported to be the largest shipyard on the East River, the center of New York shipping in the 19th century. Raised in genteel circumstances where money was no problem, they both had good educations. Homer, the older by four years, went to law school and then subsequently practiced law in a large firm for several years before he took ill and became blind and partially paralyzed; the exact diagnosis of his illness is unknown though, in today's terms, it may very well have been psychological in origin. Langley, the younger brother, graduated from college, studied music and called himself a professional musician as well as a scientist and inventor.

The two brothers moved together out of their parents' home around 1910, to a three story house on Fifth Avenue and 128th Street in Harlem, at that time a middle class neighborhood. They also owned a similar house on the other side of the avenue as well as a parcel of real estate in Jamaica, Queens, estimated to be worth $100,000 in 1938 dollars. As the years went by, first Homer and then Lan-gley stopped working and they gained a neighborhood reputation as eccentric individuals because of their reclusiveness. Although they had many cousins, they kept up with none of them. They had no friends and virtually no social life, rarely even acknowledging their neighbors. Homer was never seen because of his illness, and Langley went out only at night to perform necessary shopping and other business. Neighbors spread rumors about their having huge amounts of money hidden in the house, also claiming that they had a car in the basement and possessed human bones. Children attempted to invade their home and discover their secrets. Beginning in 1938, they became the focus of newspaper interest with stories appearing on their problems with the electric company (service was disconnected for non-payment of bills), the bank (they stopped their monthly mortgage payments) and the Department of Health (for numerous sanitary code violations). Their telephone was also cut off for non-payment, Langley explaining that he received bills for long-distance calls he never made; he requested a more accurate bill and refused to pay until a corrected one was forthcoming. All this time, the house became more and more rundown and the authorities believed that it was in danger of collapsing.

When Langley did emerge and was interviewed by the press, he appeared to be neat and clean although somewhat shabbily dressed. His clothing was at least twenty or thirty years behind the times and it was reported that he used safety pins instead of cufflinks to close his shirt sleeves. As far as behavior went, he was polite and soft-spoken, attempting to respond to his interviewer and offering seemingly logical explanations for his behavior.

Finally, in March, 1947, the police received an anonymous call (later claimed to be from a neighbor who was apparently the only individual who maintained some minimal contact with the brothers) that one of them was dead. The police forced their way into the house and found the body of Homer who had apparently died of natural causes (starvation and dehydration leading to a heart attack were considered the causes of death). However, they could not find Langley despite an extensive search for him among the accumulated debris of so many years. An all-points bulletin was put out for him but he could not be found. The police continued to search the house, going through mountains of accumulated material, dirt and stink until, lo and behold, they came upon Langley's body not eight feet from where Homer's had been found. It was determined that Langley had asphyxiated when an enormous pile of newspapers fell in on a tunnel that he had dug through the trash, trapping him. It seems that he had built a system of tunnels with booby traps to thwart possible burglars and was a victim of his own ingenuity. The final considered opinion of what had happened was that Langley had died first and was unable to care for Homer who fairly rapidly succumbed in his turn.

What remained was approximately 120 tons (that's 240,000 pounds!) of material that the brothers, mostly Langley, had hoarded over the years. Since everyone thought that they had great wealth, this material could not simply be thrown out but had to be searched through carefully for documents and objects of value among the preponderance of what could only be called worthless junk. The search had to be done very scrupulously, especially in view of the many relatives who showed up to claim their share of what was expected to be a very large estate. It was finally determined that there was much less of value than had been supposed. When taxes were paid, the expenses of the cleanup and funerals subtracted as well as accumulated debts to banks and utility companies paid, there was hardly anything left to divide up among the thirty to forty people who had claims under law as relatives.

A partial list of what was discovered, something about which everyone has some curiosity, included ten pianos, an organ, 4 violins, 2 flutes, a cello, a French horn, a cornet, a trombone, 3 radios, a phonograph, a huge musical clock, 2 ancient rifles, a brass candelabrum, a coal scuttle with its cover, a blue vase, an antique rocking chair, paintings, two trunks full of women's clothes and linens that appeared to be their mother's hope chests, 13 mantle clocks, Victorian oil lamps, white plaster heads and figures, metal figurines, dressing table bric-a-brac, empty perfume bottles, old fashioned tools, broken records, prints, worn-out towels, a broken photographic apparatus, a wooden cradle with human bones in it, bicycle lamps, 3 coffee grinders, 6 toy trains, several potato peelers, a nursery refrigerator, some lampshades, 2 dressmaker dummies, 2 old bicycles with rotten tires and crumbled leather seats, rags, the top of an old touring car, a radiator of a model T Ford, piano parts, an automobile seat, a number of leaking pails, a horse's jaw bone and all kinds of old books. But mostly, there was paper, paper, paper, endless piles of newspapers and magazines going back for over thirty years

It was not only the house that was packed full but also the yard. This was a long-time community eyesore and had attracted the attention of neighbors and authorities even earlier as a possible fire hazard. As a result, legal authorization was obtained at that time to clear away all the junk which included rotting doors and all sorts of rusting metal pieces as well as lots of papers. Newspaper accounts at the time reported that Langley wept uncontrollably as these "precious" objects were removed. Subsequently, he re-stocked the yard until it was again full at the time of his death.

Some of the items on the list are objects any of us can recognize as things we too might keep, either out of sentimental reasons or in the hopes of them coming in handy at some point but the sheer volume beats anything we could otherwise imagine, let alone the peculiarity of some of the objects, like that horse's jawbone. Reviewing the history of these two brothers in an attempt to find out just why they amassed this huge garbage dump, does not turn up much in the way of explanations. One can see that they were both somewhat shy individuals and, once Homer became ill, Langley gave up everything to care for him. He was apparently not well equipped psychologically to handle the stresses of twentieth century existence and fell back on objects as a kind of preoccupation and reassurance. When pressed for an explanation of his collecting habits, on one of his rare contacts with the press, Langley stated that he believed that Homer would eventually regain his sight, and that he, Langley, wanted him to be able to read up on all the things that he had missed over the years. Is this the real reason or is it some rationalization that he concocted just so that he could give an answer to eager reporters?

The subject of these brothers was one that fascinated a well-known novelist of the 40's and 50's, Marcia Davenport, who wrote a fictionalized version of the Collyer Brothers' story, calling it "His Brother's Keeper" which was published in 1954. She applied the ingenuity and imagination of a novelist as well as an enormous amount of research to her storytelling, and described the slow descent of two brothers (this was a fictional reconstruction, not necessarily the truth of the matter) from apparent normality through a series of drastic personal, family and external problems to the strange way they ended up. She saw the collecting as initially making some sense but gradually becoming overwhelming and assuming after a while its own perverted logic.

More recent evidence of the continuing fascination with the Collyer Brothers' story is an off-Broadway play, "The Dazzle" by Richard Greenberg, produced in the spring of 2002. Greenberg's take on the story is different from Davenport's. He sees Homer as being the reasonable one with Langley being wildly eccentric from the beginning. As Homer became ill, he could no longer restrain Langley and things rapidly got out of hand. There is one beautiful scene in which Reg Rogers who plays Langley caresses, almost sexually, a broken lacrosse bat that was thrown into the house by a neighbor. Greenberg also makes the point that both brothers had severe interpersonal difficulties and that objects came to replace people for both of them.

Such out-of-control collecting raises the question of whether there is a basic instinct for collecting and saving things hard-wired into the brain, a physically based urge to accumulate things. For an answer to this question, as they do in the search for an answer to any number of questions relating to humankind today, psychiatrists look at a number of situations which might be considered comparable in some way to what adult human beings are and how they behave at this point in our history. First, we might look at animals to see whether this behavior appears in other species. Parallels might be drawn to squirrels who store away all kinds of foods during the summer to be eaten during the cold months, and to animals called pack rats who accumulate objects that don't seem to have any intrinsic worth. (Yes, there really are such animals as pack rats; the name is not merely a phrase to describe certain people.) But, except for these examples, collecting is rare in animals and does not give support to the theory that there is some sort of instinctual basis for the behavior.

Alternatively, we might look to see whether children, even infants, collect or hoard things in support of the idea that to be human is to be born a collector. Children do have a strong sense of property and like to collect toys and other objects. Anyone who has ever observed a young child knows that he or she can becomes fixed on a favorite toy or even on several toys and doesn't want to be separated from them; sometimes even a blanket serves the purpose. Most psychiatrists believe that this sort of collecting has another meaning, being a symbol for their mothers. Holding on to the objects gives the child a sense of comfort but there is rarely anything going on that could be called active collecting.

Another way of pursuing an answer to the question is to look back on the history of the human race to see whether collecting played its part early on. Believers in the concept of an acquisitive instinct point to the caves where our earliest ancestors lived or to the ruins of ancient civilizations; archeological digs have revealed that there were, in these locations, collections of objects that may have been considered beautiful or precious, or which had religious significance. In fact, some of these collections are called hoards in archeological lingo, and most of the most famous hoards were collections of money and gold or silver objects buried to protect them intact from invading armies. The people who did the original burying never returned to unearth them, and the hoards remained in place until rediscovered hundreds or thousands of years later. It is hard to know whether other objects that may not have survived were also collected in such hoards, things made of perishable fabrics or wood. Even after we look at all these examples, it is hard to conclude beyond any shadow of a doubt that there is such a thing as a biological urge to collect. My own personal belief is that collecting or hoarding, instead of representing some sort of instinct, is instead a behavior with a number of psychological meanings.

One place to look when we want to understand the psychological meaning of a particular behavior is at seriously ill mental patients who, by the extremity of their behavior, may shed some light on motivations that make people do things. Sure enough, the phenomenon known as hoarding occurs relatively often in a large percentage of hospitalized mental patients, especially among those who have been ill for many years. While patient privacy is usually honored in psychiatric hospitals, occasionally it becomes necessary to do a ward search to look for weapons, stolen objects and contraband such as drugs. When a locker belonging to one of these hoarding patients is opened, it is usually seen to be full of bottle tops, used batteries, broken Walkmans, pieces of cardboard and so forth. All of these collections have no extrinsic worth but each, nevertheless, seems to have some precious significance for its owner. Although we can never know for certain why they collect these things, and can only wonder what these objects represent to the patients in their mentally disordered states, we may get a clue. Some of them state that these collections represent their lives and they cry, much as Langley Collyer did when, because of the fire hazard, the contents of his yard were carried away. In other words, they derive some personal identity from this, hard as that may be to imagine. This type of hoarding, however, is not limited to the inside of psychiatric hospitals.

With the growing number of discharged mental patients on the street, we have all become accustomed to the sight of filthily dressed people pushing shopping carts or carrying overstuffed paper and plastic bags through the streets. These contain their worldly possessions but what are these "valuables"? Rags, scraps of paper, empty cans and bottles, and such. I recently had an experience in the subway with one of these sad folk. She was an elderly woman who was sitting opposite me in the train and appeared to be nervous and frightened even though there was no other indication that she had a mental illness. She held on to her four large plastic bags, one of which tumbled as the train came to a sudden stop. The bag's contents began to fall out, and I tried to help her only to be greeted by a string of curse words shrieked at me, including some I hadn't heard in many years; the little old lady apparently thought I was going to steal her imagined valuables, which were for the most part pieces of (fortunately) unused toilet paper.

However, not everyone carrying a load of packages and bags full of personal belongings is a discharged mental patient. Recently, much attention has been paid to the homeless who wander the streets looking for a place to sleep or trying to find a meal. They carry with them their life possessions for lack of a better place to leave them. In contrast to the psychotics, their possessions make sense; they include clothes, bedding and important papers and other items from their lives. So, while the behavior is the same and may be called hoarding in both cases, the real life value of one person's belongings is different from the absence of value of another's.

There is a difference that should be kept in mind between hoarding and collecting. Hoarding generally suggests an exceptional amount, an excess, while collecting sounds more logical and more generally understandable. This distinction is easy enough to put into words but more difficult to separate in practice. There are some serious collectors who we may privately feel are no better than junk dealers in terms of the lack of importance of what they hold on to so proudly. Values of objects are so subjective that it may truly be said that one man's hoarding is another man's collecting.

Since hoarding occurs in a variety of circumstances, in rich people and in poor, in the elderly, the middle aged and the young, in men and women, and in the insane and the mentally sound, and may include the accumulation of money, art objects, food, real life valuables and nonsensical objects, the meaning of the practice may vary from one person to the next. I've mentioned some already but would like to discuss some of the other meanings that have come to my attention over the years although I have to admit that some cases defy my comprehension, even my wildest imaginings.

One of the easiest examples to understand is the case of food hoarding in people who were deprived at earlier periods of their lives, such as survivors of wars or concentration camps, or those who grew up in abject poverty. They may be comfortably off today but they know what starvation is and it seems to be a very real future possibility to them based on their life experiences. They tend to have full cupboards and are eternally tempted by food in stores. They purchase far more than they can eat and, when you're invited to their homes for dinner, you better come with an empty stomach. Interestingly enough, not all of these food hoarders overeat themselves; indeed some are quite thin but they feel the need to have a large supply of food on hand. Conversely not everyone who overeats and becomes obese is a food hoarder although, of course, some are.

From a biological viewpoint, the idea of overconsumption of food when it's available, makes sense and, in fact, that's what fat is all about. Remember that, in the history of mankind, things were rarely consistent, and periods of good harvests and plentiful food were often followed by periods of poor crops and famine. Mother Nature, in her wisdom, provided us with a way of storing up extra calories when things were good so that we could dig into these resources when times were bad. Social standards of our culture train us these days to look upon fat as something bad and ugly without our being aware of its very valuable function in balancing out good times and bad. So people who hoard food and people who overeat are really carrying out a natural process in many instances. Of course, as we all know, this does get carried to extremes at times and becomes the total opposite of a healthy adjustment.

People who were born into bad times often have a tendency to hoard other things as well as food. For example, the United States went through a very serious economic depression in the 1930's with real shortages of food and material goods in this usually most prosperous of countries. People who were young at that time, a generation that is gradually disappearing from the scene, were taught not to throw things out because replacements were not always available. These people tended to save all kinds of things, not even throwing out string, paper wrappings or clothing with holes, sometimes accumulating collections of these apparently useless objects. A few years after the Depression, the United States entered into World War II, and there were new shortages. People were encouraged to eat sparingly and not waste metal goods, and to collect and turn in such items as rubber bands and tinfoil. Concern for saving such things became a fixed habit that stayed with many in this generation. Their children who were born into the later generation of planned obsolescence and throw-away merchandise can never understand their parents' saving habits. This sort of saving and accumulating still occurs all over the world in poorer societies but, just so long as the society remains poor, all generations do it because they continue to face the same shortages.

Even when the society is rich, there are individuals who follow the principle of "waste not, want not" or "never throw anything away", a philosophy of frugality that is implanted in these people by their parents. This may have something to do with the parents' early experiences in life or may reflect some magical idea that the world has only a limited amount of goods to provide, and you better be careful with what you have or you'll end up doing without. Using material goods sparingly might also indicate a certain religious orientation, one example being the Shaker sect and another being nuns or monks, who save so that they can give more to charity, since there is always someone worse off and needier.

People who are poor often hoard when they have a chance to acquire things, even things they may not need. This may sometimes be food but often consists of possessions which may have no great value but serve to make the statement, both to themselves and to others, that the owners are not destitute or needy. It is a matter of maintaining pride and self-confidence by saying, in effect, that they are still able to buy things and that their poverty is not all that profound. There is logic in what they own and hoard, even if others do not share their interest in these things.

It is not uncommon for middle class and even wealthy people to be preoccupied with having a nest egg, a significant sum of money to guarantee security in the future. There is a realistic basis for the need to have sufficient funds for future comfort and for any "rainy days" that one might encounter, but some get carried away by this need. Certainly, when we see people thinking day and night about the future and financial security, when we see them sacrificing comfort in the present, and when they are already wealthy, we know that this is a problem because the concern is excessive and unrealistic. The intensity with which it is done and the lack of any real need for the hoarding expose the fact that the supposedly accurate explanation, a secure future, is just a lot of rationalizing. In fact, the explanations that people so often give for their behavior, both in the area of hoarding and in other areas as well, are no more than socially acceptable excuses. Look, for example, at Langley Collyer's statement that he was keeping all those newspapers so that Homer could catch up with the world when he eventually regained his sight. That explanation may have played a part at the beginning but then became irrelevant as the mountains of newspapers began to tower, and the slightest amount of logic would indicate that the situation is irrational, maybe to the point of insanity.

Of course, for some people, the idea of a future financial crisis is more real than it is for others. Some people seem to carry around with them an expectation of disaster as a likelihood rather than as a possibility, and it is almost impossible to talk them out of it. Somehow, in their earliest experiences in life, economic disruption and chaos must have played a part to give them this conviction. They believe that any good times must inevitably lead to bad times and they will have to pay for any good luck they have.

I am reminded here of the Biblical story of Joseph interpreting Pharaoh's two dreams, one of seven fat cows being swallowed up by seven lean cows that came after them, and the other of the seven fat ears of corn being eaten by the seven thin ears that grew after them. Joseph interpreted these dreams as meaning that Egypt would have seven years of prosperity followed by seven years of want, and he recommended that the surplus of the seven good years be stored up so that it could be used to alleviate the hardship of the oncoming seven bad years. Pharaoh was so impressed by Joseph's interpretation that he turned over to him the management of the Egyptian economy for the period covered by the dreams. Both Joseph and Pharaoh believed in dreams having predictive value (not something everybody agrees on today), and they also were susceptible to the belief that good times were followed by bad times which is the history of humankind and the physiological basis for fat. In any event, the wisdom of hoarding the food was demonstrated, and Joseph went on to further successes after that.

It is impossible to overestimate the expectation of disaster that some people carry around with them, whether it is seen as the inevitable payoff for good events or whether it reflects a dismal view of life with trouble expected just around the corner. We saw this recently when, with Y2K imminent, lots of people were convinced that computers would crash and the world come to a halt; they stocked up on food, water, money and what have you in order to hunker down and survive the debacle. Others were persuaded that the year 2000 would bring the end of the world, some other catastrophe, or the second coming of Christ, and also prepared by hoarding various necessities. It would take a huge book to describe the mental apprehensions of these people and why they hoarded while others felt comfortable about the approaching new millennium.

In this regard, it's fascinating to see what people do when a weather emergency is predicted. Some run out immediately to the supermarket to stock up on every possible food item they can think of so they won't have to forego anything during the crisis. Others never even think of doing that but just settle for what they have at home, figuring they'll manage until the crisis is past. While the reality is that there may indeed be temporary shortages of food, there's obviously a different psychology in those who hoard food compared with those who just take the matter as it comes.

I have already alluded to the fact that some poor people accumulate things as a denial of their poverty but make no mistake! Accumulation as a denial of poverty is done by wealthy people with a slightly altered purpose, to demonstrate just how wealthy they are. In a society like ours where material goods are so highly valued, the possessor is treated with respect and is admired by others. Showing off how much one had was a characteristic behavior in the late years of the 19th century when great new wealth was appearing all over the United States. It even gave rise to the label of conspicuous consumption to describe the era with people spending vast sums just to prove they had money to throw away.

While we usually don't think of collecting art objects as hoarding, for some people it is just that, a way of achieving social success and prestige, a defense against the accusation of not having enough. Of course, people of all classes like to collect objects, not for any other reason than that they find them beautiful or they enjoy being part of history. This type of collecting may even be called a healthy activity, something that has little or no neurotic motivation attached. And not only does this give the collector pleasure throughout his or her life, but the collection may be passed on intact in its beauty to others, giving the original collector a feeling of transcending death, a sort of immortality.

There is much that relates to death in the idea of hoarding things. The hoarder often has the belief that he or she can put off the inevitable by keeping busy buying new objects and amassing a collection or by piling up money. Doing so can preoccupy someone to the exclusion of having concerns about day-to-day life, and to some people, provides reassurance that they can stay alive just so long as they're collecting. You can look at the possessions which will continue to exist after you are gone and fool yourself that you also can continue indefinitely. Gold does not tarnish or deteriorate but continues in its shining, beautiful form almost no matter what is done to it. Articles and collectibles also go on, in spite of the departure of the owner. If you have the chance to review the history of precious antiquities and paintings, you will learn that they have had many owners who have come and gone while the items go on forever. Indeed, some of the previous owners, who may have been prominent figures in their times, are known today more for having owned this particular work of art than for any historical activities they may have been involved in.

For others, collecting certain objects is a way of denying the death of a loved one. These objects may relate to the departed in several ways: he or she owned them, gave them as presents or are things that he or she would have liked. At times, this kind of perpetuation leads to setting aside a corner of a room dedicated to the dead person, a veritable shrine, the purpose of which is to keep that person's memory alive in some way. While other people may scoff at the futility of such an action and point out, very coldly, that dead is dead, for the mourner such a collection is of enormous emotional significance and support.

Sentiment also plays a part in collecting. Some objects may remind people of good times and good friends that they had, and they tend to hold on to them. Of course, if there are lots of good times and lots of good friends, the few trinkets that were present at the outset soon come to be a massive accumulation. When this is large enough, the meaning of each object sometimes gets lost because most of us can't keep track of the whos and whens of a large number of pieces. I've run into people who maintain written catalogues of every object they possess in such collections and, should memory fail, they can look it up to know just what it is that they should be reminded of. In the computer era, making up spread sheets on all the objects is much easier than maintaining a batch of index cards for this purpose, and there are those who do just that.

Mark was a collector of beer bottle labels. Now 35 years old, he grew up in an upper-middle class home where alcohol played an insignificant role. When he went to college, he discovered the pleasures of drinking beer on weekends with his buddies, and soon became a connoisseur of beers. After a while, he started seeking out new and different beers, including foreign imports and the products of microbreweries, and began to collect the labels as reminders of which beers he enjoyed and which beers he didn't. He is currently employed as an executive in a large corporation and has to travel a great deal, giving him the opportunity to try beers all over the world and to add a wider selection of labels to his collection. He has also begun trying to obtain the labels from breweries that have gone out of business. At last count, he had well over 1000 labels, and the collection was still growing. While Mark gets a kick out of his collection, it is not something he spends a great deal of money on or has an enormous emotional investment in. Other people I know save wine bottle corks or soda bottle tops in much the same way that Mark pursues his collecting.

Other objects are collected because they are believed to confer good luck on the owner. Superstitious people may hoard numerous such pieces in the hope that their luck will improve but even though this is very unlikely and they can never point to any luck that derived from the collection, they are not dissuaded and they continue to collect. They tend to see any reduction in their collections, any losses, as a disaster for bad luck is sure to follow. So, even if they don't acquire good luck, they avoid bad luck by their collecting.

Learning is another goal of collecting, especially in those two classics, stamp-collecting, also called philately, and coin-collecting, called numismatics, two forms of collecting that have earned themselves special names. Many a person has learned the geography of the world and much of its history from stamps, and many have learned history from collecting ancient and not so ancient coins. Jeffrey, a 50 year old psychiatrist, became an authority on German medieval history by collecting coins from the many small German states existing during that period and researching all the aristocrats portrayed on the coins.

When people have difficulty in interpersonal relationship and when they lack a strong sense of who they are, they may turn to collecting things as a way of defining themselves. Piling up money or objects is a way of taking on an identity and giving oneself a personality, a concept which might well be stated as follows: I am the owner of these objects, these objects are me, and I matter. We saw this phenomenon in the psychiatric inpatients who had hoarded collections of things that we recognize as objectively worthless, although not to them. However, possession of objects or money can confer only superficial identities on people; whatever identity they take from their collecting is very shaky and easily threatened. Losing some thing or not being able to buy a new addition to the collection may produce severe emotional consequences by throwing these people back on to the emptiness that they feel. When such a loss occurs, severe depression and even a psychotic reaction may follow, but here the psychosis is the result of the loss to the collection, not the reason for its formation.

Lots of people do the same thing, but to a lesser extent. They live their lives without really hoarding or collecting in a serious way, but may become interested in certain types of things which they pick up once in a while. After a time, they begin to feel more internal pressure to accumulate, particularly at periods of stress or change. There is something reassuring about having possessions when things get rough. One situation that may put pressure on someone is traveling since people often feel dislocated when they leave home, being far from familiar faces and places, often in a country where the language as well as the customs are strange. Focusing on shopping is often a good way to relieve the anxiety, and spending money certainly makes the locals friendlier and one's path easier to follow.

Money spent on collecting has become a serious commercial consideration and, in our consumer society, accumulating objects is encouraged for the push it gives to some components of the economy. I've encountered any number of people who avidly collect objects that may perhaps have some intrinsic value in terms of beauty or material but are manufactured strictly to be collected, that is they are produced only to be sold to collectors. To ensure large sales, there are likely to be major publicity campaigns. As a result of a deluge of mail, magazine and television advertisements, people begin to feel that they should buy a "piece of history". Just think of all the souvenirs that were sold commemorating the year 2000; most have no real value yet people snapped them up and most will be thrown out fairly soon. A few people will take them seriously and establish substantial collections. In this case, the psychological meaning of the buying and collecting is more that it reveals the susceptibility of the purchaser to the influence of advertisement. There is no question that people differ on the basis of how much they are influenced by such commercial activity. Some run away from the ads and some embrace what the ads are pushing, gladly parting with money in order to feel that they are participants in history.

And there are those who save up all sorts of gewgaws in the belief that they are a good investment. Some day, the thought goes, these pieces will be of great value even to the point that the holder will become rich. Rarely is this the case since most trinkets have little intrinsic worth and there are enough of them around to be almost worthless, except perhaps to another collector. Yet, on the other hand, such seemingly worthless things as comic books have appreciated in value greatly over the years and bring many times their original cost when put up for sale, not millions of dollars but real money anyway. Genuine art tends to increase in value consistently but one has to have some expertise as well as luck in knowing what to choose and when. Most of those who collect with the idea of making a good return on their money are disappointed in the long run. Of course, if they stick around for maybe a hundred years, these things will have become antiques in their own right and will have acquired some value.

Not all cases of hoarding can be attributed to major psychological causes or can be interpreted as indicating personality problems. In our busy world, with piles of junk mail arriving every day, thick newspapers that you can't read through (and, therefore, put aside to read at a future date), beautiful magazines that you just can't discard, there may not be enough time to manage the material right away. These things pile up and all of a sudden, you have a huge collection of what can now be classified as trash. The higher the pile, the harder it is to clean it up. The mess is attributable to lack of time and not to any hoarding instinct. So, your home or apartment may start to resemble the Collyer Brothers' house but the reasons are different. Fortunately our computers can swallow huge amounts of material without developing indigestion.

In older age, as one slows down, there is a greater likelihood of things piling up and it's not a question of having enough time to clear it out. More probable is the fact that one lacks the energy and enthusiasm to process things and they, therefore, accumulate. There is also, as one approaches even older age, a lack of ability to go through things. The intellectual processes may slow down and become faulty, and one may lose awareness of the significance of things. On the other hand, some aged people turn, as their memories begin to fade, to amassing objects, sometimes of no value, as their memories begin to go, as a way of reasserting their identity and stating that they still are perfectly functional. Many an older person focuses on money to do this but this cannot be equated with miserliness even if the counting of money occurs in both cases.

One example of such a situation was Martha, an 85 year old widow who was brought by her family for a psychiatric consultation. She had been raised in a working class family and married a man who made a comfortable income. Throughout her life, she was economical in her spending but not a penny-pincher. As a widow, she had an adequate income and had no monetary concerns. What bothered her family was that Martha had taken to sitting at her kitchen table and counting her change (which she avidly accumulated) for hours on end. She could not explain why she did this but also kept written records of how many pennies, nickels, dimes and quarters she had. If her repeated counting produced any inconsistent results, she became highly anxious and tearful. On psychiatric examination, it was apparent that Martha had serious memory deficits and was only approximately aware of the date, both of these being classic signs of Alzheimer's Disease which was clearly the diagnosis. It was easy to conclude that Martha made up for her failing intellectual powers by losing herself in something as concrete as money. However, when she couldn't figure something out, she became extraordinarily upset almost as if she had a dim awareness of what was happening to her.

And there is a reverse phenomenon that we see in a small minority of people. They want to simplify their lives, especially as they get older. They systematically do not hoard or accumulate things but rigorously give things away. They keep their possessions under control. Entering their homes, the visitor may be struck by the spareness of the furnishings and the absence of paper piles. Such behavior goes a long way in raising questions about the concept of an acquisitive instinct unless one believes that the instinct does really exist and can be controlled by an act of will. There are also a few who make a point of giving away or even throwing out anything that might tip people off, after they have died, to anything personal in their lives; they just can't tolerate the thought that others will be poking around in their private possessions.

I've gone this far in this chapter without discussing to any great extent miserliness which is the subject with which I opened or, for that matter, stinginess which is sort of a junior version of miserliness. Stinginess is almost the opposite of collecting or hoarding and simply means that that person just does not want to spend money and always looks for bargains; he or she is not willing to spend money for anything unless sure that it is worth much more than the price asked, and that money can be made off it fairly soon. If someone is stingy enough, he or she may eventually reach the point where collecting money becomes an object unto itself, a purpose in living, again not for what it can buy but for the sheer pleasure of having it. Some of the motives for such behavior have been discussed but, to be perfectly honest, I don't understand all the reasons why people are willing to place such a high premium on the accumulation of nothing more than cold, cold cash without using it for something else that gives them pleasure.

# 8

# *Giving it Away*

One of the most interesting interactions between psychology and money is in philanthropy which is defined in Webster's Third New International Dictionary as "goodwill towards one's fellows, especially as expressed through active efforts to promote human welfare, an act or instance of deliberative generosity, a contribution made in a spirit of humanitarianism". There is no mention in that definition of how large the contribution must be to merit the term philanthropy as distinct from charity. Charity is something almost all of us participate in; the difference between it and philanthropy is one of degree with the word "philanthropy" suggesting very large amounts and charity much smaller ones. The more money involved, the greater the amount of interest it evokes in people and, very often, the more complications it entails.

While the golden age of philanthropy began, at least here in the United States, after the Civil War and continues up to the present, giving large donations to cultural, religious and social causes was certainly not unknown earlier in history. The Bible urges us to give to others to help them and preferably to give in secret so that the giver and the recipient are both unknown. An examination of ancient history reveals that wealthy people and government officials established substantial libraries, built enduring temples of architectural splendor and provided some health care for their populaces, even if the health care was dubious by modern standards. With the onset of the Dark Ages, after the fall of the Roman Empire, economies plummeted; money was less plentiful and there was a reduction, if not a total disappearance, of anything that could be called philanthropy. In the early Middle Ages, much of the work now done by philanthropists was taken over by the Catholic Church (I'm speaking in terms of European history here) including the establishment of hospitals and poorhouses, the construction of beautiful churches and other buildings of a religious nature, the collecting of art and the founding of universities. During the Renaissance, there was more money in circulation and more amassing of wealth not only by princes but also by the upcoming class of bankers and businessmen. Some of them gave from their wealth to the public welfare although most of those who collected art did so for their own enjoyment and prestige. More modern times, but still prior to the Civil War, saw the endowment of institutions such as the Smithsonian in Washington, Harvard University and other universities in the East and Midwest, and the founding of public museums, hospitals and arts organizations by people who wanted to better the world.

The explosion of philanthropy after the Civil War in the United States reflected the sudden massive accumulation of wealth as the country industrialized and railroads were laid down. A new generation of millionaires and multimillionaires appeared on the scene. Some of these men spent their huge fortunes on massive demonstrations of wealth and conspicuous consumption to show the world just how rich they were and some of them devoted their wealth to helping others and to endowing cultural, religious and educational institutions; some had enough to do both. Most of our finest museums, libraries and large scientific institutes derive from the generosity of these late nineteenth century nabobs. Andrew Carnegie, whose gifts to New York City and to Pittsburgh were legion but were only a part of what he gave away, is quoted as saying "the man who dies rich, dies disgraced" and "the amassing of wealth is one of the worst species of idolatry"; he managed to give away 90% of his fortune. And John D. Rockefeller, Sr., another contributor of vast extent to causes which have enhanced the daily lives of millions even to this day, after devoting his early years to the acquisition of money, spent his later years, giving it away or at least giving away a substantial part of his fortune.

Although cynics have criticized the motivations of these philanthropists in endowing charities, a case could be made for pure altruism on the part of both men. And there are many other examples of wealthy people who gave truly spectacular gifts in wondrous acts of generosity. One of the purest examples of such giving is that of the Havemeyers, Henry Osborne, the possessor of a huge sugar refining fortune, and his wife, Louisine. They spent their vacations around the turn of the nineteenth century visiting Paris, as did many other Americans, but they went to buy quantities of exquisite Impressionist paintings. They loved their paintings and experienced delight in their possession. When the time came for the widowed Louisine to decide what to do with their treasures, she bequeathed them to New York City's Metropolitan Museum of Art in 1929 so that others could forever share her and her husband's pleasure in these nearly one hundred spectacularly beautiful paintings.

This is just one example of philanthropy that can be matched by other contributions of art to museums and galleries across the United States: Mrs. Potter Palmer's gift of Impressionist paintings to the Art Institute of Chicago; the Cone Sisters' legacy of Matisse and other Post-Impressionist paintings to the Baltimore Museum of Art; the Andrew Mellon endowment of the National Gallery of Art in Washington with 369 old master paintings, 175 American paintings and twenty-five statues <u>and</u> the money to build and maintain a museum; as well as the later gift by his son Paul of a large number of British paintings to Yale University in addition to yet more paintings to the National Gallery of Art. Philanthropy in the Mellon family appears to be a family tradition. Likewise in the Havemeyer family with Henry and Louisine's daughter, Electra Havemeyer Webb, establishing along with her husband James Watson Webb (a scion of the Vanderbilt family, also outstanding philanthropic givers) a splendid museum of American folk art in Vermont with a large collection of cigar store Indians. These are but a few examples of the phenomenon of altruistic giving around the country.

Currently, such philanthropy continues unabated, and is not limited to paintings but includes furnishings, jewelry, sculpture and antiquities, to mention only those objects that are represented in museums. In addition, there are ongoing contributions to hospitals, to universities, to research institutes, to ballet and music organizations, and to social welfare and religious establishments.

Why would anyone want to give things away, reduce one's own financial worth, deprive one's heirs? There are many answers to these questions and the fact that there might be tax advantages in today's world is probably the least important one of all although it certainly may play a part. One of the answers is altruism but what is that and where does it come from? On the one hand, we are told that, in this cold cruel world, everybody has a selfish gene, which forces them to do only those things that enhance themselves or their descendants, to look after themselves and the hell with everyone else. On the other hand, all of us or at least most of us want to be helpful to others; we enjoy it when people stop and ask us for directions and we try to make sure that they get where they want to go. Is this helpfulness or unselfishness something that is also inherent in our genetic makeup, is there an altruistic gene, something that contributes to our individual benefit through advancing human happiness in general? Or is it something we learn as we go along, taking it in as we do other moral and ethical lessons? The answer to the question of what altruism is all about remains controversial.

What are some other reasons for giving things away? In some cases, people feel a sense of responsibility to others; quite simply, they believe that they have been given privileged positions in the world and, as part of that, it is only right that they share what they have with others, or at least some portion of it. As the Have-meyers did, they want to share the good things that they have enjoyed with as many others as possible. A large number of people give out of religious convictions, following the injunction of the Good Book to give to others who are less fortunate, to improve their difficult lives. Others want the collections on which they spent their time, money and love to continue intact, to give pleasure to others and to keep the collectors' names alive for years and generations to come, even though they are no longer alive to see it.

And then there are the tax benefits; occasionally the law makes it cheaper to give than not to give because of the complicated arithmetic involved in figuring out taxes. This is especially true when someone dies and leaves a substantial estate with a lot of valuable art objects. If the heirs receive the art, they must pay taxes on its estimated value, sometimes leaving them cash poor or requiring that they sell off half or more of the art to keep what's left. It makes more sense for a collector to leave everything to a foundation or to a museum and spare the heirs the problem. Another wrinkle in our modern high-crime times is that the high cost of providing security for a large collection of art might be prohibitive for heirs and is more easily absorbed in a museum budget.

There are also other factors in play that contribute to giving to charity. Virtually everyone I know gives to charities, maybe not a tenth of their income as in the old days and not necessarily big bucks, but something, and a study of the motivations involved in making these smaller contribution may illuminate some of the questions that arise with philanthropy where the contributions are substantial. When any of us gives to a charity, we do so because we believe that the cause is a good one and is something that we want to see carried out further. We may even become emotionally attached to certain charities over the years and feel especially close to their goals while others, equally valid, don't move us at all. We may like the people involved in the charity, we may enjoy the social functions or we may feel that it will help people we know and love.

And then there are a whole lot of other reasons that people give which have a somewhat more negative motivation. For example, we may place a desk between office and sponsored charities because our bosses want us to; we don't want to run the risk of offending them and suffering the consequences of being labeled stingy, selfish and uncooperative, spoilers of office-related activities by our co-workers. Here the giving is almost out of our hands although we can theoretically refuse. At other times, we give because we want others to think of us as generous, openhearted and openhanded people of status and wealth. And sometimes we give because the charity and its employees make us feel guilty; when they know how to make us feel this way, it means that they are using what is obviously a good technique for increasing the take.

There are also times when the charity gives us a good deal financially, enticing us with some benefit or reward that we want, something given in return for the gift of our money and our time. And sometimes it's good for our own business success to give and be known as a person with generous instincts; this not only impresses people who like this particular charity but others who like other charities as well, and even people who don't care about charity at all may come away with a better impression of us. And one should never dismiss the tax benefits of making charitable contributions. Even though we don't wind up with higher incomes, we do get credit for what we give and, in a sense, giving costs less than at first appears. It's also claimed that giving to charities is good for one's health, both physical and mental, and prolongs life into the bargain. That's something that is claimed by some people who run charities but, as a psychiatrist, I would have to see some sort of proof before I could testify that this is so.

All of these factors, both the altruistic ones and the more selfish ones, play their part in the simple act of giving to charity and all of them are also present in the more complicated act of philanthropy, charity on a much larger scale. This larger scale also means that any psychological factors present in simple charity become enormously more potent in philanthropy and, here is the difference, the size of the gift endows the giver with power.

This power is present in the relationship of the giver to the charity or cause, and may be expressed in a variety of ways. It obviously can be used in a purely beneficial way but may be used in a variety of not so socially beneficial ways. When the gift is small, for the most part, it does not give the donor any power over anyone and is usually a simple contribution to advance the goals of the charity.

One factor that plays a part, a significant one in philanthropy, is something called reaction formation. This is one of a number of mental mechanisms, processes our minds use to resolve problems and prevent or reduce stress. With reaction formation, someone has committed some wrong and ends up feeling guilty about it. In an effort to wash away the guilt, he does something good and this is the reaction against the bad, in a way an effort to undo it. Someone who had, let us say, committed injustice or hurt people by a mad and cruel climb to riches, would use some of those riches, not necessarily to help the original victims, but to benefit all mankind. It is a socially acceptable way of doing penance without ever having to state the crime or who got hurt. Not only would the guilt be cleansed but the philanthropist would emerge in a heroic light as a person of high moral values and warmth of interest in the welfare of others. He would be acknowledged as a fine human being.

One example of probable reaction formation that strikes people today as pretty funny is the British Prime Minister who almost singlehandedly presided over the latter half of the nineteenth century in Parliament. Those were the days of Queen Victoria with highly proper morals and very righteous and puritanical behavior. Well, Mr. William Ewart Gladstone was interested in the welfare of prostitutes and spent much of his non-working time searching out ladies of the night whom he attempted to help and to correct. There were no accusations made against him of improper behavior in his charitable works but, even in his own time, people smirked about these endeavors. In our own more cynical and psychologically oriented times, we might wonder why reforming prostitutes became such a strong interest on his part and we might talk about his having repressed his sexual impulses which then found an indirect and socially constructive outlet.

As I mentioned, after the Civil War, there was an enormous increase in the number of huge fortunes in this country. Suddenly, people who had previously had little money accumulated massive amounts of it and the process of acquisition may well have been cut-throat. Many of these men of extraordinary wealth, some of whom were called robber barons, became significant philanthropists, and the concept of giving money to "clean up one's act" became part of our national heritage. Although the standard psychological theories have it that these men were atoning for past misdeeds, there is no way to prove this. All we can do is speculate about their motives.

I have already referred to Andrew Carnegie, citing him as a man who was strongly committed to making large charitable donations. His life story casts light on some of the issues raised by the concept of philanthropy. He was born in Scotland in 1835, the son of an idealistic and financially comfortable master-weaver father and a tough-minded mother who saw life as a hard existence, an ongoing struggle for survival. The Industrial Revolution crippled his father's business and the family came to the United States and settled in Pittsburgh in 1848 when Andrew was 13. He went to work in a factory along with his father who had difficulty working in this job and who eventually dropped out to return to individual hand-weaving and peddling. Andrew, who had little formal education, benefitted from the generosity of a local man of means, Colonel John Anderson, who opened his library to poor children. He gradually rose from factory worker to telegraph operator to personal secretary to Thomas Scott of the Pennsylvania Railroad and then to superintendent of a division of the railroad.

As he went along, Andrew acquired financial interests in the Pullman Car Company and in a telegraph company that was absorbed by Western Union while he also invested in iron and steel manufacturing. By 1868, when he was 33, he was already quite a wealthy man and wrote that he wanted to spend his surplus funds for benevolent causes. He continued to develop his various financial interests and amassed money left and right. Unfortunately for his reputation, he became involved, along with Henry Clay Frick (also a major philanthropist and the man who established the Frick Museum in New York City) in the Homestead strike. This was one of the earliest strikes and one of the milestones in the development of the labor movement in the United States. As a result of his strike breaking and a bloody battle between striking workers and Pinkerton agents, Carnegie was called "the arch-hypocrite of the age", and his philanthropies were sneered at as an effort to restore his reputation after the deaths in the Homestead strike. In spite of all criticism, he followed his earlier plans and continued to give enormously and out of personal conviction. Altogether, he gave money to establish almost 2000 libraries in the United States, Britain and Canada, gave thousands of pipe organs to churches, set up pension funds for his workers, endowed Carnegie Hall in New York City, Carnegie University in Pittsburgh and the Carnegie Endowment for International Peace in the Netherlands, and much, much more. Yet, no matter what he gave and no matter how earnest he was in giving, Carnegie, who was incidentally a friend of William Ewart Gladstone, was constantly criticized and had his motives impugned because of the blood spilled at Homestead, Pennsylvania.

Carnegie's story reveals that he was influenced by both parents, on the one hand by his mother's toughness in her attitude towards life and the need to get ahead, and, on the other hand, by his father's idealism about bettering the lot of the human race. He himself benefitted from

Colonel Anderson's kindness in allowing him to use his library; this could explain why one of Carnegie's major contributions was helping to establish free libraries for poor people to use. In addition, the commitment to charitable giving was something that he experienced and acted upon from early in his adult life, and not something that he began later on in life as a conspicuous effort to restore his good name. Yet, no matter what he accomplished, he was never able to overcome the accusations against him and he was condemned to represent in the public mind someone evil who was trying to atone for his past sins rather than being recognized and thanked as a true benefactor.

Even in our own times, we see major contributors to charity being accused of trying to assuage their guilt by giving. One example is Michael R. Milken who was considered a Wall Street equivalent of a robber baron and who was ultimately jailed for security fraud in the early 1990's. He established, long before his legal problems began, a family foundation which has given away over 750 million dollars, mostly to medical research and to youth programs, over the last twenty years. Although he has been criticized as giving only in order to restore his soiled reputation, it does appear that his giving meets a personal altruistic motivation for which he does not get enough credit. There are also gradually accumulating numbers of instances of large charitable contributions made by, for example, the new computer billionaires where there is little or no occasion for guilt or the need to atone, but a very sincere wish to help the needy, prompted perhaps by social pressure to be humanistic and to give away some of their incredible wealth.

The social factor involved in making huge contributions cannot be underestimated. In our society, there is a distinct hierarchy with old money being at the top. The new rich, though their financial value may far exceed that of old established families, do not always find acceptance in these highest social circles. Indeed, a flat-out attempt to gain social standing often results in dismal failure. Giving philanthropically, either large amounts of money to certain causes or spending time on boards, breaks down the barriers and allows entry to the newcomers. Anyone who reads the society pages in the newspapers becomes aware pretty quickly how giving spectacularly to certain "in" causes leads to one's being included on these pages. A jaundiced viewer may say that acceptance in high society is not such a wonderful thing, certainly nothing to struggle for; nevertheless, it remains a frequent goal for the newly rich.

In addition to helping the philanthropist rise to a new social sphere, giving large amounts results in power, power over the organization and power over the staff to which one gives. The larger the contribution, the greater the power. There are even times when the amount given is so great that it keeps the charity going and keeps the staff employed. Obviously the philanthropist has power and may try to use it in whatever way gives him satisfaction. That's where the psychological needs of the donor come into the picture.

For some, the satisfaction is simply helping a good cause, one that he believes in or has come to admire. In fact, that may be there no matter what other goals are present. Another frequent and more problematic aim of the donor may be to influence the goals and direction of the cause. For example, a needy arts organization accepts a large donation from a wealthy individual. The usual policy in such cases is to honor the giver with a seat on the board of directors of the organization. We then have a situation where a person with only an amateur's knowledge of the specific art is now in a potentially decision-making role on the board and may actually not only influence but determine policy including the choice of repertory, the acquisition or rejection of a painting or the planning for future development. The officers of the organization, knowledgeable professionals in their own field, have to cede at least to some extent the right to make decisions, and have to overlook their own hard earned knowledge and wisdom to accommodate the wishes of the donor. After all, money talks and, in this case, gives the donor a power beyond his real knowledge. This kind of control of artistic policy is not limited to cases where the donor is on the board of directors although that is a more dramatic illustration of the problem. Sometimes, all the giver has to do is make a few phone calls indicating his wishes to produce the action he wants.

One unappreciated aspect of this situation is that the donor does not see himself as an amateur but rather as an untutored but extremely astute person with an inborn, instinctive appreciation of the arts. There is a great deal of ego gratification in no longer regarding oneself merely as an expert in acquiring money or inheriting it or marrying it, but seeing oneself as a natural expert, a person whose appreciation of the arts has led to widespread admiration and recognition by the arts community. In such cases, when one's self esteem is involved to this degree, it is a great and often unwinnable challenge to the real artists in the situation to do as they see fit and yet keep the donation.

Not only does the donor influence the direction that the cultural organization takes; there may even be efforts to determine the hiring practices and casting assignments of, for example, a theater, music or ballet company. These are fields where performers must undergo years of training in addition to having significant natural inborn talents, and the hiring should be done by experts who can appreciate the levels of technique and interpretive skills the performers have achieved. A wealthy donor, particularly someone on the board of directors, may have his own ideas about what excellence in the field is and may force the company to hire his favorites, no matter what their skills. If the talents of these favorites are not so great or if their charms are obvious only to the donor, the quality of the company will suffer. Thus, the charitable contribution of the philanthropist may have the opposite effect of what philanthropy is supposed to be about; it may result in a lowering of quality rather than improving it.

Another way that the donor may dilute the arts product is to use the organization as an employment bureau for friends and family members. The donor may promote one of his own for a job for which that person has no training. The work may be poorly done but it may inflate the ego of the so-called worker or sound good at a cocktail party to talk about having such a position. Some of these relatives may make an honest and sincere effort to do the job and do it well, but some others may just drop in once in a while and smile. It's very hard for the organization to criticize this individual, let alone fire him or her, and the problem often results in this person being simply ignored. This solution does not invariably succeed since feelings may be hurt and a lot of time and effort may be required to smooth over the situation and the possible loss of funding by an insulted donor.

Philanthropists may also plug their own favorite painters and paintings. While galleries and museums resist this and try to maintain high standards, they are often faced with the decision of just how much to relax them to accommodate a donor. You may have noticed, as you walk through a museum, paintings that are labeled "workshop of", "school of", "attributed to" or "from the circle of". Many of these were given by large donors who believed them to be painted by the great artist who is named after the word "of" or "to". Sometimes, the museum knows well enough that the paintings were in fact not painted by the artist in question but the staff is afraid to reject them or question their attribution for fear of alienating the donor who might not then contribute some more outstanding paintings. Initially, such paintings are declared to be by the great artists but, with the passing of years and the passing of the donors, they are reclassified more correctly.

Sometimes the donor expects benefits from the charity besides being admired and having his artistic wishes followed that are not part of the original deal. This occurs particularly in the performing arts and especially in those fields that emphasize beauty in the performing artist as in ballet. Many a donor has expected and even demanded sexual benefits from performers. Throughout this chapter, I have used he and him to characterize donors because most large donors happen to be men (with wives listed only secondarily in their capacity as Mrs.) and relatively few are women. Unfortunately, the idea of trying to obtain sexual benefits applies to both sexes. For the sex-minded contributor, there should be a realization that the performing artist is neither a prostitute nor a sexually promiscuous creature ready to supply love and sex but instead a serious and hard-working professional who takes his or her work seriously.

There are times when the issue is not one of having sex but of having a friend. A lonely donor in search of companionship may attempt to get close to either a recipient or a fund raiser; these people are concerned about obtaining the gift and are consistently polite and usually available to talk to or meet with the donor. Their hope is that this will aid in the gift-giving process but it may be used by the potential donor for personal contact with the actual donation being constantly postponed. At some point, the donor's demand may be too intrusive or the recipient/fund raiser may not be available and a crisis arises. The so-called friendship with its different meanings to the two parties involved is disrupted and it's goodbye to the donation.

The contributor, in addition to feeling very wise and very perceptive in his appreciation of art, also gets treated to a variety of other benefits such as being wined and dined, and socializing with the great names of the arts and other charitable endeavors. For someone who enjoys name-dropping, this is an almost irresistible treat. Speaking of names, one of the greatest distinctions awarded to the biggest givers is having something named after him or her. Recent years have seen the growth of this means of honoring donors and we now see buildings, rooms and even seats in theaters named after contributors. This perpetuates the tribute to the donor for decades and certainly publicizes the gift for all the world to see. Shades of the Bible telling us to give in secret! Just imagine yourself entering a hospital named after yourself! It may not change the treatment one jot but it sure must feel good. But this method of honoring the donor doesn't always achieve his goals for renown because, to the ordinary man in the street, the hospital usually continues to be known by its original name and not by the newly dubbed one. On the other hand, over a long period of time, the new name may come to replace the original one.

There are also contributors, both small and large, who prefer to keep their contributions anonymous, approximately one in three hundred contributors. Some are motivated by the Biblical injunctions to give in private so as not to obtain social benefit and credit, and so as not to embarrass the recipients. Others, though, prefer the anonymity for fear that, once they are known as serious contributors, they will be deluged with additional requests to give, to the point that it becomes harassment. All of us who have given to charity only to see the mail bring ever-increasing requests, especially at holiday times, can surely sympathize with this position.

One interesting example of a possible philanthropist was George, a 40 year old man suffering from depression related to his difficulty connecting with other people. He was the only child of highly emotional, unhappy parents. After finishing college, he left his home in the Midwest and came to New York where he buried himself in his work on Wall Street. Fifteen years later, he had amassed approximately one hundred million dollars. He continued to play the market with half this amount, and the other half was invested in tax free municipal bonds. In the course of his psychiatric treatment, he repeatedly talked about establishing a memorial for his now deceased parents. He kept looking into various possibilities: universities, research institutes and other charities. Because of his wealth, he was welcomed with open arms whenever he approached an institution with a potential donation, and he was fussed over considerably. Two stipulations that he invariably made were that he wanted to get to know the recipients as human beings and that he wanted to understand the internal operations of the organization to make sure that his contribution would be well managed and productive. Consequently, he was invited to stay at private homes and had long and earnest conversations into the night with hopeful recipients who got into personal discussions with him. Repeatedly, he returned from these inspection visits reporting that he would not give to this institute or that one because the professor in one place had an unhappy marriage and was all mixed up, or the director of another place had a child who was drug addicted. After several such reports to me, it was apparent that George had no intention of turning over any money but was using his wealth to humble leading scientists and researchers (including several Nobel Prize winners) and to feel better at their expense.

Having the power of the purse over someone else, over a whole agency, obviously gave George a strong feeling of personal power. He could feel superior to all sorts of outstanding achievers whom, in a sense, he could control, and this progressed to contemptuous disdain of all these "inferiors", mere supplicants who were fighting to get a chunk of his fortune. For someone with a weak self-esteem, this kind of control is a tremendous ego builder. It allowed George to sneer at others and treat them like money obsessed individuals turning cartwheels just to get some money. He was certainly in the driver's seat in relation to all of them.

A variant of the theme seen in George was the case of Henrietta, a sixtyish year old widow who, several years before, along with her much older husband, contributed a significant number of fine modern paintings to a large museum. She constantly talked about the donation and prided herself on still possessing several very beautiful and expensive canvases. She occasionally carried one or two around with her, casually showing them off to people she wanted to put down or to impress with her wealth and taste. One can only imagine the anguish she imposed on the museum staff before she allowed any paintings to be transferred from her hands to theirs.

I've pointed out some of the problems that arise with individual philanthropy. What about corporate giving, is this problem free? One type of corporate giving at least seems to be so and that is corporate matching grants. Here the individual worker, usually a small giver, donates a sum which is matched by his or her employer. The amount that the individual gives is too small for the giver to engage in any of the games that we see in philanthropy and the corporation itself merely supports the employee and doesn't get involved in the politics and power moves that sometimes plague giving to charities. It's a different scenario when the corporation gives on its own. Here, there is usually a senior executive in charge of giving and, even while this person is not likely to have anything named after him, just after the corporation, he can throw the weight of the contribution around in the same ways as an individual donor. He may demand to be pursued, flattered, wined and dined, have his ego massaged, and he may make sexual, social and artistic demands on the organization.

Establishing a foundation is another form of philanthropic giving, but it does not always serve to eliminate the problems I have discussed. Many foundations remain in the hands of the donors and their families with virtually the whole board of directors being related to each other. These individuals dominate the gift-giving and can play the same kinds of games that are seen in individual philanthropy. In other foundations, there are directors and staff independent of the founding families but they, too, can play the same games, not letting go of the money until their personal needs and demands are met. There is yet another abuse seen in some family foundations where its endowments are decided in advance, such as to buy up at high prices the art works of a family member who then gets listed as a highly paid painter. There may well be a great deal of playacting with possible recipient charities over the possibility of the foundation making some serious donations, but these donations are more talked about than given.

So far, I've focused on the contributor's side of the giving relationship. But the philanthropist is only one of the players in philanthropy, albeit the one with the money and the resulting power. Also involved are the recipients of the gift whom I've talked about a bit insofar as they relate to the donors and the professional fund raisers who play their parts in charities, both large and small. Let's look at these two other participants and what they go through. Although there are two distinct roles, the people involved often have much in common. The director of a charitable institution usually has a background in the field in which the institution specializes. He or she has grown up in that field and has secondarily come to the role of administrator with responsibility for keeping the organization going financially. While this person may have some previous background in obtaining grants, his or her primary interest has been to do basic work in the field rather than to obtain funds. So fund raising and dealing with potential donors is a new job function and sometimes one that must be learned as one goes along. The professional fund raiser, sometimes called the developer, may have participated in the art or had some experience in the field, and then has gone on to the new job function of obtaining money.

The director has to have a basic overview of the organization and know how it functions, both in terms of staff and in terms of day-to-day operations. He or she has to see where the need lies for additional funds or other contributions, and has to be able to express these needs to donors so that there may be a good match. George, the eternal potential philanthropist, was right to demand that he be shown how the institution operates so that he would know where his money was going. He was even right to try to establish a personal relationship with the director of the institution to which he proposed giving his money. Where he was wrong was in trying to peek into the personal life of the director. His motivation was to humiliate the director, not to give money, and a wise, experienced director would have drawn the line before confiding his or her life history.

In addition, the director may have to do some wining and dining, offer some flattery and sometimes provide a friendly ear in dealing with potential donors. Indeed, the director may have to dig into his or her staff resources to put additional employees to work in cooperating with the donor's needs and demands. All of this has to be done within limits so that the staff doesn't resent the demands and suffer a drop in its morale. Again, the wise management of a knowledgeable and experienced director will distinguish between legitimate and inappropriate potential donor requests.

When one examines the job of the fund raiser, one finds that this person has usually had, in addition to training in the special areas dealt with by the charity, special training in how to raise money. This may start with taking courses in fund-raising in universities and progress throughout life by attending workshops and seminars, reading books and articles, studying case examples and learning on the job. Fund raisers usually stand out as enthusiastic true believers in the field they are selling and in their institution in particular. They have a commitment to the cause and see their role as being activators who channel good wishes and unclear intentions into contributions to help that cause. Initially, at the start of their careers, they have great respect for donors and their wishes but, as time goes on, they become somewhat more aware of the other motivations of donors, other that is than giving money to a good cause. This may make some cynical and bitter, and end in their belittling the donors and losing faith in the cause they had held so dear; some young women fund raisers indeed refer to themselves as "tarts for the arts", pointing out their resentment of their role and its abuse by others. Other experienced fund raisers are perhaps more realistic, recognizing that mixed motivations are part of being human.

Certain techniques are used by fund raisers to obtain money. First of all is a serious explanation of the goals and virtues of the organization. Next comes the manner of presentation. As in all charitable giving, it helps when the person who solicits the gift is attractive, well dressed and charming, even sexy, and manifests a sympathetic personal style. Admiring the donor for his wit and wisdom helps as well; in other words, flattery counts. Sometimes the fund raiser must serve as a personal psychotherapist, providing emotional support and comfort. Stimulating guilt to an extent also helps. One doesn't want to overdo this, though, because creating discomfort can make the donor run in the opposite direction. Also, the donor must be entertained and amused, whether this means being treated for dinner or given special privileges or taken to the latest Broadway show.

Speaking of keeping the donor amused and entertained, the word philanthropy is often associated with fashionable social activities. Indeed, some charities are known for the large social events that they sponsor to raise funds. These may include, among other activities, balls which have special themes; the ballroom is brilliantly decorated, the food and drink are the finest, the music very danceable, and everyone has a great time. The problem is that some of these events which cater to the contributor's wish to have fun and be amused, are very expensive to set up, sometimes too expensive. There was a scandal several years ago in New York City where two professional fund raisers were famous for the spectacular events that they arranged for charitable organizations. It suddenly became known that these events raised zero for the charities because all the money that was generated was used up in expenses, including high salaries for the fund raisers. So here too a line has to be drawn just how much money, as well as time and effort, is being consumed to produce how much benefit. Another quality that is absolutely incumbent on the fund raiser is absolute integrity, not always present, as this example demonstrates.

It has to be kept in mind that obtaining funds for charity is a business that has to be studied and that uses a variety of techniques which have been shown to be successful over the years. It may not seem right to look at a charity as a business operating like any other rather than as some kind of genteel calling that is above all such considerations. Yet, if a charity did not adopt these special techniques and methods of operation, including psychological manipulation, it would soon be out of business.

Philanthropy is a one hundred and fifty billion dollar (some say the amount is closer to two hundred billion; it's impossible to know exactly) a year industry in this country alone, making it one of the largest industries in the world. There is such a large number of charities (estimated at approximately 600,000 different organizations) with so many diverse goals, and so many givers that it is impossible to list all the possible motivations, positive and negative, that play their part. Suffice it to say, as the fund raiser realists do, human weaknesses as well as strengths are in evidence. Perhaps the best part is that, after several years, the good done by the contributions persists and even blossoms further while the negative motivations tend to fall by the wayside.

# 9

# *Playing Around with Money*

The very word gambling carries with it a shiver of excitement and almost immediately stirs up interest for a number of reasons. First, it communicates a sense of high living and danger, being associated with the Mafia (supposedly the "real" power behind the scenes), and through that connection, with crime, drugs and prostitution. In its hotel/casino form, there is also a connection to the entertainment industry. Second, it conveys the prospect of winning, gaining something with virtually no effort or expense. And third, there is a feeling of personal adventure in glamorous settings and a sense of living dangerously as you enter a situation where theoretically you could lose control and ruin your life and the lives of your loved ones.

The big-time gambling business has taken pains to clean up its reputation and to try to eliminate the reputed tie to organized crime. It has changed its name to a much less exciting one, the gaming industry and, as the number of cities and areas throughout the country where gambling is legal has multiplied, it has shifted its focus from only gambling to more family oriented entertainment. This is reflected not only in the wide variety of shows geared to children at such places as Las Vegas but also in increasing hotel room rates. Just so long as gambling was the top draw and brought in the big profits, the hotel/casino owners could afford to keep room rates low as an inducement to visitors. As gambling has dropped, not in popularity but in profitability (don't worry;

they're still not losing money), the emphasis on non-gambling activities has increased with profits having to be made from rooms, restaurants and entertainment.

As interesting as the economics of the gambling business may be, as well as its relationship to show biz and to crime, my primary concern in this chapter is to focus on the other two factors that make gambling so popular, the psychological ones. What is it that provides the tingle of excitement and what leads people to lose control and to get into serious trouble?

As with so many aspects of the intermeshing of money and human psychology, I have to differentiate its positive, harmless, pleasurable aspects from its negative, harmful ones. Two different people can walk into a casino, buy their chips, and go to work on the roulette table, hit the slots or head for the craps game. One has the power to stop anytime he or she wants, and the other just can't walk away. When you first look at them, their actions are superficially the same, yet the one who loses control can get into serious trouble. Making the distinction between healthy and sick involvements is more important in gambling than in almost any other interaction of money and psychology.

There are many kinds of gambling in terms of what it means to those who do it. For example, there's the casual gambler, someone who can do it, enjoy the atmosphere and the possibility of winning but, when he or she reaches a pre-set limit, moves on to something else, a show, dinner, a stroll or back to the room to sleep. Then there are the social gamblers, people who are with a group out for a day's recreation. They certainly have nothing against winning but are really there for the companionship and society of their friends, the activity happening to be gambling instead of watching home movies or gossiping. Prime examples of this are the widespread day trips from metropolitan centers on the East Coast to Atlantic City with round trip bus fares, lunch and some gambling chips all available for a nominal cost. Many senior citizens enjoy these excursions but only a few are serious gamblers. Not only is the trip fun in itself but it provides escape from boredom, loneliness, anxiety and other worries. The more serious gamblers among the seniors settle down at the slots with buckets of change, sometimes running two or three machines simultaneously and playing with fierce determination. This raises again the question of when does fun veer into a loss of control.

Professional gamblers are also a special group. These are people who gain their livelihood by gambling and who have pretty much studied every game there is for the odds of winning (and any tricks that they must know to increase the odds in their favor). They never get caught up in a passion for gambling which might make them lose their cool and commit mistakes. Rather, they are clear thinkers who, no matter how they may pretend to be involved, are calculating what is going on every minute. No danger of them losing control! There are also criminal gamblers who know the games well and who adjust the odds in their favor, essentially cheating the poor suckers who come along. One example of this are the shell-game players or three card monte men who hang out along main streets in big cities and shift the cards or the shells to capture the attention of the very young or the unsophisticated out-of-towners who think they can outwit them.

The one who gets into trouble, who makes overcommitments and who bets more than he can afford is the problem gambler. It is he who loses control, who gets into terrible financial straits, running into debt and borrowing from family and friends. The pathological gambler is even worse, and the difficulties that much greater. There doesn't seem to be a great difference between problem and pathological gamblers, except one of degree but a lot has been written to suggest that problem gamblers are easier to pull away from gambling while pathological gamblers are particularly resistant to efforts at treatment.

Gambling of course is not limited to the big-time casinos of Las Vegas and Atlantic City. Over the last several years, more and more cities and other locales have been offering the usual casino games, as have Indian reservations and offshore sites. So many cities have horse and dog races with on-site or off-track betting. Gambling doesn't require a trip to a special locale; it comes in so many forms and is so accessible that virtually all of us have indulged in it, probably many times over. It exists in the form of state lotteries, church bingo, office pools, card games, raffles and the numbers game. Generally, these are more benign forms of gambling since amounts are smaller, the environment is more ordinary, winnings are generally smaller and most people stay within limits. There are also types of gambling that don't look like gambling. It's a difficult question to answer whether playing the stock market is gambling or whether it's based on serious studying of potential growth and profit profiles of different companies; perhaps it's a bit of both, and the money stakes are enormous. Day trading, a form of playing the market, came sharply to the attention of the whole country several years ago when a day trader in Atlanta went berserk and shot a number of people. This form of stock trading is based on buying and selling rapidly, often on rumors and hunches; the potential for large profits is there but most traders lose big time. Certainly this is more like serious problem gambling than the regular stock market and the consequences may be devastating.

However, even benign gambling has given rise to the question of whether it can lead to progressively greater loss of control in susceptible individuals, with someone who starts out in a small way gradually going on to bigger and worse situations. It is this that many reformers feel is the real danger, and they rail at the greater permissiveness toward gambling that is evident once state governments go into the gambling business. They feel that a psychological climate is created which eventually leads downhill and endangers more than a few people.

Even in locales where gambling is not currently permitted, there are discussions about changing laws in order to allow it since it's a wonderful source of tax revenues and since it also helps to invigorate the economies of the regions where it is introduced. It also brings in money to charities which sponsor it. There's a contradiction here, in a way, since many religious groups condemn gambling while at the same time sponsoring bingo games and other games of chance, admittedly not the most dangerous forms of gambling, in order to raise funds for praiseworthy causes. Very few, except for passionate religious fundamentalists, are bothered by this contradiction.

Gambling has a long history in the human species and reports of it keep turning up in ancient records and in gambling paraphernalia discovered in archeological digs; indeed it is apparent that these paraphernalia have changed little over thousands of years and look very much like today's version of what are probably the same games. Gambling devices of one sort or another have been reported in Egyptian, Greek and Roman excavations, and also in digs into other ancient cultures. When you consider that not all gambling requires such special equipment, you realize that there must have been much more gambling that left no trace at all. The presence of gambling has also been confirmed in cultures on the Pacific Ocean islands, in the Arctic, in North and South America, in Asia and in Africa, literally everywhere. Gambling has also been the subject of much literary and artistic attention, appearing in paintings and books written in many languages. Indeed, it sometimes seems as if it's a requisite in every Russian novel where its ups and downs and influence over its victims is gone into in detail, almost invariably with tragic outcomes.

Obviously, such a widespread activity became a matter of interest to psychoanalysts (those who search into human behavior, looking for its sources in personal experience dating back to childhood) from early in the history of psychoanalysis, roughly the beginning of the twentieth century. Unfortunately, while the theories offered to explain this behavior are quite colorful, they don't seem to get to the root of the matter, at least not in terms that we would recognize in the twenty-first century. Since you may hear about or read such theories, I will review them and tell you, if it's not already obvious, what I don't like about them.

One early worker, in 1902, believed that the uncertainty of gambling was necessary to our species and that risk served as a balance to over-regulation. In other words, people in a structured, over-controlled environment needed some relief. After that, the theories became more and more complicated and less and less helpful to someone wanting to understand the subject; for example, gambling was stated to be a sexualized version of other strivings. Now that's one I just can't see.

Even Sigmund Freud got into the act, attempting to explain the gambling impulse felt by Fyodor Dostoyevsky, the great Russian novelist who wrote about it and was himself a practitioner, almost always on the losing end. Freud believed that Dostoyevsky's gambling had to do with his relationship with his father and that he needed to punish himself by losing in order that he could write. Freud was perhaps a better observer than a theoretician in this instance, his description of the compulsive gambler being something we can recognize today while his explanations would produce outright laughter in our current intellectual climate. For example, he saw gambling as a kind of masturbation, a concept that astonished me when I read it while, at the same time, he accurately described the irresistible temptation, the promises made to oneself to stop, the pleasure involved and the eventual guilt.

Other psychiatrists have compared gambling to the sexual act and others to a symbolic murder of the father every time one wins. Yet others have emphasized that the gambler is deliberately, but unconsciously, trying to hurt himself. Another theory is that the gambler (who is more often, but not always, a male) wants to be overwhelmed and assume a semi-feminine role; this theory is certainly hard to comprehend today when women are no longer seen as passive shrinking violets.

There are many more theories, the nature of the theory usually reflecting the state of contemporary theories in psychoanalysis; whatever ideas were advanced to explain human behavior in general were adapted to explain gambling as well. In the 1940's, the emphasis was on the state of excitement which was compared to sexual arousal and discharge patterns. Magical thinking, which I'll discuss in more detail later, and superstition were considered important as if thoughts could influence what are essentially chance outcomes. In the 50's, the theory that was current was that the gambler was a masochist who wanted to lose as a continuation of his belief that his parents were depriving him. In the 60's, it was stated that the gambler was unsuccessful in everything he touched and, therefore, he lived in fantasies. It was also affirmed that many gamblers had poor sex lives, both before they got into gambling and especially afterwards as their marital and romantic relations soured. Also in the 60's, the theory was proposed that gambling was an attempt to defend oneself against painful emotions, burying them in the excitement of the game.

Coming into more current times, gambling is seen as a bad habit (I certainly can't disagree with this part of it) reinforced by excitement and the positive experience of the occasional win. As with any habit, there is further reinforcement when there is a high frequency of wins, when there is ready availability of the activity, when there is only a short period between the bet and the payoff, when some real skill is involved, and when gambling is socially approved and acceptable.

Simple fantasy gratification is another reason why people gamble. It is nice to think, as you go through the daily grind, that you may suddenly win a lot of money and be able to change your whole life style; no more work or problems, just whatever pleasant activities you choose. In a sense, this is a constructive aspect of gambling that is seldom sufficiently appreciated, that it provides hope to lots of people who aspire to change but don't really feel too upset when it doesn't materialize. Think of all the people who play state lotto games; they know they have little chance of winning but that doesn't stop them from dreaming and, in this way, gambling provides a very gratifying relief from money worries.

Through all this is the question of whether or not gambling is really a disease or, as psychiatrists now label everything that ails you mentally, a disorder. And here, we can get into a mess of psychiatric and psychological jargon, justifying the word "psychobabble". While it would be impossible to call the casual gambler diseased, it is easy enough to apply a label to the guy who loses control and whose gambling gets out of hand. Initially, gambling was called an impulse disorder, meaning that one had an impulse which could not be controlled, something like addiction or sexual desires.

Other students of the psychology of gambling saw it as an obsessive disorder. There clearly is an obsessive-compulsive quality in the pathological gambler who thinks of it constantly, can't wait to get back to it, and feels driven by forces beyond his control to repeat it over and over again. However, even though these characteristics are present in the gambler, labeling it an obsessive disorder doesn't really help us to understand it or do something about it.

The same problem exists with calling the gambler a masochist. Sure, he's doing something that will hurt him in the long run. Yet he doesn't want to hurt himself; that's an accidental outcome of his actions and it doesn't seem to be his purpose. People often do things which result in adverse consequences for themselves but to be a masochist you have to really want to do yourself harm. Maybe, deep down, that's the purpose but it's so far down that we have to guess it's there and then we're talking more about our guesses and theories than about what the gambler himself is really feeling.

More to the point is calling gambling a depressive disorder but, here too, there's the same problem. Most gamblers don't appear depressed, certainly not in the usual way depression shows up. I've run into gamblers who are depressed underneath it all and use gambling as a way to provide excitement and stimulation to their lives. Saying that they're depressed is, however, a gross over-simplification.

Mania is the opposite of depression, a state of excessive cheer and activity with rapid speech, easy spending and ideas pouring out, falling over each other in rapid succession. People in this "high" state lack judgment and tend to overspend. Some of that sounds like gamblers but what really defines mania is the elated mood, the wild extravagance, the non-stop hyperactivity, things that are frequently seen in gamblers.

Let's look at the case of Jimmy who was an 18 year old when his mother brought him into treatment because he rarely left the house and seemed depressed; he was also doing poorly in school. The parents were hard- working Eastern European immigrants who suffered considerable marital strife but were both loving towards Jimmy. He had had few friends as he grew up but did fairly well in school. When he started college, he felt incapable of studying and told his parents he was intellectually subnormal. When I interviewed him, he came across as a chubby, slow-moving, carelessly dressed and groomed young man with an enormous amount of self-criticism. In spite of thinking quickly and having the ability to grasp new ideas rapidly, he was convinced of his intellectual inferiority, and said he was stupid and incompetent. I diagnosed him as having a major depression but he refused to take medication, the standard treatment, or to talk about himself, another standard treatment; he stopped coming to sessions, saying that there was nothing that could help him.

About one month later, he disappeared and was found two months afterwards to be living in Las Vegas. He did not wish to return to New York but his parents insisted, and he came back. When his mother brought him for a second consultation, he spoke rapidly and fluently, and talked about the wonderful time he was having in Las Vegas. He had gone there for a "break" and initially gambled a few dollars for entertainment but he had considerable success and soon bought a high prestige car and elegant clothes, also taking a room in an expensive hotel. He met a whole new crowd of people, had innumerable "friends" and was even thinking of marrying. Most striking was his changed appearance. He had lost weight, his hair was styled, his clothing colorful, and he exuded confidence in an almost aggressive manner. His speech was so fluent that it was hard to follow him and it was full of slang. He said he was happy this way and made fun of how he had behaved in the past. The diagnosis this time was mania (when this is superimposed on a depression, it indicates a condition referred to as bipolar since it hits both the highs and the lows of emotions). Again he refused to take medication, the standard treatment for mania. He came for follow-up on two occasions during his stay with his parents, gradually returning to his previous hang-dog state. He then ran away again and refused to return home ever again. When last heard of, he was back on his high, living the good life in Las Vegas and apparently making a financial success of gambling, at least for the time being.

Saying that Jimmy had a bipolar psychosis doesn't really help us to understand why he behaved the way he did or show the way to treat a reluctant patient. But his case does demonstrate how gambling provided a sort-of cure for his depression and lack of self confidence. What was particularly sad about his "cure" was that the odds were very much against it continuing for any length of time and, inevitably, in addition to his emotional problems, he would have some very serious financial ones as well.

No matter whether gambling is a diagnosis in its own right or rather a pattern of behavior indicating another diagnosis like an underlying depression, the fact is that it is a real problem, and it affects large numbers of people. It's impossible to know how many people might be regarded as either problem or pathological gamblers but it's been said that 2.8% of all Americans have a gambling problem while 1.4% of us are pathological gamblers. These are staggering numbers when you realize that there are approximately 320,000,000 Americans. It is perhaps for this reason that the American Psychiatric Association, in 1980, decided to give it the status of an official diagnosis complete with essential features and a list of diagnostic criteria. These criteria were further refined in 1988.

The essential features of pathological gambling are chronic and progressive failure to resist impulses to gamble, and gambling behavior that compromises, disrupts or damages personal, family or vocational pursuits. You get the picture; the severity has to be great enough to have some very serious influences on your life and the lives of those around you.

Spelling this out in more detail are the actual criteria for the diagnosis. Maladaptive gambling behavior as defined by frequent preoccupation with gambling or with obtaining money to gamble, frequent gambling of large amounts of money or over a longer period of time than intended (a loss of control), a need to increase the size or frequency of bets to achieve the desired excitement, restlessness or irritability if unable to gamble, repeated loss of money by gambling and returning another day to win back losses, repeated efforts to reduce or stop gambling, frequent gambling instead of meeting social or occupational obligations, sacrifice of some important social, occupational or recreational activity in order to gamble, and continuation of gambling despite inability to pay monetary debts, or despite other significant social, occupational or legal problems that the person knows to be exacerbated by gambling.

The personality or characterology of the pathological gambler is overconfident, very energetic, easily bored and a big spender, but also someone who shows signs of personal stress, anxiety or depression at times. Generally, the disorder begins in adolescence in males, later in females, and may lead to suicide attempts, alcoholism, drug taking and myriad problems with the law. Predisposing factors are reported to be loss of parents by death, separation, divorce or desertion before age 15, inappropriate parental discipline (absence, inconsistency or harshness), exposure to gambling activity as an adolescent and a high family value placed on material and financial symbols with a lack of family emphasis on saving, planning or budgeting.

These descriptions were devised to delineate a disease entity distinct from other entities, and were based on what was observed in large number of people who were gamblers. That does not mean that every gambler has every characteristic, just most of them.

Over the years, there has been a variety of treatments offered for gambling, obviously based on the prevailing theories about what gambling really means to the gambler. Before the appearance of psychoanalysis on the scene, gambling was not considered to be a psychological problem; in fact, the concept of psychological problems was a very foggy one indeed, and gamblers usually ended up rotting in debtors' prisons or killing themselves, one way or another. However, psychoanalysis offered some treatment possibilities, and there was a serious attempt to make some sense of the problem and tie it in with the gambler's underlying personality and early childhood experiences. Descriptions of gamblers and how they behaved were accurate but some of the theories advanced to explain why they did what they did left much to be desired. In any case, treatment was rarely successful.

As the fields of psychiatry and psychology progressed, newly discovered treatments were applied to the gambler even if there was no particular theory attached. For example, electroconvulsive theory, also known as shock treatment, was first thought up and applied in the 1930's. No one knew how it worked but it seemed to be useful in the treatment of depression. It was also tested in just about every other condition you can think of: schizophrenia, alcoholism, drug addiction, homosexuality and, of course, gambling. Being subject to such a procedure was a frightening experience and it may very well have scared a number of gamblers away from the tables just thinking that they might be subjected to it. But it didn't really work.

In the 1960's, the idea of seeing human behavior as habit patterns which developed over a period of time gained currency. The goal of treatment was to reverse the habit by doing things to a person that would break it, with some education about what was going on provided as well. Deconditioning is one such component of treatment, letting the person continue the behavior but accompanying what he does with an unpleasant stimulus time and time again. After a while, the patient (or victim, if you don't like this kind of treatment) begins to associate the habit with the unpleasant stimulus and ultimately rejects the habit in order to avoid the pain of the stimulus. Giving shock treatment is one form of deconditioning; pinching and giving nauseating medications are other forms of deconditioning. The problem was that, after a period of time away from treatment, the patient resumed gambling. Also, it must be said, many physicians resisted the idea of hurting someone, even if the long term goal was supposed to be good.

As we come into the 1980's, we enter the era of self-help. People with any number of conditions have organized groups based on the principles of Alcoholics Anonymous, admitting that they are personally powerless to change but must rely on the help of a higher power to help them change, and setting up a buddy system. They attend frequent meetings, confess to the gathered group their past offenses, and get lots of support. When they feel under extreme pressure to resume the unwanted behavior, they call their buddy who hears them out or even visits them to prevent them from doing it. This approach has been successful in drug addicts, sexual compulsives, and overeaters, as well as gamblers. However, it's not possible to say that Gamblers Anonymous has been very successful because the truth is that only a small number of people respond to these methods. Compared to some of the other treatments, it's better in terms of having some beneficial outcomes.

More often used today is a combination approach in which, if at all possible, people are hospitalized in centers specializing in the treatment of gamblers. They are locked away from gambling, participate in self-help groups which continue after discharge, and receive individual counseling concerning their personal problems. Sometimes, they receive medication if another condition susceptible to medication is discovered like, for example, if a depression is present.

These days, there is an attempt to find a biological cause and cure for all disorders of behavior and personality, including gambling. The possibility that someone might have an internal psychological problem tend to be discounted, and the statement is often made that, even if we can't show the biological cause at this point in our medical knowledge, we will soon find it. Once we find the cause in some distortion of chemistry in the brain, then the drug to fix it is only a short step behind. Gambling is one of the behaviors that has been investigated for a biological, chemical explanation but that explanation has so far proven elusive. Therefore, the medications that are used in the treatment of gambling are mainly antidepressants and anti-mania drugs, occasionally anti-anxiety drugs. However, even if they treat an underlying condition quite adequately, they usually don't eliminate the gambling.

Some gamblers stay in treatment long enough for a therapist to learn a great deal about them and gambling, and there are even a few who remain long enough to benefit from treatment. Based on careful consideration of other writers and on my own clinical experience in treating such people, I've been able to formulate a picture which is fairly consistent. To begin with, gamblers possess an enormous regard for money, even greater than most people in a society which reveres money and in which people try to get as much of it as possible. The difference is really a matter of degree, with gamblers truly believing that money will solve all problems and that happiness can only be achieved with lots of money. With them, the belief in money approaches the intensity of a religious conviction and it's overwhelming and pervasive, affecting virtually every area of life. If it's true that what separates the average person from a problem gambler is a matter of degree, then the question is raised whether, given the right set of circumstances, anybody could eventually become a pathological gambler.

Gamblers also have a feeling that life is basically a dull and lackluster existence and, without the excitement of gambling, it wouldn't be worth living. They just don't seem to get interested in a whole swarm of other activities and tend to see pleasure and success as coming exclusively from gambling. What really is lacking in them is an ability to get involved in these other things and without such involvement, life may indeed look boring. Gambling fills this void for them.

Adele had been a librarian before her retirement at age 65 on a small but adequate pension. She had never married and still lived in the house where she had looked after her parents until their deaths. She had difficulty making new friends and felt bored and useless since she had retired. A cousin suggested that the two of them go to Atlantic City for a day trip just to get away, and Adele found that playing the slots was more exciting than anything she had done in years. In a short while, she was going there on a four times a week basis, neglecting her home and losing more money than she could afford. Every time she told herself she ought to stop, she seemed to win a small pot and that kept her coming back. She liked the picture of herself, sitting at the machines, negotiating two or three at a time, and smoking and drinking, activities she had very rarely done in the past. It made her feel dangerous and exciting, sitting there, hiding her emotions behind a poker face. When her cousin forced her to go for counseling, she admitted that, without her trips to Atlantic City, she was just another old maid, but gambling gave her life meaning.

Another characteristic of gamblers is that they believe in magic. They think that, in spite of all the rules of logic and probability, they can win. They deny the significance of their losses and the trouble they get into. Somehow, somewhere, if they can only find the key, their luck will turn and they will be triumphant. I mentioned earlier in this chapter the concept of magical thinking without defining it but a definition is really in order since gamblers are guided by magical thinking and superstitions. Magical thinking is defined as a belief in unreality, in things that have nothing whatsoever to do with logic or reality. For example, many people count the number of acoustic tiles in a ceiling and tell themselves that an even number in a row predicts a lucky day, while an odd number predicts a bad one. While that thought may flash through your mind as you sit bored in an overlong conference and look up to the ceiling for relief, you would hardly conduct your life according to whether the count is odd or even. Reading one's horoscope on a daily basis also represents a form of magical thinking, but fortunately most of us do not organize our day around the recommendations that we read. Astrology and the meaning of signs of the Zodiac are other examples of magical thinking, but again most of us do not let such things guide us in our daily lives even when we find them to be interesting.

Superstitions are another example of magical thinking. You've all heard about not walking under an open ladder or not letting a black cat cross your path or not breaking a mirror. If you happen to do one of these things, the bad luck that is supposed to come your way can theoretically be reversed by throwing salt over your left shoulder. These are just a few of the many superstitions that prevail in our society. Every society has such superstitions and members of that society often seem to be afraid of strange things and do some even stranger ones to prevent the bad luck that they think that they have provoked.

Gamblers have many such superstitions and create many new ones as they go along, like playing only on a certain kind of machine, gambling only with certain croupiers, entering the casino through a special "good luck" door, and so on. It seems incredible that people can believe that how the cards turn up or the way the dice fall or where the roulette wheel will point can possibly have something to do with their having gone through a certain kind of ritual before playing. Further, it is even harder for a logical person to believe that someone will risk money depending on whether such conditions are met. Yet, like I said, they believe in magic.

Luck is a real thing, but it is entirely accidental. If someone wins a big lotto jackpot, he or she is lucky. But the luck happens, statistically at least, just that once, and while the winner shares with five million or so others, an equal chance in the next go-round, it's not very likely that lightning will strike twice in the same spot. The law of averages is always in operation and has more to do with the outcome than does luck. Yet, there are people who pride themselves on being lucky, having been gifted with this particular quality from birth onward. When they go to the casinos boasting about their luck, they're riding for a fall. I've heard it so many times. People win a few dollars at lotto and are convinced their luck is turning; they then spend twice as much the next time, using up their gains and really believing their first win will influence the second, another example of magical thinking.

Of course, it's nice to think that you're a lucky person. In the same way, it's nice to think that you're specially blessed and that God is going to give you a win. God rarely involves Himself in gambling and I've never heard it said that He blessed someone to win and I've never heard any religious authority making such a statement.

It's also nice to think that one has "good hands" and knows how to role the dice in a winning way, or has some other special skill that leads to winning. One of the most dangerous beliefs the pathological gambler has is that he can figure out the system by which, say, the roulette wheel turns, so that he can bet on the right numbers and make a killing. It's these people who watch the wheel eagerly for an hour or so before placing their bets.

Since the wheel's stops are random unless it's a corrupt casino, there is really no system for predicting, just blind luck, but go tell that to someone who wants to believe that his brain has figured out a winning pattern. Worst of all is that, when the so-called system doesn't work, instead of accepting that there is no such thing, the gambler goes on to try to figure out where he went wrong that time so that he can construct a better system for the next time.

Junior was 47 when he came to my attention. He came from a home where, after years of conflict, his parents finally negotiated a sort of truce and went their separate ways. Although Junior had been a fairly good student, he had little interest in his studies and barely made it through college, after which he studied accountancy and worked in this field for several years. He felt that he had more intellectual potential than his job required and searched around for other things to do, both as hobbies and as work. In the course of time, he discovered that he liked horses and began to read up on the subject which led him into the world of horse racing. After a couple of years of going regularly to the races, Junior felt that he had learned enough about horses to be able to pick winners, and he decided to quit his job and devote his energies full time to horse races believing that, with his knowledge, he could easily support himself by choosing winners. This conviction has stayed with him for well over a decade in spite of the fact that he can barely pay his rent and basic expenses, and has estranged himself from his large extended family of cousins who have all lent him money over the years. In fact, Junior is convinced that he is still learning about horses and, with his continuously growing expertise, his ambitions will soon bear fruit and he will be a rich man.

There are, of course, some types of gambling in which some skill on the part of the gambler may increase the odds a bit in his favor. For example, in blackjack, one may be able to follow the cards that have already hit the table and be approximately correct in the next throw, but it is still a matter of chance. In other card games, including poker and bridge, watching the cards and keeping track of the action may slant the odds a little more in one's favor.

However, what I'm talking about here is the gambler's need to feel special in some way, whether it be in luck or intelligence in developing a system, or having good hands or being blessed. This need to be special gets tied in with gambling methods and winning and we should stop for a minute to ask ourselves what kind of person needs to feel special. The answer is someone who feel less than adequate to begin with. It's a long story how people develop a sense of inadequacy and it's based on a variety of things: poor parental support, lots of criticism, failure in various life endeavors, having been or seemed defective in some way. And someone who feels this way about himself will undertake to rebuild an image to make up for the feelings of inadequacy, sometimes going in the other direction, trying to feel superior. Gambling is unfortunately the way some choose, unfortunate because it can never lead to success; the odds are against you. So, on top of all the other factors that contribute to feelings of inadequacy, add on the losses at the table and the defeat of the mental mechanisms that were used to build up an image. The gambler ends up back where he started, and in fact worse off.

Raymond was 35 at the time he came to my attention for treatment. He was born the seventh child in a lower-middle class home and never gained much attention from his hard-working and hard-drinking parents. His school performance was mediocre and he seemed to be eternally a follower in all his friendships, having no close friends but always being a hanger on in a larger group. When he finished high school, barely completing the requirements, he got a low level office job with little opportunity for advancement, and he plugged away at this for four years before getting married. He adored his wife and wanted to have children even though there would be financial problems. She realized that he was shy and lacked confidence, and she hoped that she could help him overcome these problems. Things moved along fairly well in the marriage but, with the birth of their third child, the shortage of money became an overwhelming problem and necessitated that Raymond's wife take on a job. He felt ashamed that he was not able to earn more money, particularly since he felt that he had more potential than he was using. Although he had never gambled before, he went along on an office excursion to a gambling resort and found himself caught up in a whole new world. He felt that he would no longer have to struggle on a daily basis just to earn a poor income but could use his intelligence to figure out a system and bring home buckets of money, more than enough to take care of his wife and children. Things didn't work out that way and he began to borrow money to tide him over until his system worked. It never did, and eventually his wife took the three children and left him. Even that didn't change his new style of life but it did add alcoholism to his problems.

When a therapist tries to work with a gambler to "cure" the disease, it's important at some point to make him see that he has these feelings of inadequacy, that he has difficulty getting involved in things around him, that he can't make a religion out of money and that there is no magical cure for his problems. But that's like asking him to be depressed and to give up his religion and his whole belief system which is probably one reason why most gamblers flee therapy. It's just too much to take.

My own treatment for gambling which I developed over a period of years is to use what is essentially a psychotherapeutic approach. I try not to follow any of the psychoanalytic formulations I have already described for two good reasons, they don't make sense to me and they're not very successful. The gambler is a tricky patient who, for one thing, usually doesn't come willingly to treatment. He is most often pressured by his family or may be forced to come by the court system. He may not even admit that he has a problem and he often establishes a pattern of lying to the therapist, something which makes treatment extremely difficult. Reluctant patients find may reasons to skip appointments and rarely have any interest in continuing. However, the one thing they cannot deny is that they are in trouble and have managed to get themselves into debt and create havoc in their families. Even then, they believe that the best cure for the problem is to go out and win the money back, and they're always casting fond glances in the direction of the tables.

The first step in working with a gambler is for the therapist to establish some rules for the treatment and to take the stand that gambling is a psychological problem with a psychological cure. Two of the rules are that sessions must be kept on a regular basis and that payment for services must also be regular. It might seem crass to raise the question of payment so early in treatment and so forcefully but the gambler has a tendency to gamble away every dollar including money allocated for the therapist's fees. Excuses are then made as in all other life situations. Eventually, this results in a contemptuous attitude towards anyone who swallows these excuses, and contempt is hardly a good attitude for a patient to feel towards a therapist.

It is important for the therapist to remain sympathetic to the problems experienced by the gambler but it is also important not to focus too much on the details of the gambling which may be very colorful and very interesting but are not relevant to the therapist's work. It is preferable to talk about problems in living beginning with those that result from gambling and moving on gradually to those that preceded the slippage into dangerous gambling. While doing this, a therapist should never depart from the stance that gambling is a problem that has to be overcome but should not come across as rigid or judgmental in taking this stance. Hopefully, the gambler eventually comes around to gain a more objective view of what gambling means to him, and with that awareness, develops greater control over his urges and sees more clearly his relationship to the world and how gambling has come to replace other areas of his life. He should also be made aware just what in his psyche prevents him from getting pleasure from the usual sources of gratification that are provided by society: his family, his friends and his job. This type of awareness is essential to the abandonment of the illusions provided by gambling and leads to a more satisfying and more realistic existence.

# 10

# *Money Transactions in Everyday Life*

So far, I've stayed pretty close to home and the family in considering money from a psychological perspective but don't get the impression that difficulties occur only there. There are any number of areas of life in which psychology interacts with money, and they may occur within families, between friends, between coworkers, between buyers and sellers, and between employers and employees, not to mention between masters and servants or slaves. In fact, problems relating to money occur in almost any relationship you can imagine. Just staying alive depends upon money transactions all day every day, so it is little wonder that people's personalities and money styles are right there playing their part, sometimes directly and sometimes incidentally. No matter what you do to eliminate concerns about money, they're with you throughout your life in practically everything you touch. In fact money issues are so prevalent in everyday life that they are worth a chapter in their own right.

What are these situations that I'm referring to? They are things like saving, advertising and shopping, buying and selling, conspicuous consumption, borrowing and lending, nepotism, debt, servitude, gift-giving and bribery, paying or avoiding taxes, insurance, litigation and the whole question of psychological damages as determined by the legal system. While it fortunately is not part of everyday life, money management at times of crisis is also worth some attention. I'd like to look into this panoply of subjects with you, recognizing that they are only the most frequent ways money and psychology interact as we go through out adult years.

First, let's look at saving money. We are instructed from our early years that it's a good idea to save part of our income for future needs whether that means for luxuries, for retirement or for the proverbial "rainy day". We are constantly reminded that Americans save less of their incomes in percentage terms than do people in other countries, and Japan is held up to us an example of a country where saving is much greater than here; in fact, when Japan not too long ago was experiencing its years of greatest prosperity, we were told that the reason for their success was that the Japanese saved so carefully; we were less frequently told that their formal pensions are smaller than ours and an individual's savings are much more important to the style of life that will be maintained after retirement than they are here. Nevertheless, in spite of their continuing to save money, that nation subsequently ran into serious economic problems, and their economy is still in a tailspin. Saving money scrupulously is still considered to be a good idea but, like many good ideas, it can be carried to extremes and people can become so addicted to saving money that they forget that they also have to live in the present.

Harriet is one example of this; she was a successful businesswoman who made a religion out of saving at least 10% of her after-tax income, quite an achievement. She was careful about every penny she spent and kept telling her relatives who tried to convince her to treat herself better that she wanted to have something to fall back on in case of an emergency. When she developed cancer at age 63 and had to undergo chemotherapy, her family begged her to take in a health aide to help her in her weakened condition. Harriet was adamant in her refusal to do so but not because she didn't have the money. She was worried more about the fact that, with her poor health, she was not able to earn her usual income and keep putting aside money for the rainy day. It's hard to understand Harriet's stubbornness since it was apparent to everyone that the rainy day had arrived. Even when you accept that her denying that fact was one way of defending herself against the idea that she might have a fatal illness, one still would have to admit that Harriet had become addicted to saving money to the point that it no longer made sense.

Advertising is a major industry in this country and indeed in most parts of the world. The purpose of advertising is to get the customer to buy something by convincing him or her that it is the best product on the market, that its price is right and that he or she really needs it. It's the last one that relies on psychology since proving that someone needs something means that that someone is in trouble without it. His or her feelings of inadequacy, fears of being defective and other aspects of lack of self confidence are exploited by the advertiser who promises to relieve these problems. Perfumes, for example, not only smell nice but are meant to disguise one's natural odors. Most people are self-conscious about smelling bad and turn to soaps and deodorants, as well as to perfumes, to combat this. Women are specially susceptible to these fears and turn to items to enhance "feminine hygiene". On the other hand, I once saw a young adult male patient in consultation (a one-time evaluation visit) who came to my office reeking of cologne. He believed that, every time he masturbated, he began to stink, and then needed all the help he could get in covering up the odor. This, of course, is a delusional extreme of an idea that many people have to a much lesser extent, that in the course of living their daily lives, they produce socially unacceptable smells which have to be concealed from the rest of the world or they will be socially ostracized.

Another goal of advertising is to convince you that you should have every new product that comes on the market. It used to be said that people "kept up with the Joneses" in the sense that they too had to have every luxury that their neighbors had. That seems to have been replaced with "being the first on your block to have one", indicating that you have become the one who sets the standard for everyone else. Each of these slogans is based on the assumption that you need whatever they're promoting to maintain your social position which might otherwise be threatened, another jab at your feelings of self-confidence.

It's not that advertising does not serve a useful purpose in keeping us abreast of new developments in a rapidly changing world and helping us to find the best prices for the things we want, but it so often capitalizes on negative feelings about ourselves to achieve its goal, which is to make money for the advertiser. A potential buyer has to regard commercials with a wary eye and try very hard not to get caught up in spending excessive amounts of money in an effort to overcome some real or imagined defect.

Shopping, which is intimately tied up with advertising, is the great American pastime. Whether we are at home or on vacation, we are constantly urged to shop every time we open a magazine or look at television. Some of what we see are useful and necessary goods, and buying them makes sense. But we are also urged to shop for the sheer fun of it, to buy things just for the pleasure of spending money after roaming the stores or the mall for hours. Circulating money is good for business, and every good businessman is happy to encourage shopping. The question that arises is whether the purpose of the shopping is to give you something to fill up your time or whether its purpose is to search out something you truly need or want. Keeping yourself busy touring the stores generally means that you don't have other things to do with your time and are using shopping as a sport or hobby.

Not only have I met people who shop to occupy empty hours and avert possible boredom but I hear almost every day someone say that she (women are greater shoppers than men) wanted to treat herself well and went out looking to see what would do the job. I have also heard many times that someone was feeling depressed and wanted to go out shopping as a way of feeling better. This is when shopping starts to have psychological significance; when people use the act of spending money on something to produce a good feeling that is otherwise absent, shopping becomes therapy for an unpleasant mood. In fact, there are those who become addicted to spending money in this way as a treatment for depression; it would, of course, be better to work out whatever may be the psychological problems and not have to rely on shopping to make yourself feel better. Writing these criticisms of advertising and shopping does not mean that I'm against them; it just means that I don't think spending is the best treatment for psychological problems and, like other treatments that relieve symptoms, it reduces the distress without doing anything about the real causes of the distress. In that sense, shopping is like aspirin which takes the fever down and removes the pain while the underlying illness keeps going and can kill you in the end.

Another common thing we all participate in is buying and selling. These are transactions that each of us does several times every day, sometimes on a small scale and sometimes on a large one. We can't avoid doing so since it is impossible for any of us to personally produce everything that we need to get along; therefore, we have to buy things that we need and can't make on our own from someone else. Also, just as we need things from others, there are things that we can either produce or provide that somebody else needs and wants from us. Occasionally, we trade with each other but most often money is used to accomplish the transaction. There is, almost always, a fixed price for whatever the goods or services are, and we know in advance that that is the cost; so we pay the price and walk away with what we want. Frequently enough, the price is subject to discussion (bargaining), particularly when many are competing with each other to sell and there are relatively few who want to buy; each of us tries to get the best deal we can, either by paying the smallest amount possible if we are buyers or acquiring the largest amount possible if we are selling. That is the nature of business, and has been so since the beginning of time in economies all over the world. Where then do emotions come into the picture?

For some, walking away with a "bargain" means that we put one over on the other guy, that we outfoxed him which proves that we are the smarter one in the transaction. While it's healthy to try to get the most for one's money or to make the most profit possible in a business deal, problems arise when we need that to boost our poor self-esteem; without constant proof of our intelligence, aggressivity and business acumen, we feel that something is missing and we walk away from the deal with a sense of loss and a feeling that we are no good. Even depression may ensue from such a situation. To be competitive in life has its advantages but not when every deal results in either exultation or defeat; then it's overdoing it.

Americans by and large do not like to bargain although it is pretty much the way business is practiced all over the world in transactions large and small. For example, people who travel to other countries and go to flea markets request the price of an object, hear it and pay the price requested. They feel that to offer less and discuss the price over a period of a few minutes is insulting to the vendor and they hesitate to do so. The vendor has usually built in to his or her asking price an extra amount to allow for bargaining and, while he or she may enjoy making the extra profit if there is no bargaining, feels contempt for the purchaser as a fool who deserves to be parted from his or her money. There are even times when the price is rigged extremely high for the ignorant tourist to permit a major drop in price during the bargaining process. This gives the tourist satisfaction and yet still gives the merchant a large profit. The poor unsuspecting tourist feels great until he or she has a chance to check the price in a store with fixed prices and finds that, even with all the bargaining, the price paid was still twice what the store charges. Then anger sets in at having been fleeced.

Conspicuous consumption is the name given to show-off purchases when people buy things to prove to their friend and neighbors that they have lots of money, and deserve the respect that comes with being rich. The term was first used in the late nineteenth century to describe the buying patterns of newly rich Americans who wanted to impress their friends and neighbors, and who spent huge sums of money on things they didn't need and often couldn't appreciate. The term was new then, but the phenomenon has a long history and has probably been part of humankind since private property first became a fact of life. Today, for example, we have people building huge mansions that have space far beyond their needs (these have been called megamansions) and the needs of even their large extended families. It may not be needed but it sure impresses the neighbors. People often buy large cars and expensive furs for the same reasons.

Sometimes, one encounters the phenomenon of someone who has an expensive property but is otherwise poor. They are called land-rich to indicate that the property which is on view to others belongs to them but that they lack other resources, including the money to take care of it. The New York City equivalent is someone who buys or rents a large and expensive apartment at a good address but then has no money left to buy furniture and fixtures. No one is ever invited home to see the inside of the apartment because it's furnished with little better than the wooden crates in which oranges are shipped.

Another transaction that often arises in daily life is the question of borrowing and lending money, both within families and outside them.

One person feels an acute shortage of money, a crisis if you will, and turns to a close friend or family member, explains the circumstances and states how much money is needed. The lender often feels flattered by the request since it suggests a certain degree of intimacy as well as a recognition on the borrower's part that the lender is a solvent, responsible individual: the usual response is to comply and lend the money. The check is written and the money passes from one party to the other with some agreement about how re-payment will occur, this agreement being either verbal or written. For example, payment will be due in total at a certain specified time or will be paid in installments over a certain duration of time. But the matter is not so simple and, more often than not, problems arise.

In most of these informal borrowing arrangements, interest is not charged by the lender although he or she would be earning some amount if the money was left untouched in the bank. So the lender is really doing a double favor, providing the money and dispensing with whatever profit he or she would make on it otherwise. For the borrower, not having to pay interest means that he or she is really getting a bargain, money to use with no extra charge attached.

The borrower is faced with the fact, however, that he or she has to pay back the money, something that will consume a part of future earnings and be burdensome, a nuisance hanging over his or her head. (This is not to say that all borrowers are this way; many have a distinct sense of obligation about the matter and pay it in total as soon as possible with no ill feelings occurring on either one's part.) The borrower forgets that at some point the loan was a great help and may even have been a life saver and, instead of feeling gratitude, begins to dislike the lender, finding reasons to avoid him or her and certainly not paying the money back, at least not willingly. The lender, on his or her part, feels hesitant about pursuing repayment, not wanting to pressure the borrower or create an uncomfortable situation between the two. As time goes by, the borrower goes blissfully along, conveniently forgetting about the debt, and the creditor becomes increasingly angry at the non-payment. The lender is faced with the problem of how to reclaim his or her money, a frontal approach or a roundabout one, but whatever method is chosen, it turns out to be wrong since the borrower really doesn't want to pay, and even feels that the other is imposing on him or her by reminding that a debt exists.

A couple of examples will illustrate the points I am making. Silvia was an unmarried middle level administrator in a large corporation who had managed to put away a fair amount of money for her retirement. Her sister had several children who all hit college and postgraduate school with large tuition bills at the same time, and the sister and her husband found themselves in a money squeeze. Three of their children turned to Silvia for loans to help with tuition expenses, and two of the three repaid these loans as soon as their financial positions had stabilized. The third, a niece, obtained a postgraduate degree, married a man with a good, well-paying job, and went about her life with no effort to return the loan. Silvia became increasingly concerned about what to do, and finally wrote a gently worded note to her niece who responded by asking whether Silvia indeed had proof that the loan was made. Since Silvia was an extremely well organized person, she had saved the original check and sent her niece a copy. What followed was an offer by the niece to pay fifty dollars a month (on a $5000 interest free loan, that would mean 100 months or over eight years until the loan was paid in full). While she was well organized, Silvia was reluctant to engage in this sort of delay and all the accompanying extra bookkeeping, especially since a negative atmosphere had been created and there was every likelihood of skipped payments along the way, and she denied the request. Matters were at a level of high family stress with phone calls going back and forth but the niece finally came across with complete payment, largely because she was concerned that the matter might extend beyond the family limits and be brought to the attention of her employer or even lead to a lawsuit. Needless to say, aunt and niece have not spoken since, and this has proven awkward at family gatherings.

It's been said that one should not lend money to a relative unless one is willing to do without it and, alternatively, that one should present the money as a gift if that is possible and avoid all the discomfort and ill will that a loan will give rise to. One might well ask what factors made this niece different from her two siblings who returned their loans promptly, and one is forced to consider the in-law factor since the niece had married, and her husband participated in the decision either to not return the money or to drag out payments to a ridiculous extent. It may well be that the husband and his family of origin had a different approach to the handling of money than did the niece's family of origin.

Things are not always so simple as they first appear, though. Further knowledge of the facts of this case revealed that Silvia's niece had profound and longstanding grievances against her mother who she felt should have paid all her tuition bills. The niece felt that, by not doing so, her mother had forced her into the situation in which she had to ask for the loan. It was her intention to precipitate a crisis between her mother and her aunt which would be resolved by her mother's paying the money, but she handled the matter clumsily and this intention did not work out the way she wanted. Also, her husband, while he earned a good income, liked to gamble and frequently found himself short of ready cash; it was fine with him if the money never got repaid since he had other uses for it. In addition, it came as a shock to him to realize that, when he married, in addition to acquiring a wife, he also acquired responsibility for her debts. Most cases of family borrowing and lending are superimposed upon family histories that go way back, and the loan tends to revive all the old problems that preceded it.

Another case of a painful loan situation occurred with Frank. He and Don had grown up and gone to college together, remaining friends over the years and socializing together fairly frequently. Don came from a small family, having only one cousin who had several children and whose husband was not a regular breadwinner; Don himself worked as a loan officer in one of New York's big banks. What happened was that Don's cousin called him in tears because her husband had started to gamble and was in debt to some rather dangerous characters who finally gave him a deadline for payment or else. The cousin turned to Don who had little ready cash, and he turned to Frank who, like Silvia, was known to be a regular worker in a good job who was conservative about expenditures. Frank lent the money, also $5000 (which seems to be a favorite amount for friend and family loans), and drew up a letter of agreement with Don that there would be regular monthly payments. The first several months brought payments at the expected time, then there was a one-month skip, then a few delayed payments, then they stopped altogether. Frank called Don who became highly indignant and asked what did Frank want from him, suggesting that he go chase his cousin instead. Frank persisted in his request for regular payment and was cursed out in no mild terms by Don until things reached the point that Frank threatened to bring the letter of agreement to the attention of Don's employers. With this threat, payment was immediately delivered in full. Needless to say, the friendship was finished and there was no further contact between the former good friends.

Marked alterations occur in a relationship when the question of a loan arises. Instead of there being an association of two equal people, one is making a demand on the other. It's almost as if, to prove that your heart's in the right place, you have to come across with some money, otherwise it's you who will damage the relationship. I usually tell patients who present such problems to me that the relationship is already changed at the moment the loan is requested and that they're better off denying the request, unless they are absolutely convinced they are dealing with someone honest and reliable (and one may learn to the contrary only after the fact). At least they will still have their money. It is the person who is requesting the loan who is damaging the relationship, not the person who denies it, but that's something people find hard to accept, especially when the proposed borrower is a close relative or a long-term friend.

Lenders also may have agendas of their own, especially when they are sure they will be paid back. Having helped people out with money and having them in your debt represents a kind of power over them. One can remind them frequently and publicly that the money is owed and one appoint oneself a judge over their entire budget, deciding how they should spend money and criticizing their life style. For as long as the debt is not paid off, this power is retained. Even afterwards, it can be thrown up to the borrowers, privately or publicly, that they were rescued financially, and the lender can wonder out loud what would have happened if not for his or her generosity.

Trust Shakespeare to have a phrase of advice on the subject of borrowing. In Hamlet, Polonius, a minister of state for the king of Denmark and a constant provider of cliches, warns his son, "neither a borrower or a lender be". One should certainly follow this advice and leave the matter to the professionals, the banks and insurance companies which lend money at interest to ensure that they make a profit. Anyone who has a reasonable credit rating and who is worth trusting with the money can obtain a loan, and should not have to turn to friends or relatives. I say this to assuage the guilt of those who feel bad when they don't come through for a friend or a relative; remember that they do have other places to go and you are not depriving them of the education that paying the tuition assures or placing them in dangerous situations.

Another form of lending money, on a much more minor scale but still having psychological consequences is laying it out for someone else. This may involve buying a movie ticket for the other person because you happen to be there first, ordering theater or concert tickets by mail as a convenience for a friend, or buying groceries for a neighbor. Ordinarily, you're paid back on the spot but there are times when, for any number of reasons, this doesn't happen and repayment is postponed. You may be left holding the bag because the other party to the transaction forgets about it, and indeed you yourself may sort of forget about it. The sums involved are usually small and are of no great consequence, although it is irritating to have paid someone else's way and then have him or her proceed as if nothing happened. It's embarrassing to ask to be repaid later on since it makes you feel cheap and excessively finicky about money rather than relaxed about it. It can be also be embarrassing to the other guy who has been careless about his or her debts, no matter how small they may be. What most people do is let the matter drop even though they may feel some annoyance, but watch out if the situation comes up again! At that point, there may be a refusal to undertake the favor and a reminder to the debtor that he or she did not pay the last time around. This can even lead to one of those endless discussions where you're sure that they didn't pay and they insist that they did. Both parties are left with unpleasant feeling about the other and the friendship may be destroyed.

A variation on this theme of laying out money is having lunch or dinner with someone who invariably forgets his or her wallet and credit card, forcing you to pay for the meal. What happens next, do you remind him or her or do you let it ride and just write it off to the ups and downs of a friendship? Most of us let it ride rather than make a fuss over a few dollars but we soon begin to realize who the chronic offenders are and avoid eating out with them rather than get stuck repeatedly.

People who often eat out together resort, for convenience sake, to alternating payment with one picking up the tab one time and the other picking it up the next time around. That generally works out okay even if the cost is not shared totally equally; there are, of course, some who make sure that, when it's their turn to pay, the restaurant chosen is considerably cheaper than when the other guy pays. It doesn't take too long for the other person to realize what's going on and to build up resentment at the situation, resentment which continues to grow until it finds verbal expression so severe that it might even be called a confrontation.

A similar situation arises when a group of people eat out together. They agree to split the bill evenly, dividing it by the number of people present. In every crowd, there's one who invariably orders the most expensive items on the menu, in this way allowing the others to treat him or her by picking up more than their fair share of the meal's cost. Again, it doesn't take too long for the others to realize that they're being taken advantage of with the result that dining out together stops or some sort of confrontation ensues.

One has to wonder about the motives of the free-loader, the person who is taking advantage of another's spontaneous generosity and helpfulness. Doesn't he or she realize that the other guy has to get wise to this behavior and eventually give up on, if not the friendship, at least a willingness to be helpful? Most freeloaders enjoy the feeling that they are saving money by outsmarting others and that their charms can be turned to financial advantage, no matter how small the amounts. They take pride to the point of arrogance in what they see as the fact that others are willing to take care of them and their needs and pay for their friendship even if they do so only out of politeness. Free-loaders lack respect for the intelligence of others and their ability to see what is happening. This disrespect verges on contempt for their gullibility and their inability to defend themselves against such exploitation. Getting away with it only makes them feel that they are better than the other guy in the same way that a businessman gets a charge out of fooling a customer or a bargainer feels that he or she has outsmarted the other party in the transaction.

Nepotism (which has the same Latin origin as the word for nephew) refers to the hiring or obtaining a job for someone in the family, not limited to nephews. A person in a position of wealth or influence recommends a relative for a job and that person is hired preferentially over others as a result. This creates problems with other workers but it also creates problems with the provider of the job who has to accept criticism if the worker doesn't perform well, and creates problems with the worker himself or herself since that person has to demonstrate that he or she can do a decent day's work to gain approval. Alternatively, the hired "nephew" may not want to do too much and may coast along on the relative's influence. Such hiring practices usually lead to trouble, not only outside the family, but inside as well since the influential relative may be embarrassed by the "nephew's" poor performance and feel that it reflects badly on him or her.

Being in debt is a frequent phenomenon with a substantial percentage of the American population owing money at any given time. Some of it is based on credit card accumulations but more significant is that most cars and most houses are bought on credit, meaning that the owner of the property is not a full owner but is in debt to some financial institution or other. Such companies are fairly astute in determining who is reliable and likely to pay off the debt and who is not able to do so. However, every year, there is a certain number who fail to pay and become bankrupt. Theoretically, they are no longer able to obtain credit and are forever at a disadvantage. But there is hope for them since some institutions will issue credit cards to almost anyone, no matter what the circumstances, tying them down to a lifetime of having to pay past bills. While most people attempt to handle debt carefully to maintain their creditworthiness for the future, others do not and remain at a disadvantage forever.

Servitude, the situation in which one person works for another for money, comes in many degrees, but there are some things that the masters (or employers) have in common, just as there are some things that the servers (or employees) have in common. In general, masters often get the notion that, because they pay a salary, either in money or in room and board, they have unlimited rights over the body and soul of those who work for them. Servers, on the other hand, try very hard to preserve their sense of self and define the limits of the relationship; when it is overstepped, they become resentful and angry, and may take steps to retaliate. They are also concerned about maintaining their own sense of self-esteem and not appearing to be mere cogs in the wheels of the "great ones" whom they serve.

In the most extreme case of servitude, one person is another person's slave, not receiving money and being at the total whim of the master in every sense of the word. The slave has no rights and is seen as mere property; in many societies throughout history (and this is the case in some part of the world even today), the slave was happy to be alive and didn't begin to dream of having wishes and desires of his or her own. That situation happily no longer exists in this country although we are still dealing with the legacy that treating people in this way has left behind.

The next category of servitude is being a servant for someone else, doing a set job for a set salary. Fewer people do this today than one hundred years ago but very wealthy people still have several servants, and even middle class families have nannies and maids as well as cleaning staff, especially when both husband and wife work. Usually, each party to the relationship understands where responsibilities begin and end, and the servant is free to pick up and go elsewhere if unhappy. However, many employers abuse their servants, not physically, at least not usually, but in terms of making demands on them, giving them additional job functions or asking them to work longer hours. Sometimes, they expect the servants to abandon their own families and responsibilities to travel with the employer, even on short notice. Employers may feel that they have the right to make such claims on servants since they are paying the bills and supporting them, forgetting that services are being rendered by mutual agreement. Many employers also assume that their servants are intrinsically lazy and try to get away with less work than contracted and they feel justified in making these extra demands.

The person who serves, no matter what the capacity, is still a person with feelings who has definite ideas about his or her part in the relationship. For most, it's a job and a respectable one at that, and the worker wants to be able to hold up his or her head at the end of the day. Others dislike having to do someone else's bidding, and feel sullen or resentful about being in that situation. All, at least in an open democratic society, want respect for what they do and even appreciation, although this is not always forthcoming with the master feeling that the respect and appreciation are restricted to the weekly salary check.

The servant situation in this country is complicated by the fact that many are illegal immigrants and can't fight for their legal rights; they are, therefore, much more at the mercy of their employers than people with appropriate documentation. They often come from societies where servitude is an accepted way of life and they are accustomed to taking orders and not having their feelings consulted.

However, we do occasionally hear on the news about illegal immigrants working in slave-like conditions, forced into this condition by bosses who know that they can get away with it. Sometimes, the illegals are able to escape, and sometimes the situation leads to violence against the employers, a pay back for what they have been doing to their servants.

Employers of servants, even in legitimate situations often get strange notions about the relationship. For example, a member of the British royal family, now no longer with us, was reported to pay very low salaries to her servants; at one point, her maid who had her own family and expenses to worry about, requested a small raise, and the Royal was totally flabbergasted, saying that the honor of working for her more than made up for any salary deficiency. This report suggests the lack of sophistication in daily money matters on the part of the Royal as well as a certain amount of indifference to the woman who served her. It's almost as if the days of slavery are not in fact over. Little wonder that fewer and fewer people find lives as servants interesting or rewarding.

The situation is not always dreadful. There are nannies and housekeepers, as well as chauffeurs and butlers who, over a period of many years, practically become members of the family even if they are never really accepted as such. They live with the family after retirement and have no financial worries, their needs continuing to be looked after. Such an outcome requires a suitable frame of mind on the part of the worker and on the part of the family, and only rarely happens.

What is true about masters and servants has relevance to the relationships that exist between bosses and employees. We have all heard too many horror stories over the last few years about the sexual harassment of female employees by male bosses (and occasionally male employees by female bosses) to be ignorant of the fact that some bosses feel that they are entitled to other services from their employees than the strictly business ones. Fortunately, that situation is changing with governmental assistance but too many bosses still feel that being in the position of paying people's salaries gives them special claims on their bodies as well as their souls.

Unfortunately, even with the progress made over the last few years in dealing with issues of sexual harassment in the workplace, the problem continues and the worker can't always fight back. She is dependent upon the salary and there may not be another worker in her family who can carry the financial load if she walks off the job. She may also not be able to find an alternate job that easily and would have to explain in some fashion her sudden departure from her previous position. Even if she takes the case to court, she still has bills to pay in the meantime such as mortgage or car payments that cannot be put off while the rights and wrongs of her case are being adjudicated. As a result, she may feel intimidated to go along with outrageous requests on the boss's part, disliking herself, hating the situation and wondering in frustration how, if at all, she can get out of it.

Being master is not limited to being an employer, however. There is one situation that occurs fairly frequently in which we all of us are, if only briefly, the master, and have a servant to take care of us, and that is when we go into a restaurant. The waiter or waitress is there to serve us and make sure that our requests are met and that we feel comfortable. In return for this service, we are expected to leave a tip to express our appreciation. Yet, there is a master-servant relationship in this situation and it is interesting to see how people handle it. Jack, for example, gave every waiter and waitress a hard time, demanding that his water glass be filled every time he sipped from it, asking the server any number of questions about just how the food was prepared, returning food that he claimed was not properly cooked or was not the right degree of doneness. He invariably requested a new napkin and silverware, claiming that the ones that were on the table to begin with were stained. Furthermore, he repeatedly snickered at the server, claiming that he or she was stupid, and couldn't read or write correctly, let alone total the bill accurately. It was embarrassing for others to dine with Jack since he mistreated waiters and waitresses who initially attempted to please him and took his criticisms seriously. But he was the master in the situation since he not only used the server's services, but the server depended upon him for that tip. On one occasion, a waiter got so angry with Jack that he threw a glass of water over him, something that no doubt cost the him his job. On another occasion, a waiter managed to drip some sauce on Jack's suit which infuriated Jack but this waiter didn't lose his job since it was an "accident". Servers have been known to spit in the food they serve to difficult and demanding patrons and I know of at least one case where the waiter who did the spitting was HIV positive. This story only goes to show that people, whether they be in service to others or not, resent being mistreated, and no amount of money can make them put up with such maltreatment.

In a service-oriented society such as the one we live in, many workers including many professionals get a fee for service. The service is based on knowledge accumulated during many years of special study and is usually charged on the basis of how much time is spent serving the client. When the client receives the bill, particularly in the case of attorneys where even the time spent on the phone doing work for the client or in dictating letters to a secretary is calculated in, there is usually a gasp of shock and a reluctance to pay. The amount seems just too high and no explanation on the part of the lawyer suffices to calm the outraged client who may be satisfied with the outcome of the lawyer's work but not with the bill. As a consequence, many attorneys prefer to work on a contingency basis, getting a certain percentage of whatever damages may be collected from winning a case. If the case is lost, there is no payment but, if the case is won, there's quite a chunk of money going to the lawyer and then, too, the client feels outraged at the amount. The odd thing about all this is that the client is paying someone with whom he or she has had face-to-face contact, someone who was originally liked and regarded as a friend and supporter and now suddenly is placed in the role of rapacious villain. Perhaps it is the fact that the relationship started off in such a friendly fashion that made the client forget that this was a business arrangement and that eventually a bill would be submitted. The same client may buy expensive furniture, paying the dealer and the manufacturer huge profits without a murmur because these people remain distant and faceless.

Physician fees and psychiatrist fees, the second creating perhaps more anger than the first, also produce outrage. This is somewhat mitigated in this age of managed care where faceless third parties determine how much will be paid, leaving the patient with only a small amount, nicely called a co-payment, left for the patient. In psychiatry, while managed care has made its inroads and numerous practitioners work exclusively for whatever fees the managed care corporations set, others, especially the ones who do psychotherapy and psychoanalysis, work out their own arrangements with patients. Since the amount of time the therapist spends with a patient is considerable, the fee charged reflects this and only the relatively well-fixed can afford to pay. Questions arise when a patient runs into financial difficulties during a treatment and can no longer afford to pay these high fees.

There is quite a bit of controversy about what the therapist should do under such circumstances. My own personal feeling about the matter is that the therapist has to look at it from the position of his or her overall income, to which any individual fee doesn't contribute all that much. Doing this permits one to reduce a fee when the case necessitates it without a significant loss of overall income but, obviously, this is not a practice that one can do again and again without having one's income drop precipitously. Other therapists strongly disagree with this position, feeling that it entails giving the reduced-fee patient preferential treatment, something which would cause problems for other patients if they learned about it. Another response to a patient's having economic hardship is to terminate the treatment if the patient can't pay, and refer him or her on to a lower cost clinic.

Fees are also paid for services that are quite unrelated to mental health assistance, and that is the situation that prevails when clients buy prostitutes or at any rate a certain amount of their time. An unwritten contract exists between the employer and the employee about what will be provided for how much money. There is a whole range of services, almost a price list, with the more odd-ball activities costing more. In these cases, there is rarely argument over the fee and whatever has been agreed upon is usually handed over without protest. However, since such arrangements are outside the law, things can go wrong on either one's part. The prostitute, usually a woman is at the mercy of her "john" who may get rough with her. On the other hand, a fair number of prostitutes of both sexes manage to supplement the original bargain by robbing or mugging their clients. These clients rarely report the crime to the police because of embarrassment over the situation.

One example of an enterprising and creative almost-prostitute (I could never figure out what to call her) that I encountered was a young woman who lived in a public shelter. She was quite attractive and went out every evening to patrol the area near the shelter for customers who drove up and down the streets there, knowing it was a pick-up zone. She got into their cars and alerted the guys that she had HIV (she really didn't), and then would ask that they give her some money for having warned them in advance so they could protect themselves. She was invariably asked to leave the car but managed to make a fairly good living without providing any services at all.

I have referred to gift-giving in family situations in the chapter on Marriage. Yet gift-giving also plays a part in many other relationships. Viewed quite simply, it may be an expression of affection or appreciation but it can take on other meanings depending upon the relationship. In an office or business, it is customary to give a present to one's employees at Christmas time, and this is probably the simplest case of pure appreciation. Giving a gift to a business associate may mean appreciation for a good working relationship, an acknowledgment that you like and appreciate him or her and also a statement that you hope the relationship continues. It is a given that the person who benefits the most from the business relationship gives the larger gift. Is this a subtle bribe to continue the relationship and its profitability? It is certainly hard to separate out the two components, and some people who are supremely ethical may refuse any gift at all or may set a low maximum price on any gift they accept. I had an experience several years back when one of my foreign students, a not very good one at that, presented me with a gift of a chess set consisting of mother of pearl pieces; it was obviously very expensive. I did not accept it, considering it a bribe to pass him, a bribe under the guise of a gift. I subsequently learned that, in his native country, it was customary to give substantial gifts to one's teachers and that there, my refusal would have been considered rude, almost to the point of insult. I have never been clear on what his intentions were but I did feel comfortable about my reaction since the two of us were operating in this country, and the norms and standards practiced here are what should prevail. For those of you who are curious, he managed to master the essentials of the course and squeak through with a marginal pass.

It is not only in this example that bribery touches on the subject of psychological meanings of money. In our country, bribery is considered a crime but this is hardly the case in the rest of the world where it is frequently considered the normal state of affairs for someone to give a large gift of money or some other valuable in order to obtain a favor; the favor may be a judge dismissing charges or an executive granting a contract or almost anyone in any position of authority doing something to increase the bank account of the briber. Some American corporations have complained that our laws against bribery prevent them from competing in foreign countries where the practice is prevalent. Even though it's against the law here, there are almost daily reports in the papers of bribes being given to public officials, if not in money, then in football tickets, expensive vacations, the use of private planes, and so forth. Internationally, too, American corporations have learned to manage in the countries where they operate.

Bribery probably comes easier to those who were acquainted with bribing tactics in their homes when they were children and their parents gave them things to gain their compliance. These people still use the technique in their personal lives and don't see much wrong with doing it in their business lives as well. Even those who were not raised by bribing families and who initially are reluctant to go along with the practice find their resistance breaking down when they see it going on all around them and realize that strict morality will result in their losing business. As far as the law goes, they're all willing to take their chances if they get caught.

Cheating on taxes is something that all of us would love to do since probably each and every one of us feels that the government is taking away too much of what we earn, leaving us with too little. Yet, actual cheating comes more easily to some than to others, even though anyone who does so is subject to legal retribution. I'm not talking about small amounts that many people fudge as they work out their returns but large sums of money that go unreported or fake donations that reduce the tax bill. What differentiates those who cheat to the point of fraud is a kind of arrogant self- confidence that they can get away with it while the humbler ones among us feel that we will probably be caught and that the punishment is not worth whatever we might save. There is a famous case of a hotel and real estate tycoon who claimed that paying taxes was only for little people. She was caught in her tax evasion, found guilty of fraud and served time in a Federal prison.

Insurance is yet another subject in which psychology and money interact. We are all required to have insurance on our cars, and most of us have life insurance and health insurance as well. In addition, we may have homeowner's insurance, mortgage insurance and insurance for our businesses. There are also other, more esoteric insurances that few of us have. Obviously, the more insecure we are, whether because we are in a vulnerable position or because we feel vulnerable, the more types of insurance we carry and the higher the amounts of coverage we maintain. At times, this can get wild. Take the example of Norman, a former patient of mine, who had been a student in a highly respected medical school when he had a nervous breakdown. In spite of the fact that we psychiatrists take the position that mental illness is like all other illnesses, there was no way that the school would accept him back after he had recovered. Norman went on to other graduate studies and established a different career for himself. Yet, he was so fearful of another breakdown (which has yet to happen twenty- seven years later) that he insured himself heavily against the possibility, ending up with four different policies to pay his medical and hospital expenses, if necessary, and to replace any lost income. He searched out policies that would pay in spite of his having other coverage, and he experienced the satisfaction of knowing that, should he ever again have a mental illness, he would make a profit on the experience. Of course, he did pay a huge amount of money every year in insurance premiums, enough that he had to make sacrifices in other areas of his life.

We have been called a litigious nation, going to court seemingly at the drop of a hat. Certainly, other countries' courts do not have such huge case loads of people making claims against each other for all sorts of hurts and injuries. We believe that everyone is entitled to his or her day in court in order to obtain justice. It is an interesting phenomenon that the salve for all these hurts is almost invariably money, and that the justice desired is monetary. There are people who are willing to sue over the slightest injury while others just want to get away from the whole thing and not think at all in terms of monetary awards. There are also those who sue every chance they get in the hopes that, even if the case does not go to a jury, the sued party will provide some financial compensation to them just to have the case terminated and be free of any further bother. In these cases, the person who sues is trying to supplement his or her income almost as if this is a business by itself.

Every now and then, we hear of a case in which someone sued another and collected a huge payment based on psychological damages, over and above any actual physical injury. These psychological damages are usually for pain and suffering, mental anguish and loss of companionship of a loved one. It is difficult to calculate how much such psychological damages are worth in money terms, and courts have trouble setting amounts when such cases come up. It really depends on how generous a jury feels. In any event, there has to be some proof that real mental pain exists and is of sufficient duration and severity as to warrant financial compensation, such proof being frequently hard to deliver.

When there is a major crisis, such as occurred with the ghastly destruction of the World Trade Center, people have a tendency to hunker down and not spend their money although they may tend to buy certain eternally valuable money equivalents such as gold and precious stones. We saw this holding back on spending occurring in the months following the attack in spite of the fact that all our national leaders encouraged us to continue life as normal and keep the money in circulation, something which would keep the economy active and prosperous. However, people were fearful of what the future held in store, and wanted to be sure that they were solvent, although a few hardy souls did continue to travel, buy consumer goods, go to entertainments and to restaurants. This conservatism about money matters is a very common response to uncertainty.

In this case, there has followed a gradual loosening up of spending and a gradual return to normal with increasing easing of anxiety.

As you can see, the money question and its multitudinous psychological significances arise in so many areas of adult life that they truly affect every one of us. It is hard to say whether the problems come first and then get expressed in money terms or whether the money issues come first and so influence what we feel that we act on them without doing much thinking about the subject, sometimes committing crimes as we do so and sometimes getting ourselves into remarkably entangling situations.

# 11

# *Parenting and Grandparenting*

Virtually all parents want their children to have things better than they did in their own childhoods, both as far as being loved goes and as far as having a plentiful supply of material goods. We all know of parents who sacrifice their own well-being to put enough food on the table or who work double shifts to make sure that their children get a quality education, one which will allow them to get better jobs and make their future lives brighter and easier than their parents had it. They want their children to have all the advantages and to enjoy all the good things in life. So they work hard and hope that this will accomplish their goals. While most parents don't go to the length of having two jobs to make their children successful and happy, they still hope that things will work out trouble-free for their children.

But, as so often happens, things aren't always that simple and, in spite of their good wishes, parents often create problems for their children, establishing in spite of themselves an unhealthy atmosphere which is reflected in the area of money as well as in the area of emotions. I have made the point several times already that each of us is influenced in our own childhoods and teen-age years by the attitudes towards money and towards all aspects of life that were held by our parents and other significant relatives, friends and other people of importance to us. Every parent carries around within himself or herself a trunkload of such attitudes which inevitably influences the ways that the parent treats his or her children. These attitudes may be passed on from one generation to the next virtually unchanged or they may produce opposing and rebellious attitudes on the part of the younger generation. No matter how these attitudes eventually show up in the children, they are the direct product of what parents felt and thought, and then said and did.

In addition to these unconscious attitudes which are passed on to children, there are other situations which influence how parents treat children, both in terms of money and in terms of affection. The two are not always easily separated since what a parent feels in terms of affection or dislike is almost always expressed as well in terms of money and its equivalents, specifically what parents give to their children and what they withhold, and why. The children may also be influenced by parental personality traits like consistency and tendency to tease.

We tend to think in terms of the so-called typical family in which the parents live together in one household with their children. However, in these days of alternate family situations, parenting comes in a number of styles: single parent families with a totally absent parent of either sex, divorced couples with the children living with one parent and the other one somewhere in the background, a parent living with a homosexual companion, and the presence of other relatives on the scene. These different situations don't necessarily have implications for the child's eventual attitudes towards money but the other adults present in the household also play their part in shaping future attitudes.

Although what I want to talk about here has some overlap with the problems I presented in the chapter on childhood, I will devote this chapter to discussing the situation from the parents' position. They are the ones who are the senior parties in the relationship, they are the ones who create the situations and they are the ones who can do something about it if they realize that they are hurting their children by setting them up with problems for the rest of their lives.

Sometimes, you can see negative personal vibes arising even before the child is born. While the parents very much want the new baby, they might have some reservations about what this interloper will mean in their own lives. They have worked out, more or less, the problems and adjustments involved in the marital state that confront every new couple and, with luck, they have made themselves into a unit. There comes a change, however, with the discovery that the wife is pregnant, and this new situation requires a readjustment on both parts. The wife becomes preoccupied with the physical changes going on in her body, and with the realization that she will soon become a mother and everything that that means to her. Questions assail her as to whether the baby will be healthy and whether, after it is born, she will prove to be a good mother. Her worries about the child's health and development through the prenatal months are shared with the father, but she generally keeps to herself any doubts she may have about her abilities to raise a child. She is also thrust back at this point into memories of her own childhood and her relations with her own parents for better or for worse. If she feels that her parents short-changed her, she will vow to do better and if she feels she was well-treated, she tries to model herself on her mother and father.

The husband, for his part, is usually enthusiastic about the idea of becoming a father but also has some reservations, particularly when he sees his wife, who formerly was attentive to him over all others, becoming less concerned about his needs and putting his wishes into second place even before the baby is born. Depending on the father's sense of security, he may recognize that his wife's behavior is natural or he may become resentful of the child. Just as his wife worries about being an adequate mother, he too will worry about being an adequate father. So, even before it is born, the child has evoked some negative and anxious reactions in each of its parents.

In addition, both parents realize that the child will require a great deal of time and expense if they are to do right by it. This necessitates, especially in families with limited finances, a major review of just where the money has been going up to this point and decisions about what expenses will have to stop. This may also entail changes in the couple's life style with no vacations for several years after the child's arrival, fewer nights on the town and perhaps even adjustments of work schedules to accommodate the fact that the child needs someone around at all times. Even the search for suitable nursery care, if both parents must be away at the same time, may create a stressful situation.

What happens with all these reactions is most important; do the negative reactions get lost in the excitement of the new arrival and all the positive emotions relating to the baby, or do they remain, creating conscious awareness in both parents of their own mixed feelings towards it? At times, the negative feelings go underground and influence what the parents do in relation to the baby without them having any idea that they are expressing anger, resentment, jealousy or other negative emotions.

There is a condition which used to be called postpartum depression which occurs in some women shortly after they give birth. Its symptoms are a pronounced feeling of sadness, a feeling of inadequacy about being able to take care of the child, an inability to actually perform the necessary care, and a fear on the mother's part that she will injure the child, either through negligence or through overt violence, a fear which at times is carried out. Only recently have we seen a case in Texas where a mother drowned her five children while under the influence of such a condition. There is another psychological condition which may also appear at this time, probably precipitated by the postpartum state, but looking quite different. A mother suffering from this condition becomes motionless and remains mute; this condition is called catatonia.

Both postpartum mental illnesses are usually self-limited in the sense that the mother generally gets over them on her own after a short while and is able to fulfill all her responsibilities. Although they still appear with regularity, it's a curious fact that neither of these symptom pictures are reported much in the medical literature anymore. Perhaps this is because, as more effective antipsychotic and antidepressive medications came on the scene, postpartum reactions proved fairly easy to treat. Nevertheless, in spite of mostly good responses to treatment, there has always been a small percentage of women who never snap out of it. While postpartum reactions occur most commonly after the birth of the first child, they may also occur after the birth of other children even when the mother has previously done well.

Another reason that we don't hear the term postpartum much any more is because, as diagnoses wax and wane in popularity over the years, these conditions have been absorbed into other diagnostic categories of depression or psychosis. Even when things are not severe enough for the mother to be given a formal diagnosis, the fact remains that a large percentage of women do have much milder, but nevertheless upsetting emotional reactions, after giving birth; these are usually blamed on the hormonal instability occurring during the weeks following delivery.

Those psychiatrists and psychologists who are inclined to look for causes of emotional distress in life circumstances rather than in chemical imbalances blame these postpartum reactions on the pressures the new mother is subject to. She feels overwhelmed by her new responsibilities at the same time that she is already suffering from severe doubts about her ability to accomplish those quintessential womanly jobs, getting through a pregnancy, giving birth, and child-rearing. It's been speculated that some women completely avoid becoming pregnant to avert any such crisis without being consciously aware of the reasons why they don't want to have children. In any event, the mother who has suffered a severe emotional response to the birth of a child may very well go on to having mixed feelings about that child, feelings which will be communicated to the child in one way or another, but also in the giving freely of love and money equivalents or holding back on them.

Edna was a woman of 40 who had had three children prior to the one which triggered off her postpartum psychosis, a psychosis of major proportions, necessitating long term hospitalization because of violent behavior that could not be completely controlled by any antipsychotic medications. According to her husband and family, she sailed through her previous pregnancies with no trouble although one sister did notice that she had seemed to become more and more moody over the years. After the fourth delivery, when she returned home, she attempted to throw the baby out of a fourth story window since she believed that it was a devil-child and she, as a God-fearing woman, shouldn't be forced to take care of it. She drifted into an extensive delusional (a delusion is a fixed belief contrary to reality) system of religious content, and nothing, psychotherapy or medication, touched her or relieved her disordered thought processes. Anyone who attempted to talk to her rationally or even to try to get her to bathe was greeted, at the best, by hymn singing and, at the worst, by being attacked. Edna was the subject of many conferences and consultations but no one could determine just why this particular delivery started off such a major reaction while the others had gone off uneventfully.

While Edna represents an extreme case of postpartum reaction, milder versions abound, as I said, and many mothers feel overwhelmed and moody during the several months after giving birth. They feel awkward about handling the child and tend to pass as much responsibility for its care onto others as they can get away with. Some relatives criticize them as abnormal mothers because they don't take care of their newborns, an approach which does not help matters, and this criticism may persist in the family history, providing an ongoing stress for the mother. The infant usually gets its basic care one way or another and, after several months, things seem to straighten out. This early avoidance of care-giving does not affect the child's attitude to money in and of itself but it does establish a pattern in which the mother feels guilty in relation to that particular child (or to any and all children from whom she has withdrawn from basic care-giving) and will try to over- compensate as the child gets older; she may, alternatively remain aloof and uninterested in what the child does. Those reactions which continue into the years during which the child gains awareness of the world around it are much more likely to influence its attitudes towards money and towards gifts as well as its feeling wanted, accepted and worth-while.

Much less frequently mentioned than postpartum reaction in mothers are postpartum reactions in fathers, although I have encountered this condition several times over the years. This reaction is a state of anxiety of some severity which has a duration of several months after the birth until events settle down. The father feels not only inadequate to fulfill the responsibilities imposed upon him by the newborn but may also experience the strange idea that, by the very fact of fathering, he has lost a certain amount of a very limited quantity of life energy that he had prior to generating this new life. One such case was Walter who, at the age of 35, became a father for the first time. He was married to a woman three years older than he and he had never wanted to have children at all but she pushed him into it because she felt the biological clock was running out for her. Walter had a transient psychosis lasting two weeks after his son was born and his delusions were unusual. He came to my office on a beautiful spring afternoon, having walked through New York City's Central Park to get there, and he complained to me that there was a television system set up in the men's room there which spied on him as he urinated. He felt that privacy had become a thing of the past in our technological society and that even his performance of this natural function was being observed by someone who had sexual designs upon him. I asked several questions about his experience and what led him to this conclusion, and he let me know that he had been feeling weak since his son was born; he had never previously had any thoughts or feelings that could remotely have been considered homosexual and he was not really interested in such experiences except for one reason. He believed in a magical way that he could replace the vital force he had lost in fathering a son by receiving an amount of vital energy from another male in a one-time semen-receiving experience. He remained concerned about his "loss" of privacy and mused about having a one-time homosexual experience for several weeks. Then these thoughts disappeared and he went on to fulfill his role as a father although in a somewhat cautious and distant manner. Indeed, he found many reasons to work late or stay away from home and he showed the child little love.

When a father feels that he has lost precious vital energy in the very act of becoming a father, a psychological situation that doesn't arise too often and certainly has no basis in fact, he may become stingy in his gifts to the child. The belief is that what is lost in giving rise to life can be made up for by holding on to other valuable commodities. Fathers who have this idea, even to a very minor degree, tend to withhold love and other gifts from the child, coming across as miserly and cheap in relation to that particular child or, as a matter of fact, to all their children if the same reaction to the birth occurred on each occasion.

Nevertheless, most parents weather the birth of the first child well and go on to weather the birth of following children well without experiencing undue anxiety and without developing "complexes" in relation to their children, attitudes which inflict psychological damage upon their children and have ramifications for how generous the parents will be to them. There are always a few who lapse into a permanent state of resentment underneath the superficial happiness that they show to the rest of the world. It's this underlying resentment that is damaging since it is reflected, not in the basic care given to the newborn, but in the treatment that parents deliver without being aware of it. While I think it can be taken for granted that, in the vast majority of cases, there will be enough of the necessities, plenty of food, secure surroundings, decent clothing and appropriate medical care, deprivation will show up in the area of extras such as money and its equivalents such as presents, gifts, or toys.

Surprise treats that parents give children on the spur of the moment are perhaps one of the greatest joys in childhood. For no apparent reason other than love, a father or mother brings home something that they think their child will like and enjoy. If anything proves to the child that their parent loves them and approves of them, it is this sort of surprise, and naturally such surprises build self-esteem and self-confidence. It is just this sort of treat that is missing when parents feel stingy towards their children because their love is contaminated with other feelings; as a result, they don't bring treats, and the child misses out on what is one of the most pleasant aspects of childhood.

Largely based on their own early experiences, there are parents who maintain very severe attitudes towards their children. They feel that giving allowances or even simple gifts, unless they have been earned by hard work, means that they are indulging the child who will, as a result, become spoiled. It's hard to define exactly what the concept of spoiling is all about but it usually means that the child has too many good things and does not learn to appreciate that the world is a tough place where you have to sweat for anything good that comes your way. Most parents hear the word spoiling and worry whether they are giving the child too much; they should consider that it is possible to give the child a great deal and still have it be aware that money is something that one works for. In other words, giving money or gifts to children tends to make them happier and does not rule out any current or future learning about the realities of money.

There is a whole variety of factors that produce favoritism on the part of parents to children, in the sense that they prefer one child to another, or its contrary, dislike one child more than the others. I have already mentioned that there may be some residual distress in either or both parents resulting from a mild form of postpartum reaction. There may also be reactions to particularly stressful births with parents feeling angry that that particular child caused the mother a dangerous and painful labor with the father fearing for the well-being of his wife; the child who, quite unconsciously, contributed to this may be placed in the category of least favored child. On the other hand, some parents are so thrilled that the baby made it after all that they treat that child with special consideration and prefer it over their other children.

Some children remind their parents of someone very dear to them, often someone who has died, and the child serves as a substitute for that loss. This reminding may be due to a physical resemblance or to personal characteristics similar to those of the deceased. Sometimes the child is even named after the dead person. While everyone acknowledges that the child is a separate entity, to be cherished for itself, the parent may feel that it is a reincarnation of the deceased, especially when the child bears the same name, and he or she will shower it with love and gifts. This is all great for the favorite child who feels super-loved but it's not so great for the other children who have to face life watching someone else constantly getting preferred over them, receiving gifts and money, while they have to do with second best.

Actually, it may not be all that great for the favored child who realizes that he or she is getting things at the expense of siblings, and may feel some guilt at the situation even though he or she didn't create it. There may also be active resentment on the part of the others to the favorite which can find expression in teasing and in physical rough handling. So, being preferred can work out to be a double-edged sword.

In situations where a child is least favored, it may be because it looks like or has the characteristics of a disliked parent or grandparent, or because it reminds a parent of someone else whom they couldn't stand. The innocent child is made to bear the negative treatment that would have been shown to the disliked relative, and that includes getting less than its share of money and other gifts. It will have to do with hand-me-down clothing and second best toys rather than going first class along with its siblings.

Sibling rivalry may also be consciously stimulated by a parent who wants the children to compete, believing that it's good for them, preparing them for a world in which people have to struggle to get ahead. Parents who follow this line of thinking will set up competitive situations between their children and will reward the winner and disparage the loser. Contrary to their belief, doing this only produces negative feelings in their children toward each other and toward the parent who introduces such negativism into the home.

Other parents enjoy the fact that their children compete and, whether they set it up or not, like the idea that the children are striving with each other to gain parental approval. It makes the parent feel important to have the kids compete for his or her attention. Obviously, this too is not a healthy situation; it reveals feelings of inadequacy on the part of the parent and turns the home into a sort of battleground the purpose of which is to make that parent feel better, stronger and more important.

Something that I've encountered from time to time is the parent's giving the child gifts that are expensive to the point of lavishness, not out of love or out of favoritism but as a bribe to cover up the abuse of that child, sexual or physical. The parent, usually the father, becomes alarmed after the deed has been done that the child will talk and, in order to prevent this, makes an unspoken bargain with the child that, in return for silence, presents will be given. This compounds the psychological damage of the abuse since the child is now involved in an ongoing economic transaction with the father. If the abuse wasn't damaging enough, there is now an ongoing conspiracy of silence based on the child's making a profit out of his or her victimhood. The child becomes aware of the role that bribery and manipulation play in human relationships, and learns how to be a player in such situations. Although it's nice to believe that the home is a model of direct and open communication, that is hardly the case here.

There is such a thing as doing too much for a child to make up for parents' fears that they're not doing enough. For example, in the case of wealthy parents who were once poor and who want to make sure that their children don't experience the want and deprivation that they themselves experienced when they were children. There is a story told about Aristotle Onassis who was Jackie Kennedy's second husband and a man of great wealth, the owner of a fleet of merchant ships. He too had been married previously and had two children, whom he adored and indulged, by his first wife. He was very concerned that they never experience an unfulfilled wish as he had in his impoverished childhood, and he bought both son and daughter large numbers of toys. When the toys broke (which seems to be the inevitable fate of toys in the hands of children), no matter where he was, he sent a helicopter to buy replacements so that his children would not have to do without, even briefly.

One hears such a story and wonder whether a life without even brief deprivation is a good and constructive experience for children or whether it too has its damaging effects. Life, even for the very rich, requires that one be prepared for hardships since there are uncontrollable hazards and stresses such as illness, death and unhappy love affairs. That doesn't mean that parents have to keep emphasizing that life is hard and keep warning their children to be ready for problems later on. Being aware, though, that life brings with it some unhappiness, some frustration, as one goes along is an accurate perception, and perhaps a little deprivation in childhood helps to fortify someone in weathering such events when they arise later on.

There are many ways for parents to handle incidents of broken toys or torn clothes and injuries as well as such commonplace occurrences as spilt milk or stains on clothes, tablecloths, walls and carpets, and the response to these events is important. Toys first! Some parents replace the toys with no comment, some make a fuss over the breakage, and some decide to teach the children a lesson that they have to be more careful, making them do without. My advice to parents who encounter this situation (and that is virtually every parent) is never to make too much of a fuss over the damages; the child who already feels bad at the loss of the toy or the clothing or about the spills will feel that he or she is clumsy and can't be trusted with anything. A more relaxed approach puts the matter into a proper perspective since, really, it's not that important in the total scheme of things if something spills or gets broken; certainly, it's not worth getting upset about or contributing to damaging a person's self esteem.

It's probably a good idea not to spend too much money on any single toy but to buy enough varied toys so that the child will remain interested and have choices. Also, if the toy is not expensive, it's no great tragedy if it breaks. Advertisers who push expensive toys and manufacturers who produce them might not agree with this viewpoint and, no matter what my opinion in the matter is, toys have become more and more expensive these days, particularly those related to computers, so parents do have to educate the child to be careful in the way it handles things. Of course, for the younger child, my advice still holds good since they are pre-computer and they still enjoy cheap toys and have yet to be too influenced by advertisers.

When it comes to reactions over other damages, many parents make a great to-do over the incident and believe that they are training the child to be more careful by denying it things it wants. The statement is made to the child that, "as long as you're so careless, we're not going to give you anything, you have to learn the value of things." It's hard to believe that any parents really believe that this sort of treatment is helpful in training the child to be more careful since it's in the nature of childhood not to have the physical skills to control everything it does; such reactions probably indicate more the parents' own frustration and anger at the wasted expense. Children also tend to be more exuberant when they are younger and, as a result, will break more things than later on when they are more controlled and more able to be careful. What the child usually takes away from this sort of parental condemnation is a feeling that he or she is somehow bad and does bad things which parents have to punish in order to help them become good when they get older.

It's been said by more than one wise observer that you never truly know someone else until you've seen them in a position of power over others. This is certainly true of employers who, when they have control over subordinates, begin to reveal previously unexpected aspects of their personalities, characteristics that are often not for the better. Personal traits that were kept hidden, were perhaps even unknown to the individual, start to appear as the powerful person realizes that he or she can do whatever he or she wishes and get away with it. The same is true with parents and, while they may be delighted to have children and want the very best for them, they now find themselves in a position of power over others and they let this dimension of their personalities come out. This may show up in the parents being rigid and punitive disciplinarians. On the other hand, there are parents who use their power to support, encourage and even indulge their children.

It's also not a very good idea to promise a child a reward for some accomplishment or even to promise that something the child wishes will be delivered at a later date, and then not come across with the present, whether it be money or something else. The child responds to the promise with the desired behavior and acts "good" but, in the meantime, the parent has either forgotten that the promise was made or had no intention of ever fulfilling it. While the child can tolerate, even if impatiently, a delay in getting what it wants, it finds it difficult to accept that the whole situation was a lie meant to fool it. The result is not only a loss of faith in the parent but also a loss of faith in promises from others. It may sound like a very large consequence, losing faith in other people's promises for the rest of one's life and it does not happen if it's only a one-time breach of faith. When the lack of fulfilling promises is ongoing, then it does have a significant influence on the future adult's sense of trust in others.

The issue of how to train a child from ignorance and from immediate gratification of its needs and wishes to greater knowledge and the ability to wait is an extensive one and only one part of it gets played out in the arena of money and its equivalents. Parents promise to reward the child for good behavior (that is, the behavior that the parents want) and punish it for poor behavior (whatever it is that the parents don't want). I have no objection to a system of rewards but I do have some reservations about a system of punishment since it would be preferable to discuss matters with the child, granted that it has only a small degree of comprehension at a very early age, and this comprehension grow rather slowly. I believe it is okay to rap a child on the wrist when, in its infantile exploration, it wants to play with the electric outlet or touch a hot radiator. In the absence of verbal comprehension, a physically emphasized "no" is very effective and may save the child some real pain in the long run. But, as the children get older, have greater command of language and understand more complicated ideas, parents should switch to discussion as the best way of training, and remove themselves from physical and monetary rewards and punishments.

What I do find troubling is that there are many parents who, while loving in other ways, tend to take out their tempers and upsets on their children. Too often, when they come home from the job, for example, and are in a rotten mood, they act nasty to their children who had nothing to do with causing that mood, and this ill-temper is expressed in money and gift withholding as well as verbal nastiness and sometimes physical mistreatment. Displacing one's miserable mood from a boss or a co-worker onto a defenseless child is neither an effective way of handling the work situation nor of being a good parent. Unfortunately, it is easy to tease or criticize one's child or to withhold gifts and love, and the child's understanding of what is going on is not great enough to see the reality of the situation.

Anyone who has observed youngsters knows that they like regularity and consistency, predictability if you will, and they do not like changing circumstances. They are in a period of life where they are learning norms of behavior and are trying to conform to what is expected of them. Parental inconsistency, then, becomes a major problem for children to deal with, and when the rules keep changing because the parents are moody or because they are constantly changing their minds, the children become confused and doubting. Parental alternation between being indulgent one minute and withholding the next, makes the child blame itself for the variability and feel guilty for upsetting its parents. It is probably easier for a child to tolerate a consistently withholding parent than to deal with someone who keeps turning on and off. Again, doing this once or twice will hardly have lifelong consequences, but repeated inconsistency on the parent's part will contribute to a child's lack of belief in the sincerity and trustworthiness of others, not very good equipment with which to face the world as it grows older.

Another form of subtle mistreatment of children consists of making fun of them and their lack of skills. Sometimes, it's just a bad joke on the parent's part and sometimes it's a sadistic criticism masked as humor but the effect is the same, to make the child feel that it is inadequate and unable to meet parental expectations. Children experience depression, just as adults do, and these situations involving criticism, mocking, withholding love and gifts, and being the least favorite all contribute their share to creating depression on the spot and providing a foundation for depression in the future.

Of course, most parents mean well but they become parents not because they are perfect or because they represent sterling examples for their children to follow. They tend in fact to treat their children in the way they were treated; this is true not only in the handling of money matters but in disciplinary matters as well. Without having fully appreciated the fact, parents have generally absorbed the attitudes to money that their own parents had, and they tend to pass these on to the next generation. Rarely, though, do these attitudes get transmitted without modifications of one sort or another.

One of the modifications that we might see is that there are two parents and they are not always compatible in styles of relating to their children as well as to managing money; as a result the child is exposed to the values of the mother, the values of the father and the values that the two of them have agreed to or, if not exactly agreed to, compromised on. It can get somewhat confusing which attitudes to adopt, not only for the children but for the parents themselves.

As a rule, the same kinds of treatment that children experience at the hands of their mother and father will be experienced at the hands of a single parent, no matter of which sex. Here the child has no other parent to turn to for validation, but on the other hand, there are still a number of relatives around who contribute their share to where the child ends up. The situation for the child becomes much more complicated when the parents are divorced and when he or she lives with one, usually the mother, while the other, usually the father, is merely an occasional visitor to the household. For the most part, the visitor comes on weekends and takes the child or the children out for the day or for the whole weekend. This parent feels the obligation to entertain the children which usually entails spending money on them, and this entertainment can easily become more important than the time that they spend together. Many a father gradually decreases the frequency of his visits, eventually losing contact with his children because of the burden of providing something new and different every weekend they're together as well as the very significant expenses over and above what he is paying for child support. For their part, the children learn to judge the weekend, not on the quality of the relationship with their father but on where they went, how entertaining it was and how much money he spent on them.

Depending upon the bitterness of the breakup the mother, who usually is the one with custody of the children and who spends the vastly greater amount of time with them, may set up a scenario which is essentially a no-win situation for the father. She may encourage expensive outings and emphasize the financial aspect of the father's efforts, belittling everything he does for the children, cheapening their experience with him and making them reluctant to spend more time with him. She may also set up alternate entertainments for the children on weekends, making them reluctant to leave her and go off with their father. Much of this is based on the spending of money to influence the children's reactions, and they learn early in their lives to respond to these manipulations and also to set up some manipulations of their own, telling each parent how much the other is doing for them and, in this way, challenging that parent to do better.

In the last few years, there has been a great deal of attention paid to the children of parents who discover that they are homosexual and subsequently divorce their spouses. Aside from the problems that occur following any divorce, there do not seem to be any greater problems for these children and, as occurs with heterosexual parents, things are generally better when the homosexual parent is in a stable relationship rather than being a solitary. However, the heterosexual parent is often so angry and feels so rejected by the homosexual parent that she will turn the child or children against the father, using financial weapons among others to do so.

As we as a society have moved away to a great extent from the norm of a two-parent family to many alternate situations, the role of grandparents has changed as well. First let's look at the role of grandparents in the standard situation which has its positive and its negatives. One tends to think of being a grandparent as an unalloyed pleasure just as one tends to think of retirement as a situation with few or no problems. People at this stage of life are assumed to have accomplished their goals, both at work and at home, have successfully raised their children and are theoretically able to sit back and enjoy their grandchildren without having the day-to-day headaches of paying the bills and changing the diapers.

In this ideal view of the relationship between grandparents and grandchildren, the older folks live nearby, are cheerfully available as baby sitters, and have a special soft spot in their hearts for their grandchildren. We see adds on television extolling the grandparent's relationship with their grandchildren; they take them to vacation spots or share sports and hobbies with them. Somehow, we are given the impression that there are things that grandparents can do with the youngsters that are just not doable by the parents themselves. This is true in the best of circumstances, and grandparents often have the extra funds to treat their grandchildren to all sorts of goodies that the parents who are stuck with paying the necessities cannot afford.

However, as we have looked at the relationships between people, particularly what goes on between parents and children, things don't always proceed according to the idealized view of how they should work out. There are often snakes in the garden of Eden which upset and complicate matters, producing outcomes which are quite contrary to what is presented as ideal. Grandparents naturally have their own attitudes towards money, attitudes which may be the same as the parents' and serve as a reinforcement for them or which may be quite different. Not only might the parents have rebelled against their own parents' monetary habits but they have also worked out new compromises with their spouses. In addition, over the years, the grandparents' attitudes and ideas may have changed as their own financial picture evolved, and they may no longer be in harmony with what their children, the parents, feel. This can be quite confusing to the youngsters who are not sure which are right and which are wrong, and what should they themselves do, other than get the most for themselves.

Yvonne and Richard were well off parents who maintained a financially very high standard of living with only the best that money could buy. They were not happy when their daughter Virginia criticized them for their wasteful ways and sympathized with the poor and downtrodden of the world, advocating a simple and impoverished life style. They were even less happy when she married a man of another race whose attitudes towards money matched hers. His family, who was solidly middle class, was also upset with the attitudes of the young couple. As time went by, Virginia and her husband had three children and, although they earned little money and still advocated a simple existence, they did accept help from both sets of parents so that the grandchildren would have decent food, clothing and toys. The children were taught to laugh at their grandparents' attitudes towards money but the fact is that they enjoyed everything they were given and even wanted more while denying this to their parents. Imagine the confused attitude to money and material goods experienced by these children, and the conflict engendered in them by the clash in attitudes between their parents and grandparents. It's tempting to predict ahead that these three children will end up with attitudes towards money closer to their grandparents' than to their parents'.

Grandparents rarely have problems feeling that they are inadequate in the role of looking after children since they've been through it before and they don't provide direct care, but they still may have their most favored and their least favored among their grandchildren and are likely to show these preferences one way or another in the way they give gifts and other treats to them. One patient I treated vividly recalled an episode in which her grandmother gave candy to her cousin and not to her, and reported that, twenty years later, she still hated both her grandmother and her preferred cousin. Grandparents may carry over their favoritism to the children of their favorite child, or dislike the children of their least favored child. They may also have grandchildren who, regardless of whether their parents were favored or not, may become most favored or least favored in their own right, usually for no action of their own but merely because they represent someone else or were born at a certain time in the family's history. Remember that some people who don't want to grow old or have others think they're old try to disguise the fact that they are grandparents and dislike the living proof that they're not as young as they claim to be.

As is the case with parents, some grandparents may encourage competition between their grandchildren for their favor which finds expression in the handing out of money and such. They feel more important and more vital if the grandchildren compete with each other for their attention; instead of feeling lonely and somewhat outside the family situation, they feel more loved when the kids try to please them and do things for them, not being willing to admit that what's being done is for the rewards they hand out. Obviously, stimulating a competitive situation is not a healthy activity but that fact gets obscured by the need which gives rise to it.

There is also a triangularity in the relationship between grandparents and grandchildren with the parents providing the third component. In terms of evaluating what is going on, I would have to know how the parents and the grandparents get along as well as how the children and the parents get along before I could draw any conclusions about the role that the grandparents play in their grandchildren's lives. If, for example, there have been lifelong strains between the grandparents and their own children, this will have an influence on what happens between the older folks and the grandchildren. Grandparents who dislike their own children, and there are plenty of them, under superficial friendliness and warmth, often attempt to establish primary relationships with their grandchildren with the single goal of outdoing the parents, trying to become more important to the grandchildren than their own parents.

Since the grandparents often have more money for free spending, they may attempt to buy the affections of the grandchildren at the expense of the parents. Situations are set up where children are forced to choose between the two, where to spend time, whom to go on vacation with, and so forth. The children may very likely make their decisions based on who will give them more or who will spend more time with them. The advantage here goes to the grandparents who have the free time and the extra money. When there is a subtle hostile relationship, the grandparents take a triumphant satisfaction in beating out the parents, even though this may never be stated. The parents, on their part, feel anger towards their own parents and resentment, sensing that their children are being stolen from them by underhanded methods. Too often, since there is nothing overt being stated, what occurs is a repeat of the original relationship established between the grandparents and their own children, the parents, dating way back.

When the children's parents are divorced, grandparents are often faced with a difficult challenge. Some, a minority, don't like their own child and are glad at any inconvenience he or she may suffer. They side with the in- law and tend to support any actions against their own child, legal or emotional. More often, though, they become spokespersons for their own child and attempt to fill his or her place with their grandchildren. This is perhaps one of the reasons that parents who have custody rights either try to eliminate totally or significantly reduce the frequency of contacts with the ex-spouse's parents. They are treated as if they are secret agents who have been uncovered for what they are and who can't be trusted. No matter how much love these grandparents may have for their grandchildren, they often wind up being excluded from visiting or having any share in their grandchildren's upbringing.

On the other hand, when the parent is single, there is greater reliance on grandparents. Usually, in the case of an absent father, his parents have little to do with the rearing of the children, but some grandparents make a forceful approach to join the mother's parents in filling in for the absentee, both in physical presence and in financial assistance. More problems arise when a spouse has died and the remaining spouse wants to get on with life by remarrying. No matter what the parents of the deceased spouse do, they are often unwanted reminders of the past and are not welcome, no matter what they do. Children may have questions about their absent parents and grandparents but these can be put to rest, and the children go about their new lives.

Once the situation gets complicated and we move more and more away from the ideal script of how grandparents relate to their grandchildren, money and equivalents become more and more important. Children are naturally intuitive and sense the conflictful situations in which they are in the middle. It is not surprising that they respond by playing one set of adults against the other in order to get more of what they want. However, when they do so, it means that some of the natural bonds of love that should tie families together are being replaced by questions of who can provide them with more material benefits.

# 12

# *Breaking up*

At no time in history has divorce been so prevalent as it is today with an estimated 50% of marriages in this country ending up on the rocks. About 75% of divorced people re-marry and, of these, 60% divorce again. As a matter of fact, a substantial number goes on to get married and divorced again and again, something called serial marriage and serial divorce. Divorce is so common that social scientists feel compelled to come up with explanations for this sorry state of affairs. It has been attributed to a breakdown in our society's moral structure which allows people to divorce so much more easily, and also to the fact that women are now earners on their own and can afford to undertake actions leading to divorce to get out of intolerable situations, something only men were able to do in the past.

Whatever the wider social causes that contribute to making divorces easier to obtain, my focus will be on the psychological reasons that contribute to it and the ways that these find expression in money matters. Although money may have been a problem in the marriage, most divorces are not specifically the result of irreconcilable approaches to it on the part of the husband and the wife, but come about from other irreconcilable problems. These include sexual incompatibility, minor personal irritations that grow slowly over a period of time into hatred, in-law interference, a variety of differences in personal style, and personal growth away from each other. Sometimes these find expression in monetary terms along the way but this does not always happen.

Whether or not money plays a crucial role in bringing about a divorce, it becomes one of the primary issues that arise as things get played out in legal proceedings and decisions about who gets what. Even when the couple starts out amicably enough on the road to divorce, recognizing that their marriage is not working and that the best thing is a quick parting of the ways so that they can get on with other things and other people, somehow or other, money enters the picture and becomes a pivotal issue. It's often claimed that divorce lawyers are to blame for stimulating the frenzy over money and the bitterness which we all too often see. While lawyers may play their part, it's been my observation that virtually all other problems get funneled into financial considerations since it's easier to think in concrete money terms than it is to go into the convoluted emotions that have evolved between two people. In other words, the stored up anger and bitterness, the disappointed expectations and feelings of failure, the jealousies and sexual hurts, all get translated into money, at least that's what happens these days in our society.

In spite of the fact that divorce is so common today and gets so much attention, it is hardly new in the history of humankind. Records from ancient times indicate that it occurred way back with different societies handling it differently, largely depending upon how each one viewed the roles and status of men and women. Ancient Egypt appears to have been quite casual about divorce as well as about marriage, at least among the common people. A man and a woman simply moved in together with no formal wedding agreement and then separated when the relationship no longer worked, again with no formalities. Nevertheless, even then, there were rules about the division of property between the pair; laws about the ownership of property seem to be an essential feature in any country that warrants being called civilized. Not only did the Egyptians have property laws applicable to "divorce", they even had a form of prenuptial agreement with the parties stating in advance which property belonged to each member of the pair; it was expected that, if they separated, each one would resume ownership of what belonged to him or her before. Of course, what was true among the lower classes was not the same as what occurred among the wealthy and the aristocracy, where marriage was much more of a contractual affair and where different rules prevailed in relation to property. In these classes, marriages were alliances between families and between nations, and any rupture could have had grave consequences, including war.

When ancient societies had more formal arrangements and when records of these still exist, it seems that throughout history it was the husband who divorced the wife with her having little say in the matter. His reason for divorcing her may have been that she did not bear him a son or even any child at all, or because he just didn't like her any more, or because he wanted another woman, that particular society permitting only one wife per man. In other societies, the wife might just as well have been divorced since she was pushed into a corner while the husband went his own way, bringing home additional wives and concubines regardless of the women's feelings.

Most of the time, it's women who've gotten the bad end of the deal financially when there is trouble in a marriage because their needs and rights have mattered less in a male-dominated world, something we hear about a great deal these days as attempts are made to reverse that situation and come up with more equitable solutions. Nevertheless, even with women earning more money than ever before and having greater autonomy, while they may feel freer to file for divorce, they still seem to get the worst of it when divorce occurs. It takes a long time for established attitudes and practices to change.

There have been some high profile divorces in history, perhaps the highest profile of all leading to the establishment of a new religion when Henry VIII of England got rid of the older Catherine of Aragon and replaced her with his younger and more beautiful girlfriend, Ann Boleyn, who was pregnant by him. His divorcing Catherine was not well received by her brother, the King of Spain, or by the Pope and, rather than change his mind and accept their wishes, Henry declared himself free of Roman Catholicism. He made himself the leader of his own church and the exclusive master of his own country. That divorce initiated an almost 200 year on-and-off war between English Protestants and Catholics, with outside forces periodically intervening. More blood was probably spilled than in any other divorce in history, although some of today's divorces seem bitter enough to equal that. I might add that Henry, in addition to unloading his unwanted wife, also managed to make a financial profit on the deal, closing Catholic monasteries and convents, and adopting their real estate, money and gold religious objects as his own.

A brief history of divorce in the United States may come in handy here since it has contributed its share to today's situation. Here, too, there have been differences between the wealthy and the poor, and more difficulties for women than for men. Before the twentieth century, divorce was, in any case, a very infrequent phenomenon, and people either stayed together unhappily or separated without any legal proceedings. In the early years of the twentieth century, divorce was considered scandalous among the upper classes and a woman was expected to put up with any and all sorts of marital mistreatment rather than go her own way; if she did, she was shunned socially and, provided she could afford it, was better off moving to Europe where her status as a divorcee was not held against her and where she could maintain a social life. This situation provided the plot for many a novel and was a subject of the great novelist Edith Wharton in several of her books and short stories.

A bit later on, divorce became somewhat more acceptable but, prior to the Second World War, that is in the 1930's, it remained difficult to obtain in most states. Rich women whose husbands wanted to marry someone else went off to Reno, Nevada, the divorce capitol of the country, where they could become legal residents of the state after a brief stay and then obtain a divorce (a divorce in any state is recognized in all other states), returning afterwards to their homes while their husbands married their girlfriends. The whole business was quite expensive, making divorces something that only the wealthy could undertake; if you were poor, you just put up with the bad situation or parted informally.

One factor that plays a part in the increased divorce rate is the phenomenon I mentioned earlier, serial marriages and serial divorces. Here, marriages are undertaken as a form of escape from bad situations. Both partners may have been unhappy before they got married, frequently being at odds with their own families, not having rewarding friendships, not obtaining satisfaction from jobs or other activities, and having financial problems as well. Into this mess comes a new person who stimulates enthusiasm and seems to promise relief from all the troubles that existed before. (This doesn't usually turn out to be the case as Henry VIII discovered when Anne Boleyn gave birth to a daughter and not to the desired son. He went on to four more wives after her.) In the case of most people, the enthusiasm and excitement they experience are interpreted as love even when the attraction is based on a negative, running away from unhappiness, and the hopes for a better life are based more on wishful thinking than on fact.

People bring their own unhappiness along with them and what usually happens is that the enthusiasm that was there at the start wanes quickly as their hopes are not met. So, after a short while, each party relapses into the same unhappiness that he or she knew before, and there is disappointment and anger over the new defeats. These are directed toward the spouse who never lived up to expectations, and with a bitterness that is sometimes extreme. I don't want to sound too pessimistic since on occasion the two can work out their problems and manage a fairly good marriage. However, the truth remains that "he or she who marries in haste repents at leisure", and such marriages all too frequently lead to divorce. Part of the reason that people like this marry and divorce again and again is that they never stop to examine themselves but keep looking for partners who will be the salvation for all their problems and bring them happiness in an almost magical wishing will make it so scenario. Some of the nastiest divorces stem from such defeated expectations, and wrecked hopes and fantasies. Of course, sometimes they're so glad to get rid of each other that any money considerations are mere afterthoughts. What they want is freedom.

The case of Nan and Marty illustrates the type of situation in which both partners were trying to escape unpleasant lives. Nan was raised in a chaotic family, her father being a heavy drinker who was suspected of having abused her sexually, while her mother was a highly anxious woman who never really wanted to have children. In spite of the chaos, Nan managed to complete a college education and go on to graduate school; her feelings about herself were hardly very confident and she had severe problems with self-esteem. Marty's family background was also troubled, his father having severe depressions and his mother struggling to hold a job and provide the basics for her three children with little emotional energy left over to demonstrate much affection. As a result of their experiences during childhood, both Nan and Marty were severely deprived emotionally and needed tons of positive input. Nan wanted a man who would look after her and protect her from all kinds of stressful situations and Marty wanted a woman who could give him reassurance and comfort. When they first met through friends, Nan was impressed by Marty's many courtesies such as opening doors for her, bringing her flowers and candy, and always soliciting her opinions as to where they should go on dates. He, for his part, loved the fact that she took him seriously and admired him. Theirs was a whirlwind courtship and they married three months after they met.

Things went well for a while and they seemed to meet each other's needs. Then, Marty began to have problems at work due to his company being taken over by another firm with the possibility of future layoffs. He became worried and irritable, and no longer bothered to show Nan the attentions she wanted. She began to get angry at him for his "neglect" and created scenes with him, undercutting all the support and affection he had grown accustomed to receiving from her. This situation worsened and they began to wonder what they had seen in each other from the beginning. Marty began to stay out late just to avoid contact with Nan and, although he claimed there was no other woman in the picture, Nan was none too sure of that. On her part, she became romantically interested in a man at work who seemed to embody the courtesy and stability she had once seen in Marty. They were both relieved when they decided to divorce and move on to new relationships. Their divorce was one in which money arrangements played no part, largely because there was little money and partly because they wanted relief from each other. Just not having to deal with each other was reward enough.

Looking at this sad story, perhaps the saddest part of it is that neither of them had any real understanding of the intensity of the needs they brought to their marriage, needs that were so great that they were unlikely to survive the stresses of life together. More to the point is the likelihood that they would have the same experience in their next relationship and would probably move on to several more before giving up on the whole subject of romantic relationships. However, as the story repeats itself, there is invariably increased bitterness with each failure and an increasing with to hurt the other in any way possible, especially in the pocket-book or wallet.

Actually, one doesn't have to be married to get a "divorce" in view of the fact that there are so many informal relationships all over the world, including in this country, in which a man moves in with a woman. Probably the reason she provides the home is that she's the one who takes care of the children while the man doesn't always feel that responsibility, let alone assume it. They stay together for a while until things begin to go sour and then he picks up and leaves, sometimes remaining in touch and sometimes totally disappearing from the scene. In these arrangements, since there is no marriage, there can be no divorce and there is usually no dispute about property and who gets what; he just goes and whatever property there is stays with her. Ideally, that is, since he may take whatever appeals to him when he departs and she has little recourse in the matter. However, if they have lived together for more than a specified amount of time, often seven years, but that may vary from state to state, theirs might be considered a common-law marriage and, in that case, the woman does have distinct rights just as if they were legally married. There are some states, though, like New York, which do not recognize the entity of common-law marriage, no matter how long the pair have been together.

A new category of live-in pals, as distinct from a real marriage and from a common-law marriage has recently been acknowledged. Here two people live together for a while and give out no claim to be married, being accepted by their friends and relatives as a pleasant couple with no commitments. Questions arise, though, when the relationship breaks up, as to whether the poorer of the two is entitled to some sort of financial compensation, and this is a question which still remains unanswered.

There are those who regard divorce as just another business deal in which one tries to get the most money possible out of the other. But, over and above that, it's as if by getting more money, one of the spouses gets revenge on the other for all the troubles in the marriage; in addition, the more one takes away financially, the greater the proof that the problems leading up to the divorce were caused by the other. Not only is the financial winner supposedly innocent of contributing to the disharmony that led to the breakup, but also is rewarded for all that he or she (usually she) had to put up with. This is a belief held by a large percentage of the population, that the evil-doer must pay and the victim deserves compensation, but the fact is that fault is not an issue for judges as they decide monetary awards. With rare exceptions, they try to allocate division of the property on the basis of real needs and incomes, and not on the basis of past misdeeds.

Even though lawyers may not initiate the battles over money, they do play a prominent role in what goes on, and it would be incorrect to minimize their share in the bitterness that accompanies financial arrangements. Every lawyer who takes on a case wants to win, both for the ego gratification that a big win brings as well as for the financial rewards. Lawyers have their own reputations to maintain, and the more big amounts they get for their clients, the better known they become and the higher the fees they can command. However, these fees are not based on getting a percentage of what their client gets; instead, the attorneys get paid on a per hour basis. Of course, the more complicated things are and the more points at dispute, the more time they are required to spend on the case and the more they will take away for themselves. Here is where you can tell the difference between a lawyer who is scrupulous and one who churns up as much time as possible, making motions and fighting them before the judge.

Any divorce is difficult emotionally and monetarily but it becomes more so when there is a third party involved and the original spouse is being literally dumped for someone else, evoking feelings of rejection and lowered self esteem. They can't help but feel that they just weren't attractive enough or good enough to hold on to their spouses who were, as a result, driven to find someone better. When there are children, that too complicates matters as does the presence of grandparents and other relatives who play their role in what eventuates. Even prenuptial agreements do not guarantee a quick resolution of matters, nor does that even newer phenomenon, a post-nuptial agreement. The post-nuptial, as its name suggests, is an agreement about allocation of money that the couple agrees upon after the marriage. It usually occurs in a good marriage where the partners realize that they do not want to accept whatever decisions the government or a judge may impose and that they have ideas of their own about what they want done with their money in case of divorce (or in case of death).

Marriage is a legal arrangement between two people and so also is its rupture, and the process of breaking up is one that goes through many stages. In order to understand some of the money aspects that relate to this breaking up process, I'd like to review some of the legalities involved in the process and demonstrate where emotions play their part. This is more complicated than may first appear since there are so many factors at play in every divorce and since each state has different laws regulating what happens in divorce (not that there are fifty completely different sets of rules but what applies in one state does not necessarily apply in another).

Current legal and financial arrangements concerning divorce have changed significantly during the past generation to the point that things are much easier in most cases than they were fifty years ago. In most states, mutual agreement between the spouses that the marriage is not working, that there are irreconcilable differences, is now sufficient to obtain a divorce although some states require that there be a period of legal separation between the spouses in an attempt to overcome and resolve problems; such divorces by mutual agreement are called no-fault, just as with car accidents. Mediation of the issues between the spouses used to be required by some states but has pretty much fallen by the wayside.

If one of the partners does not wish the divorce to go ahead, then things change. In New York State, the rules are fairly stringent and, if one spouse wants a divorce and the other doesn't, the spouse who wants it must prove some failing on the part of the other, something severe enough to necessitate an escape from the marriage. Four reasons are considered to meet the bill: 1) cruel and inhuman treatment (and that means real hurtful stuff), which is seen in the most bitter divorces and which requires a trial by jury rather than leaving matters in the hands of the judge alone; 2) abandonment, which may involve desertion or which may be something called constructive in the sense that, although the spouse is present, abandonment may be construed because of the denial of sexual contact; 3) imprisonment, and 4) adultery, this not being taken very seriously at present. Not only does the accusation have to be made but it has to be provable in a court of law, not that most divorces come to trial. What usually happens is that the couple meet with their lawyers all together to work things out. When this proves too difficult to accomplish, then a judge reviews the case and may impose financial conditions. In practice, judges much prefer that both sides work thing out for themselves with their contribution being to confirm the arrangements.

One outstanding example of the extremes that people go to in obtaining divorces was the recent break-up of the marriage of New York City's ex- mayor, Rudy Giuliani and his wife, the television personality, Donna Hanover. She accused him of adultery following his accusations against her of cruel and inhuman treatment. Both sides held fast to their positions and the case seemed destined to come to a bitter trial when they settled at the very last moment before it was scheduled to begin. There must have been a very happy judge as well as a very disappointed press when this happened.

Of the four acceptable causes, imprisonment is easy to demonstrate, but the others are much harder to define and to prove. The odd thing is that it's often the spouse who wants out and may have a playmate on the side who goes to great lengths to prove that it's the other spouse who is committing the infidelity; that's because the guilty party feels at a psychological disadvantage throughout the divorce proceedings and wonders whether his or her actions may impress the judge adversely resulting in financial consequences as well as having implications for which spouse is considered the more suitable one to have custody of the children.

Here, again, the popular belief that one partner will be punished for the errors of his or her ways is erroneous since judges are, for the most part, concerned with coming up with fair decisions rather than with penalties. Nevertheless, lawyers keep trying to convince the judge that their clients are angels and the opposite side is the very devil, a tactic which generally does not impress a judge who has been through the scene countless times before. But it has the benefit (to the lawyer) of making the client feel that he or she is doing everything possible and is a real buddy. However, if both sides agree on the divorce and on all the financial arrangements, they can live apart for one year under mutually agreed upon terms, and the divorce will be granted.

Naturally, as I previously mentioned, no divorce is a sudden event but results from problems which have been brewing for some time. When divorce comes, there is already a long history of slights, angers and irritations which have reached the boiling point and are no longer tolerable. In spite of this accumulation of grievances, many couples decide to see what it would be like to stay married but to live apart for a while in the hope that, somehow, tempers will cool and the positives that originally led to the marriage will prevail over the negatives that arose along the way. This is a trial separation which is really only possible if the couple has enough money to maintain two households for the period during which decisions about the long term fate of the relationship are made. Couples may seek counseling help during this phase, and sometimes they are able to resume their lives together fairly happily. Because of the difficulties entailed in setting up separate residences including the expense involved, many a couple who is undergoing a trial separation continue to live together for a while; it is also not unknown for sexual activity to continue throughout the trial separation period. There are no statistics available to indicate how many of these arrangements actually go on to divorce and how many just settle down instead.

Sometimes the settling down together is not too happy a state of affairs because the problems persist and may even become worse, the ties holding the couple together including fears of being alone, wanting to put on a good show for their community or wanting to provide a home for their children. This was the case with Ted and Peggy. They were childhood sweethearts who married as soon as they finished their education and who settled in a pleasant suburban town not far from New York City. Ted taught at the local schools and Peggy stayed home to raise their two sons but she also did some sales work in a local antique store. Since Ted had no head for business, Peggy handled all the finances. Everything looked great to outsiders but Ted discovered that he was attracted to younger men and went in for this in a big way, heading to the city where he frequented gay bars and baths, constantly on the search for new partners. Along with these activities, he totally lost sexual interest in Peggy who, whether because of Ted's indifference and his increasing verbal abuse or for other reasons, turned to alcohol. This situation went on for a long time and became even more extreme after he retired by which time, Peggy had become a confirmed alcoholic who underwent cures on a regular basis but always returned to her addiction.

A crisis arose when Ted learned that Peggy was seeing another woman from her alcoholism group. His jealousy was aroused and his distress was compounded when he discovered that their joint savings and retirement funds were down the astonishing sum of $400,000. Peggy couldn't account for the lost money but it became clear that her girlfriend had a share in the disappearance since Peggy often was too befuddled to handle their affairs. One stormy session followed another and both promised to give up their misbehavior in order to salvage what was left of their marriage. However, their good resolutions didn't last long and both returned to their extramarital activities. They decided, though, that they still loved each other and would continue to stay together. Contributing to this decision were their feeling that the marriage kept them somewhat heterosexual and helped to maintain the facade they presented to their community as well as wanting to continue to provide a home for their two college age sons. The disappearance of the $400,000 was still a fact and they couldn't figure out what had happened to it, but it certainly was too great to have been spent on groceries or even on liquor. The question arose whether Chrissie was providing for her future with Peggy, with Ted pushed out of the picture, or even just looking out for her own future although nothing was ever proven. Nevertheless, as of this moment, the couple remains together with divorce not even being considered. One can't imagine a more separated couple and one can only wonder whether ultimately there will be any money left at all. One can also speculate whether retaliation for Ted's frequent and well announced (to Peggy) infidelities contributed to her helping to "lose" so much money.

They face a future still together but not really together and much impoverished.

Their case is not unique and lawyers' files are full of stories of all sorts of misappropriations and mismanagement of money in order to get around the legal division of property that occurs with divorce. At times, as Ted and Peggy's case demonstrates, these maneuvers occur even when no divorce is contemplated with each partner attempting to better his or her financial situation at the other's expense since the real bonds that tie a marriage together are no longer in place.

Once matters progress beyond the stage of trial separation, divorce is next, and here we encounter a whole series of problems in which money is a major issue and the emotional attitudes towards money play a very great role. You may recall, from the chapter on marriage, that I said that some couples maintain totally separated financial lives while others keep all their property in common and yet others have a mix of these. Should the situation deteriorate into divorce, how are those funds handled? Even though the original intention may have been to preserve each one's financial independence, the fact is that the law has its own ideas about things.

Joint ownership is the term used to describe all assets that the couple has in common, that is all manner of things that are registered in both names, although it also includes everything that was earned or acquired during their life together. There are also possessions that belong to each member of the couple individually and this is indicated by the fact that it is legally listed in that one's name without the other one being mentioned at all, though a judge's decision can overrule that. Property acquired during the marriage (except by gift or inheritance) is considered joint marital property, no matter in whose name it is listed and, as such, has to be divided exactly in half when the divorce occurs.

But a simple statement that everything should be divided in half does not completely resolve the issue since some things can't easily be split down the middle. How does one divide a house into two halves? What about cars, pets, appliances? Pension plans and social security tend to be considered the property of whoever's name they're in though there's some question about this in the case of pension money added during the marriage. Also, look at the debit side instead of the assets! How does one divide up the accumulated debt the couple has run up over the years? What about the debt that one partner brought to the marriage which the other partner assumed some responsibility for? And what about the debt that a spouse runs up during the divorce process? No matter how a judge struggles to be fair in the division of assets and debts, it is almost impossible to come up with results that are completely split down the middle. If you add on the spite factor in which one partner wants to hurt the other, it becomes even more difficult to split things in two since almost any intangible asset can be overvalued or undervalued. Even when one of the partners does not like some particular object, he or she may claim to want it with a burning desire just to bug the other who may really want it. Sometimes it requires the wisdom of a King Solomon to know which of the two really wants or needs the object in question and which one is just creating a storm.

Even when the wife works, there are usually significant income differences between the two spouses with the husband almost always earning the higher amount, at least during the child-bearing years. In situations where the wife started out generating more income, the chances are that she had to cut back her working hours to have enough time to be a wife and mother. After divorce, she is at a disadvantage in returning to the job market since she has been out of work for a while and may not be able to resume her previous employment at its previous level of income.

Nora was a nurse when she first met Bart who was a medical student at the university hospital where she worked. They started to date and, after a year, they married with Bart continuing his studies and Nora continuing to work. Both worked hard for several years, Bart to complete his training and Nora to make ends meet; finances became even more difficult with the arrival of twins during this period. Eventually, Bart finished his training and established himself as a surgeon in a suburb of the city where they worked. Within a short period of time, he was earning a substantial income, and Nora wanted to quit work and look after her home and children. At just this point, Bart told her that he had fallen in love with someone else and wanted a divorce. Nora was devastated at this and was further devastated by all suggested financial arrangements along with the divorce. She felt that she had enabled Bart to become a surgeon and she was entitled, in addition to half his current assets, to a share in his future earnings over the years, as well as in any pension arrangements that he would acquire. While she got half his current assets, she had to settle for much less income than she felt entitled to via alimony and child care payments in the future, and was disqualified from a share in his pension plan. She felt that she had been used and ultimately thrown away when Bart had no more use for her as he moved into a higher income and into more elevated social circles.

Even when all financial factors seem to be decided, there are still many loose ends which contribute to the messiness of the divorce and the financial arrangements. In his eagerness to obtain a divorce, a husband may commit himself to open-ended expenses which may come back to haunt him. For example, he agrees to pay the children's educational expenses, and then finds that he is responsible for paying tuition in the highest priced private high schools and universities with enormous graduate school costs as well. Or he may agree to pay for a daughter's wedding, only to find, when the time comes, that his ex-wife has arranged for the most luxurious wedding party in history. Yet, he is legally bound to pick up all the expenses since he committed himself to do so.

One of the interesting eventualities that may occur as divorce is considered is the absolute refusal of one spouse to agree to a divorce, necessitating complicated legal action to achieve it. This sort of situation might arise when a husband (usually it's the man rather than woman) has found a younger girlfriend whom he wishes to marry. He attempts to get his wife to grant him a divorce but she is so outraged that she digs in her heels and absolutely refuses; either that or she tries to make the financial conditions so stringent that he simply can't meet them. Because obtaining a divorce is more difficult when the parties are not in agreement about it, this behavior on the part of the wife may make divorcing virtually impossible as the cost can exceed the husband's capacity to pay. He is then in the position of either remaining with his wife and living a life of hellish tension or moving out to be with his hoped-for second wife. The other woman, for her part, usually is unwilling to accept the role of permanent girlfriend, no matter how strong her feelings for him might be, and she eventually leaves; sometimes her departure has a lot to do with the fact that the man is so financially strapped after fulfilling his commitments to his former wife and children that there's little left for a new home and a second marriage. What ensues is essentially a legal separation with the two parties going their separate ways, and lots of unresolved problems involving finances and child-rearing practices.

Another variation on the theme of divorce which is the reverse of this arises in some Orthodox Jewish families; according to tradition, it is only the husband who can initiate a divorce, called a "get". He may dislike his wife so much that, instead of starting the procedure leading to a get, he refuses to do so, leaving her in marital limbo, even though he may continue to support her and his children (although that is by no means a sure thing). She is left in a position where she cannot establish a new relationship but is locked into the current empty and meaningless one until such time as he agrees. What makes it worse is that some husbands not only refuse to support their wives and children, but agree to file for a get only when and if the wives comes up with sufficient money to buy them off. Civil law, not religious law, has been instituted to direct the husband to take definitive action, but that gets us into the issue of church vs. state and the imposition of state law on religious matters. However, with growing awareness on the part of the Orthodox community of the strangling situation these women find themselves in, there has been mounting pressure by religious leaders on the husbands to do the compassionate thing and free the wives from this forced connection and allow them to move on.

When a divorce looks like it's going to take place, the next important step after dealing with current assets is figuring out financial arrangements for the ensuing years, these being based on the usual situation where the man is the major breadwinner, and the woman either earns less or stays home taking care of children. Generally, there are two kinds of payments that an ex-wife receives, one is alimony, the more modern word for which is maintenance, and the other is child support. Both of these come from the husband's pocket but under different circumstances. Alimony is paid to the wife to keep her in the style to which she was accustomed. It is deducted from the ex-husband's before-tax income and, for tax purposes, is counted as the wife's income, meaning that she has to pay taxes on this as if it was money that she worked for. Child support, which may continue until the child reaches the age of 18, finishes his or her education or some other specified point in time, comes out of the father's income after taxes, meaning that the wife doesn't have to pay taxes on this income. A shrewd wife advised by a knowledgeable lawyer may attempt to get more in child support and less in alimony so that her tax burden is less and she keeps more of what she gets. On the other hand, child support payments do lapse at some point while alimony goes on forever (occasionally there are some time limitations).

Alimony generally continues until death of one or the other or until the wife re-marries, with the idea being that her next husband becomes responsible for her future care. There are occasions when an ex-wife decides that she will never remarry in order to keep on receiving alimony for the rest of her life regardless of the fact that she may enter into relationships that are marriages in all but name. She and her boyfriend live together and benefit from the income received from her first husband. Of course, if he gets wind of this and can prove that she and her boyfriend are virtually married, he may be able to negotiate a termination of his alimony responsibilities. However, proving that they are indeed living together is easier said than done, and may involve the services of a private detective to obtain proof of the situation.

All of this is based on the assumption that the husband is the major breadwinner in the family and the wife earns little or nothing. What happens in those cases where the wife earns much more than her husband, and he puts in a claim for alimony? The courts have not come up with a clear answer to this question because our society takes a dim view of a husband living off his wife's money, he theoretically being the one who has greater income potential and theoretically not needing anything from her. Some cases have resulted in the husband's getting alimony and some have not; no one can predict the future of this particular issue although it is sure to arise more and more often as increasing numbers of women attain higher executive positions and earn higher incomes.

When there are children in the marriage, no matter which parent gains custody (usually the mother), the other parent (usually the father) is placed in an awkward situation since visits are limited with the children's day-in, day-out home being with their mother. Paternal visits are limited to weekends, occasional holidays and sometimes part of the summer. On these occasions, which take the children away from their homes, the father is forced to provide entertainment for them and to work out a schedule of activities in advance. Even though he tries very hard, the situation is artificial and proves to be a great strain for all concerned. Most fathers fall back on doing things which means spending money to the point that it becomes a burden on them. Even when the children enjoy being with their father, they start to look forward more and more to the entertainments. Eventually the success of the visits has a great deal to do with the amount of money spent. In any case, the children are removed from their usual activities and friends, and are placed in a highly artificial situation.

The situation is aggravated when the mother remains angry with the father and bitter over the events that led up to the divorce, no matter what the justice of the situation. This certainly was true with Nora who could never bring herself to forgive Bart and did what she could to make his life more painful. These mothers frequently influence the children against their fathers, suggesting all sorts of wonderful activities that they could be doing if they stayed home. They may even go as far as making nasty comments about the fathers and encouraging the children to share their negative opinions of them. In these efforts, they may be supported by their own parents who have it in for their former sons-in-law. They may also be supported by their former in-laws who may realize what is going on but don't want to lost contact with their grandchildren; they go out of their way to cater to the mother. At times, knocking fathers down goes so far that these mothers help the children to "realize" that their fathers are making sexual overtures towards them, in this way re-opening the question of visitation rights.

One example of this sort of behavior occurred in the case of Roger, a 40 year old stock broker who had been married for ten years to Rosalie. They both entered the marriage with great expectations of a happy life together, particularly since both had played the field and been disappointed many times previously. Each felt that this marriage would be redemptive for them and that from that moment on, there would be no problems. Things didn't work out quite that way with Roger devoting his time and energy primarily to the "market", and Rosalie her time and energy to her wardrobe. They had one daughter, Angelica, and kept up a superficial cheerfulness to the outside world even though they were enormously disappointed in each other. Eventually, they realized that their marriage was a failure and decided to divorce. Rosalie was furious with Roger, not only because of her disappointed expectations but because she was embarrassed in front of her friends that her marriage had failed and because her parents kept telling her that they had warned her he was no good. Rosalie obtained very generous child support and alimony as well as more than her share of their jointly held property, and Roger was left with weekend visits with Angelica.

Rosalie did everything she could to turn Angelica against her father, criticizing his weekend plans, calling him cheap, delaying the hours that he could pick up Angelica and so further limiting their time together, as well as performing any other spiteful tricks she could think up. When

Roger bought Angelica clothes, Rosalie would subject them to careful examination, pulling at the fabric until it tore and then telling Angelica that her father bought her junk. She also ended up breaking most of the toys he bought and she told Angelica that the toys too were garbage. Her parents, who had maintained a strong influence on Rosalie, supported her in her criticism of her ex-husband. Roger attempted to keep up the connection although he reduced the frequency of his visits with his daughter when, out of the blue, he received a summons to court because of charges that he was sexually abusing his daughter. When the court heard the case, it was apparent that there was no truth to the story and that Angelica was reciting a script that her mother had rehearsed with her. Nevertheless, the point was made that she was not happy with her father's visits and they were cut back in frequency and in duration; there was also provision made that a chaperone would be with them at all times, just in case.

Roger felt that he had been framed and eventually almost discontinued his visits to Angelica. The only question that remained was whether, at some future point, she would realize that she had been unduly influenced by her mother and maternal grandparents, and had been unfair to her father or whether he would just recede into the background as a man that had once been around and then disappeared. The answer to this question depended on how much influence her mother and grandparents brought to bear on her, and whether it was enough to stifle any curiosity about him or whether, to the contrary, it made her realize that she was being denied the opportunity to form her own judgments.

One of the more recent developments in the break-up scenario is the payment of what is called palimony. This comes up when a couple has lived together for a number of years in an informal arrangement. They are generally recognized by friends and families on both sides as a pair, and they are invited places together, go on vacations together and share many of the things that a married couple does. There are many explanations for their not getting married, but the fact is that they never do. Eventually, they come to a parting of the ways and separate. The woman who usually has the lower income sues the man who usually has the higher income for financial support, claiming that the relationship was almost a marriage and she is entitled to a share in his income. She might advance the argument that, without her being there, he would never have reached the income level he attained and that, therefore, some of his money by rights should go to her. Courts are inconsistent about their support of such claims and decisions vary from state to state and from one court to the next. In California, notably, in some such cases, awards have been made to the woman and the word palimony has been coined to suggest that it is the reward for being a pal over the years.

There is another way of breaking up a marriage, very effective if also illegal and immoral, and that is to murder the spouse. While not that common, it probably occurs more frequently than we realize, and it certainly happens enough in books and movies. What leads up to it is usually a combination of several factors though not all of them have to be present: vicious hatred, lack of conscience, money problems and the inability to terminate the relationship any other way. If done successfully, it avoids all the legalities involved in the divorce process and all the concerns about who gets what in the division of the couple's assets.

Don't make the mistake of thinking that it's only in our country that murder resolves these issues. It also occurs in other parts of the world, for example, in some parts of India. Here, a wife brings a dowry to the marriage which reverts to the husband if she dies. Many a wife who doesn't please her husband has a fatal "accident" and he winds up the richer for it. Of course, this can't happen repeatedly since the families of potential brides learn of such "accidents" and avoid the groom like the plague. Other societies have other traditions involving doweries but you can be sure that there are fewer accidents of a fatal nature in those societies where the dowry returns to the bride's family. Also the husband is likely to be more cooperative when he knows that, in case of a break-up, the money will leave with the wife. In yet other societies, the groom's family pays a bride price and buys the wife from her family. In these cases, she's treated much better since she is worth money over and above any personal value as a human being she possesses.

There are, without a doubt, many more variations on the theme of breaking up a marital relationship in which money and emotions play such vital roles. Suffice it to say that, since divorce is so turbulent, it might have been better in the long run to have worked out more of the couple's personal problems before legal entanglements complicated the picture rather than have to go through the hell of a divorce and all its monetary ramifications.

# 13

# *Retirement*

Once upon a time, not very long ago, retirement was considered just one phase of old age and not a very important one at that. When someone reached the age of sixty-five, he or very occasionally she (women seldom worked outside their homes) was given a farewell party by an employer or by co-workers and then went off to pass the few remaining years of life being yet one more elderly person, sitting around and waiting for illness and death. But that is no longer the case since increased wealth in our society and advances in health care have made retirement a distinct component of the life cycle with its own spectrum of delights and problems. Depending upon your personality and expectations, it can be a positive experience or a negative one.

Retirement is regarded by many as something to be enjoyed. No longer do you have daily work obligations; instead you have plenty of time to be with your family and friends, the freedom to travel and the opportunity to pursue personal interests. You can take up hobbies, look after your grandchildren, acquire new skills and knowledge, and resume interests and activities which previously had to take second place to work. You even have the option of moving to an ideal climate where the world lines up to meet, even anticipate, your every wish. In this scenario, good health persists for many years and there are no money worries whatsoever.

Others doubt that this paradise exists and don't believe that all the wonderful expectations occur to the extent that is hoped for. These people focus on the other side of the retirement coin; for them, it is viewed as a period of boredom, a pathway which leads, more or less quickly, to illness and death. They see it as a continuing diminution of involvement in life, a period of make-work with no real rewards and lots of losses and suffering, and they view it with foreboding and fear.

This contrast in expectations only goes to show how we are each of us different in terms of personality; lifelong relationship to work, family and friends; external circumstances; health and interests, all of which play a part in decisions about retirement such as when and how it occurs, and what anyone ends up doing with the so-called golden years. In addition, all sort of chance occurrences and just plain good or bad luck play their part. And then, there's the big question of how much money you have and how that stacks up against what you may need. Money, in fact, is one of the major determinants in what you do in retirement, how you go about planning for it, and how you adjust to it, but it is far from being the only consideration, and it is a mistake to think of it in those terms.

Although retirement traditionally occurs at 65, it may take place earlier or later. But the question of retirement comes up very much earlier in one's life than age 65, and some people think about it actively even before they start their work lives. Such early attention is partly due to the situation of parents and grandparents whose retirement lives and satisfactions are on display to the younger generation. Partly it is due to the fact that there has been an increasing emphasis on retirement with new laws and new programs coming along fairly regularly and with experts at the workplace explaining all these options to employees on an ongoing basis. Also a very large and well-organized retirement industry has arisen which encourages retirement and constantly comes up with creative and enjoyable ways for you to utilize your money and new-found free time.

While most of us start our work lives with concerns about the nature of the job, the people we will work with, the setting and the salary, there are always a few who feel the need to meet first and foremost with the Personnel Department to learn about benefits and retirement options. To other workers, these people seem a little crazy, planning for the end of their work lives before they have even started. These people are not so strange as it may seem since it's not a bad idea to start planning for retirement long before you get to the age where anything you can do about it no longer matters very much. Too many of us wake up to the inevitability that we must retire only when we reach our fifties and become painfully aware of the realities of life, death and long-term illness, starting to see them up close in our parents' generation and hearing of the occasional death of one of our contemporaries. By this time, it's a bit late to start planning although, if you want to retire at 70, maybe twenty years of planning would be enough. But starting retirement planning in your fifties probably will not let you accumulate enough for you to stop working in your sixties. Every financial consultant you see on television or hear at lectures on the subject emphasizes that a little money invested per month starting at an early age will add up to a pretty large amount when you reach retirement age, much more than a larger amount invested regularly beginning when you're older.

These days, there's lots of room for individual planning in what you do with the money accumulating in your job's retirement plan. Up to about thirty years ago, you had money deducted from your income before or after taxes, and it went into the company's standard plan. You had virtually no control over how it would be invested or what would be done with it, and you were generally granted a relatively low rate of interest on the amount. Subsequently, competition and changing rules in the financial organizations that hold your pension funds allowed you to move your money from one type of investment to another, but only a little at a time and no more than a certain amount each year. Your choices were to obtain a fixed interest, to receive money market rates or to have the money invested in some basket of stocks. More recently this has been further liberalized to the extent that you now have a multitude of choices in how your money will be handled, sometimes a dizzying number of choices including conservative stock portfolios and aggressive growth (not that they always grow so aggressively, but it feels good to the investor to think that he or she is acting aggressively to increase retirement income), mutual funds and everything in between. You may not be a great financier or terribly knowledgeable about the stock market but having a wide choice allows you to become more involved in what happens to your money. People who are more passive tend to let the corporation do their thinking for them and they do little more than glance at the annual statements they receive. Those who are more financially enterprising tend to review their account statements regularly and switch funds around to what seem to be better investments. If you can manage to do this over the years while still keeping up with all the demands of your job and family responsibilities, you may wind up with a retirement nest egg several times larger than the person who just lets matters slide.

Psychological factors obviously play an active role in early thinking about retirement. Those who are more cautious about planning their lives and are fearful for the future are certain to be among the people who start their retirement planning even before they take their first jobs. People who like compulsive organization in their affairs will also start their planning early as well as those who are driven by pessimism; if you expect bad things to happen in the future, you are more likely to take whatever actions you can to make your life better even though you may keep on doubting that anything you can do will make a difference.

On the other hand, there are those who just can never settle into thinking about retirement. No matter how often people around them, friends, family and co-workers, tell them they ought to do some planning for the future, they can't bring themselves to think about it and, if they are forced to do so, quickly escape back to their previous avoidance. Although psychiatrists call this type of behavior avoidance, that may be too strong a word since some individuals are so involved in their work and current issues such as job development, promotions and salary increases that the whole idea of retirement is too remote to grab their attention. Some are so afraid to look ahead at what they consider the end of their lives that they don't prepare for it, and some are so busy living in the moment that any plans for the future seem unreal and unnecessary. Also, there are those whose job situations are so insecure and their incomes so unpredictable that they don't have the luxury of giving any serious consideration to retirement; their efforts are concentrated at just holding on to the here and now, the current job and whatever security it promises for the moment.

Obviously, then, there are extremes in thinking about retirement while one is still young, from being overly preoccupied with it to the extent that current job and activities are seen exclusively in terms of future savings, to the opposite, not even thinking about it at all. What you should do is examine retirement packages every time you start a new job, making sure that there are good long-term benefits while focusing on whether you really like this job and what the salary is. In other words, the most appropriate approach is to take a job for itself while checking to make sure that your future is being provided for.

Early awareness of retirement is the beginning of the process of retirement, the first phase which may be called the planning phase. The second phase, partly dependent on how much planning in advance one has done, is the actual decision when and how to retire, and the third phase is what to do with the long period of retirement after one stops working on a full-time basis.

The question of how much money you have is perhaps the key consideration you take into account when deciding just when to retire. It is of course impossible to predict for how many years of life you are accumulating resources and how much will be needed. It is also impossible to know what the rate of inflation will be and how much your money will actually buy as the years unfold. It is also impossible to know when and how deeply medical expenses will cut into your savings. Many experts suggest that returns of 70—75% of pre-retirement income per year is adequate. However, this is just a ball-park figure since it is based on the assumption that you will spend less on clothing and commuting expenses after retirement and will probably have lower standing monthly expenses, having paid off your mortgage, completed tuition payments for your children's education and have discontinued your life insurance policies as no longer necessary, saving yourself the substantial cost of the annual premium or its monthly installments. You probably are in a lower tax bracket as well. On the other hand, once liberated from the daily grind with its restrictions on how much playing you can do, you might spend much more than you did in the past in pursuit of enjoyment, at least in the early days of retirement. There is even a theoretical possibility that you will have more money than you know what to do with, and that brings with it its own dilemmas, especially for the person with a life-long addiction to watching every penny that goes out.

While there are those who are afraid of outliving their money, others are more concerned about leaving as large an inheritance as possible to their heirs, sometimes because they know the heirs will need it and sometimes because they want people to think that they were rich. It is so important to them to give this impression that they live very frugally, spending money only where it will show and otherwise living a spartan existence. Furthermore, they hold on to this supposed distinction, being rich, as if it really mattered once they have left this world. Reality based factors concerning money often take a back seat to psychological factors in retirement as well as in other phases of life.

People often reveal previously hidden personality characteristics under the stresses of retirement and their attitudes and behavior cannot always be predicted. The subject is so emotional and so weighted with significance that optimists may become pessimists and pessimists may become optimists. The optimist who expects to have a long life expectancy is the person who is more likely to worry that his or her money will not last out a lifetime and who becomes more fearful about what the long-term future may hold in store; cheerfulness, the usual approach to life, turns into worry. The pessimist who expects to have a short and unhappy life after retirement may feel more inclined to spend money and engage in expensive and adventurous undertakings to make the best of the limited time that is expected, sometimes revealing a previously hidden zest for life. Such reversals in personality are not unusual as people enter retirement mode.

Another factor that may play a part in estimating whether one has enough for the rest of one's life is the idea that one will live forever, an idea secretly held by a significant number of people. While none of us likes to think about dying and we all tend to deny that it can happen to us, there are some who simply cannot accept it and somehow believe that they are different from the rest of us. Their thinking in terms of money as they decide on retirement reflects this belief and they can never conceive of having sufficient funds because they are anticipating an extremely long future.

When one retires, there are usually several sources of income available; one that is markedly different from one person to the next is how much money you have managed to save during the course of your lifetime. There are those who are lucky enough to have plenty of cash, in which case money is not a real problem while others have put little aside and are more dependent on pensions and social security. The ones with plenty of cash are not always the ones who were born rich or who made huge salaries; instead they may have earned relatively little but stinted on spending throughout their lives, planning for retirement by constantly restricting the outflow and carefully supervising their various investments and pensions; these are future-oriented people who deny the present and its demands. Similarly, the ones with little money in the bank are not always the ones who earned less; they may have made a lot and spent a lot, enjoying the present with little thought for the future.

There are many kinds of retirement income other than those based on savings. There is social security which brings in a monthly check as long as one lives. Some people have government or other pensions which also go on for as long as they live. However, once you enter the big wide, wonderful world of pensions, there are enough options to test your personality and expectations. You can choose a pension payment which allows a higher amount per month for as long as you live but these payments end the moment you die and the account dies with you with nothing left for your family, no matter how much you put in and no matter how little you received back; this option is usually selected by single people, by those who want to have as good a time as possible in terms of spending money, by those who believe that they will live a long time and by those who want their families to have nothing; yes, some people dislike their families enough to want none of their relatives to benefit by their deaths. There are other payment arrangements which also give high monthly payments but stop after a designated period of time; these are generally chosen by people who don't expect to live too long. Yet other pension pay-offs provide less per month but go on as long as you live, and whatever remains from your contributions and accumulated interest payments goes to your heirs; these are for people who are concerned about protecting the interests of their families and legatees. There are still other arrangements. By the time you figure in your spouse's pension plan with all of its provisions, and which amounts are before taxes and which are after taxes, there is a confusing and often overwhelming number of choices but there is something for almost every personality and way of life.

Deciding when to retire is not based exclusively on how much money you have stashed away. Although the decision to retire at a designated time may have been carefully planned for years in advance, it may happen suddenly, sometimes for reasons beyond your control such as the failure of a business or a major change in your health. In a way, your age is an almost secondary concern even though it does shape the attitudes that predispose to earlier or later retirement.

What are some of the other situations that contribute to a relatively abrupt decision to retire? Technological developments, such as computerization, which provide challenges to the older worker that feel overwhelming and insurmountable, is one. Social changes in the world also contribute to the decision to retire, as do cultural developments. For example, the rise of managed care has led many physicians to decide, if they can swing it financially, to retire rather than function under the new circumstances which have replaced the former professional style to which they were accustomed. Popular musicians who achieved recognition in one musical style may not be able to keep up with different styles as they come along and may prefer to leave the scene gracefully rather than struggle to hold on and lose out in the end, anyway.

At some point in the years or months approaching retirement, there is also the realization that you're no longer as employable as you used to be. Formerly, in the golden years of being a younger worker, you could search for a new job and be a welcome applicant, someone whose services an employer would be glad to obtain. Now, when you go for a job interview, no matter what the laws are against bias based on age, you know that your age is against you and you feel the pitying looks the interviewers give you, that is if you get the interview. Even though an employer is not supposed to ask your age or birth date, your resume points pretty accurately to how old you are and new job opportunities vanish without your ever being told exactly why. After a while, you realize that your choices are limited to staying on in a job that no longer turns you on or throwing in the towel completely and retiring.

In the current job market, one hears much about downsizing to increase profitability. When you're downsized into retirement, what is actually being said is that you are of no further use to the organization and it's not worthwhile for the organization to continue to pay you. No matter how alluring a buyout may be, it takes a very strong sense of who you are and your value both as a person and as a worker to remain buoyant and confident when your boss attacks your working identity. Golden parachutes, providing very ample pensions and retirement benefits, make the same statement about uselessness, even if it is on a higher financial plane.

The situation may be somewhat different for the person in a power position, he or she who owns and controls the business or department. As the determining force on the job, it is unlikely that this individual can be compelled to retire. However, even here, there may be children or younger executives who want their time at the top and who see the chief as an impediment to their advancement. Intergenerational conflict, battles between parents and children with the parents eventually losing, rears its ugly head and leads to the inevitable "youth must be served". It is hard for anyone to resist even subtle pressure when it is continuous and progressive, and even harder when you're older.

When people have been forced to bow out of a work situation for such reasons, they usually end up with some feelings of defeat and inadequacy. Feeling this way often leads to a need to prove the opposite, that one is no slouch but has value and abilities that continue unimpaired. People in this situation may be inclined to attempt to prove their value by undertaking new and sometimes costly ventures, often investing in hare-brained schemes with the hope that success here will justify their existence. Even when they don't do such foolish things, they carry around sad hearts and are sometimes sitting ducks for serious depression, serious in the sense that treatment may be required.

Health is another factor that goes into the decision to retire but, while illness and disability may be related to age, they do not necessarily parallel it. There is usually some slowing down and loss of energy with advancing age but this may not be apparent until well after 65 and even less so in a sedentary job where physical energy and extensive traveling are not major considerations. However, as one grows older, there is a greater likelihood of debilitating illness which may make further work impossible and necessitate retirement. Alternatively, there may be an accumulation of many minor problems requiring frequent visits to doctors, dentists and the like. It is even possible that the time involved in making all these visits, doing all the associated bookkeeping, and filling out of insurance forms prevent one from meeting the obligations of a full time job and raise the question of retiring just to keep up with doctors' appointments. Not only does one have to accept the physical problems associated with getting older but, to add insult to injury, one has to give up important and meaningful job satisfactions.

One further health consideration is the feeling of pessimism that may be aroused in some by test results which predict future disease. Elevated blood pressure, blood sugar, cholesterol and triglycerides serve as reminders that life is finite and force one to look at the questions of retirement and how to spend the rest of one's anticipated shortened existence. Of course, depending on personality style, many people will work hard to lower the high numbers and not even consider the possibility of a health precipitated retirement. Others will use their time searching out new and unusual, possibly dangerous, treatments, spending piles of money in the effort. Even when one remains healthy, there is the spouse's health to consider. When a spouse has seriously failing health, retirement may be forced on a worker in spite of excellent health and job circumstances on his or her part.

Speaking of health considerations raises the question of health insurance. This usually comes and goes with the job, and may be provided to a greater or lesser extent in early buyouts. However, not every early retiree will have automatic coverage upon retirement until Medicare kicks in at age 65, and not every coverage is meaningful in terms of what it allows. Sometimes, one may be covered by the health insurance of a working spouse, but this is not always the case. The cost of independently maintaining health insurance may be insurmountable for some and may lead to delaying retirement rather than having to dig deeply into one's pocket and the limited and shrinking resources available when regular job income stops. That is the reality but, again, people's psyches play strange tricks and there are always those who totally ignore considerations of insurance because they feel that they are indestructible.

Obviously, there are no easy, universally applicable answers to the questions that deciding to retire raises. It helps to have plenty of money, enough at any rate that you don't have to worry about where the next dime is coming from. Even that is no sure cure since what someone feels about the money can make it seem to one person that there is plenty and to another person that there's not much at all; that the glass is half full or half empty, even when the amounts are the same.

One case of a botched retirement which illustrates that there are other considerations than money is that of Paula, a woman who was born with a physical handicap. She was a highly intelligent person who, in spite of her deformity and the restrictions it imposed on her, persisted in her pursuit of an education. She obtained a professional degree and, armed with this, she got a good, well-paying job. For her whole working life, she struggled to get to work daily in spite of bad weather and travel difficulties as well as the many illnesses that resulted from her deformity. Her co-workers admired her fortitude and she was popular and well-liked individual, someone others turned to for advice. She dreamed about retirement as a time when she would no longer have to face the difficulties that she had experienced working on a daily basis, and she carefully monitored her savings and her pension funds. She never married and finally, at the age of 65, retired as planned. Her next step was a move to Florida where she had bought a condominium in a very desirable community that she knew from having spent several winter vacations there. On her agenda was inviting her many friends and her extensive family to visit her for long vacations, but these plans never quite worked out; she also found it difficult to make new friends. Initially, Paula wrote to her family and friends raving about the wonderful time she was having and how great it was to be free from job pressures, how things were so easy and comfortable in the warmer climate. Suddenly, communications to her friends and co-workers stopped and, two months later, her family let it be known that she had committed suicide by jumping out the window. What went wrong with Paula's retirement that led to this horrifying outcome?

While Paula's circumstances, in view of her handicap, were somewhat special, it is pretty clear that she made some mistakes in planning her retirement. She had spent her time and energies worrying about having enough money when the time came to retire but she had not thought enough about what would come afterwards. Her focus was on the better weather in Florida and the greater liberty that would provide her but she had underestimated the importance to her of her job, her family and her friends, and the interests and activities that had filled her years of working. Suddenly, she had good weather but little else of the important things that had meant so much to her, what we call her support system, and that had sustained her through so many years of struggle.

Let's look at what is necessary besides money to make a retirement successful. One of the major factors to be considered is a person's attitude to the work to which he or she has devoted a lifetime. For those who enjoy their work, their jobs represent a personal expression, a form of creativity which contributes to making life more exciting and stimulating. When people stop working, there ensues a major re-adjustment to their sense of who they are. It may also signify to these individuals the end of meaningfulness as members of society and the onset of a drone-like series of years with nothing to look forward to, feelings associated with depression.

Even when people detest their jobs and regard work as sheer drudgery, a necessary evil to make a living, and retirement is seen as a relief from daily pressures, some adjustment to one's self image is required. This sort of retiree also loses some purpose in living even if that purpose is only the pleasure of cursing out the job, the boss and the co-workers. Over and above any work accomplished, the day-to-day routine of a job provides structure and organization to life. You have a place to go and a pattern to follow. Not only are the weeks organized with five days on and two days off but even the year consists of a regular pattern of holidays and vacations. Without that structure, you may wind up feeling lost.

Daily interpersonal contacts at work are important components of life whether they involve exchanging words about the weather with the coffee vendor, discussing ball games, politics or movies with co-workers, or participating in meetings with peers, supervisors and subordinates. There is also the thrill of watching real life dramas among one's fellow workers including sex scandals, legal and illegal doings, financial fiddlings, and life and death events. Work also provides a school of continual learning to the employee who becomes aware of new developments and new techniques in the field. While formal educational programs offered by the employer may be less than scintillating and are often a focus of sarcastic humor, just being there and hearing what is going on are ways of remaining intellectually alive.

Again, the retiree is deprived of these stimuli and must find alternate means of staying in touch with the world.

For another thing, it is vital to have a support system in terms of family, friends and non-work-related social life and activities. If there is a strong system in place with many relationships and interests, the potential retiree is better able to accept the loss of the support and interests supplied by the job. However, if the support system is limited or is in the process of imminent reduction (the death of a loved one or having someone move to a far-away location), the loss of the support provided by the job will be felt more acutely; if you have a choice in the matter, retirement should be postponed.

Incidentally, even strong support systems may undergo changes after retirement and no longer be what you expected. You may have great friendships but there's a difference when you go out with people for fun and when you desperately feel a need for their company to keep boredom and loneliness at bay. You change from being an equal as a friend to someone who makes demands, someone who feels slighted when others are not available and someone who starts to complain about not being treated well. People will accuse you of being too demanding and a whiner.

Housing and the familiarity with a neighborhood or a town are also part of the support system although this is not always appreciated. At a time of major change in life such as retirement, it's good to have other things remain stable. Nevertheless, many build a move into their retirement plans just as Paula did, changing locations immediately after they retire, sometimes just across town and sometimes clear across the country or even abroad. When the move puts the retiree into increased social or family contact, such as being nearer to children and grandchildren, it substitutes one type of support for another. However, even the shortest move, with all its attendant fuss, can be dislocating and stressful at a time of already great stress. And even moving to be near one's children may prove disappointing since the parents' lives and their children's have already gone their separate ways, and it may prove difficult to restore the former closeness.

Retirement brings with it a reduction in stimulation coming from the outside and from others but this does not mean that there has to be a loss of stimulation.

Rather, the stimulation must come from within and one is thrown back on one's own resources. It obviously helps when there's a lot of money available to purchase new forms of stimulation but money is not necessary. At times, instead, money provides the illusion of having things to do in the sense that it enables one to run around all day long being busy and looking involved, but basically doing and accomplishing nothing. Deep down, one realizes that there's a difference between activity that is genuinely interesting and worthwhile and activity that merely fills in the hours and provides a false sense of doing something. Killing time is not a good way to spend your retirement; in fact, it leads to a sense of desperation and barely controlled depression which, not so coincidentally, is found frequently in the retired population.

In Paula's case, we will never know exactly what wrong since she confided her unhappiness in no one but it is pretty clear that her social and family support networks were absent and she was also removed from the cultural activities that had played so large a part in her working years. It is likely that, as she went through these years, she was more aware of her daily struggle than she was of the pleasures that she had managed to create for herself all through those years. We should also remember that she gave up the position of being an admired worker and all that that meant to her in terms of the affection of her co-workers and the approval of her supervisors, and it looks as if she couldn't come close to creating for herself an alternate social and cultural life.

So far, we've talked about retirement primarily as it relates to the retiree. But in most cases, retirement involves couples. The generation approaching retirement at this point in time is possibly the last in which the husband worked and the wife stayed home to take care of the children and maintain the household. She rarely was employed and, if so, only later on in life. If she is currently unemployed, her husband's retirement may impose on her yet another adjustment to his changing needs with him being home all the time and underfoot. But, if she is employed, usually being younger than her husband, she might not be ready to stop working just because he is stopping; it may also not be to her best advantage financially, let alone emotionally. It was certainly easier in the old days when there was only one retiree in the family (although that may be simplifying the case since both halves of the couple still had to adjust), but now the fact that there are two workers, each with his or her own set of financial problems and realities, makes matter more complicated and may stress the relationship to the breaking point.

In one case that came to my attention, a long term marriage in which the husband was five years older than the wife and had retired before her, a rather bizarre situation had arisen which illustrates some of the money issues that arise. Jerry, the husband, worried about finances while Marge, the wife who was still working, remained relaxed about the matter. He was reluctant to raise the issue so he decided to siphon off some of the money that came in just in case there would be a rainy day coming up. Over a couple of years, he had put aside several thousand dollars in a separate account and Marge was wondering why the cash seemed to disappear so rapidly. She learned what was happening only when a careful accountant picked up the fact that there was an extra account generating interest and requiring that additional taxes be paid. The worst marital crisis of their lives followed.

Consider also the case of Josephine and Albert who had been married for thirty-three years when Albert retired from his upper level management position at age 65. Josephine was 57 at this point and fully enjoying her career as a lawyer, a career she began only at the age of 39 when the youngest of their three children was old enough to get along without her being at home. At the time of Albert's retirement, all three children were adults and out on their own. Josephine had made rapid progress in her law firm and she was earning more than her husband when he retired. Albert enjoyed the first few months of his freedom from daily employment and assumed many of the household tasks that they had formerly shared or delegated to hired help. He gradually, however, became restless with his free time and began to urge Josephine to retire too so that they could travel or move elsewhere. She felt torn between his requests and the pleasure she derived from her job. Albert, like Jerry, was worried about finances while Josephine not only needed a good wardrobe for her job but also wanted some of the perks that her income could buy: elegant restaurants, a luxury car, even a new house; no way did she want to retire. They began to have arguments with a frequency and bitterness that they had never previously known.

Their situation became even more complicated by the deterioration in health of Josephine's mother who had severe cardiac problems as well as Alzheimer's Disease. These required that she have live-in assistance needing some family supervision as well as someone to manage her financial affairs. Albert refused to assume any such responsibility and Josephine was faced with the possibility that she might have to take an indefinite leave of absence from work or retire earlier than she wanted to. Either of these alternatives would have serious repercussions in her eventual retirement package as well as her current situation. She felt that Albert was worse than useless to her in her time of need and began to think in terms of divorce just to get rid of the nuisance that he was turning into. Because of the length of their marriage, their previous good relationship and the distress of their children, they sought counseling, and were able to come up with some ways of lessening the stress by arranging priorities though "cure" was not possible.

This is an example of a discordant retirement which worked fairly well for one spouse but not for the other, in contrast to a reciprocal retirement which satisfies the need of both partners. While Josephine and Albert's case demonstrates many of the grounds for a discordant retirement situation, it does not include one of the most common and most problematic issues of retirement in couples, the amount of time that they now have to spend together. Previously, one or both worked and they were out of contact with each other for ten or more hours a day. When they got together, there was a lot to talk about in a limited amount of time. Now, unless they build in safeguards, they are together constantly, sharing virtually everything to the extent that they have little or no news to bring to each other. To put it bluntly, they get on each other's nerves. Such a situation can be predicted if the couple had trouble spending time together on weekends during their work lives.

Josephine's situation also demonstrates that women, in or out of marriage, face different problems than do men in approaching retirement. For one thing, they have generally worked fewer years than men and have usually earned lower salaries than their male counterparts. They are also more likely to have interrupted their careers along the way to care for sick relatives or to handle other family emergencies, another factor lowering their eventual pensions. To compound their problems they have greater longevity than men, and the sum that they have accumulated has to last longer; the result is that many retired women face increasing poverty as they grow older. In the course of their retirement, if they were married, they learned to depend on the combined social security and pension payments due the couple; however, this sum is much reduced when the husband passes away, again increasing the financial stresses on the wife. Similarly, the husband's terminal illness may have used up a good portion of their savings, leaving the wife even more strapped for money. There's no question that women have it tougher in retirement that men do.

Look at Albert's situation! He didn't have enough to do and became restless but clearly did not want to assume certain family tasks. What do you do after retirement if you stay in the same place and have the same family and social support systems or, even if you move? One of the first issues is how you spend your time. The choices range from working full time, either in the old line of work or a new one, working part time, again either in a new job or doing the same type of work, doing volunteer work or simply spending your time on hobbies, sports and other interests. There are financial implications to working full or part time in terms of obtaining pension payments and, until recently, one's social security payments were reduced if one had an income.

Doing volunteer work is another option but it is not always so rewarding as it initially seemed when someone had the fantasy of being appreciated for oneself and being able to come or go as he or she pleased. Volunteer agencies are businesses in their own right with their own organizational frameworks and, of necessity, demand structure from all participants. Unless you are very cautious, you can wind up being enslaved in this new formal structure without having a say in how it functions and without even being paid for it. There are of course a wide variety of volunteer situations, and some allow for more creativity and freedom from excessive time demands.

One of the advantages of moving to a new structure of employment or endeavor is that you become exposed to new people. While retirement entails many interpersonal losses, it also enables the formation of new relationships provided that you do not retreat to a narrow environment such as your four walls. However, you should not expect new relationships and friendships to resemble or replace old ones. When you are younger, you have the expectation that someone you meet will be around a long time and that there will be a lifetime of experiences to share. Time is not an issue and you expect the years to increase intimacy.

With friendships made in the older years, particularly post-retirement, there is an awareness that the duration of the relationship will be shorter and there is a diminished expectation of the depth and intimacy that take many years to ripen. Nevertheless, new relationships are still potentially full of interest and enthusiasm, particularly when values and interests are shared and when you have freedom of choice. There is a transition of expectation toward sharing and companionship and away from long term satisfactions, but new and valid social experiences can occur at any time in life.

Moving, while a potentially disruptive event, may also provide exposure to new and exciting experiences provided that you are open to them. This is a matter of personal accessibility and attitude. If you change geography and people with the expectation that you will only be filling in time till summoned to the Beyond, you are likely to experience defeat, isolation, loneliness and depression. If you, on the other hand, approach these issues with the anticipation that new and exciting things will happen, you are much more likely to enjoy new locations, new jobs and new people.

Retirement is obviously a mixed blessing, something that proves both the optimists and the pessimists correct. It should be planned for meticulously and people should try to retire at an age when they are young enough to enjoy its benefits, being careful to avoid the pitfalls that might contribute to serious emotional consequences. Since it usually occurs at ages when physical problems are possibilities, these possibilities have to be taken into consideration and have to be factored into one's planning. If there is denial of the realities of life, painful and tragic events may occur but, if the realities are factored in, retirement can be as enjoyable as the optimists would have us believe.

# 14

# *Getting Old*

Once the retirement hurdle has been passed and its problems been solved or at least brought under control, people are generally considered to have entered the phase of life called old age. Even at this point, with most of the storms of life behind one and with quiet and tranquility anticipated for the future, money remains an issue and there are still many emotional entanglements with it; indeed experience only proves that, for as long as one lives, money is a source of trouble and life's problems continue to be expressed in terms of money.

Since not all old people are the same, one can't generalize about these problems. As with any group that includes millions of individuals, there are diverse personalities, varying family settings and a wide range of financial situations among the ranks of the elderly, and these differences are expressed in a wide variety of behaviors, some of which may seem strange to other people and some of which may be constructive or destructive in relation to the elderly themselves, their families and their immediate social groups, and to society at large. Nevertheless, there are a number of things that the elderly have in common with each other which make them different from other age groups.

For one thing, even though someone is elderly (a nicer way of saying old), it does not mean that his or her attitudes towards money and the ways it's been dealt with, problems and all, throughout life, invariably undergo major changes. Character traits generally remain with one all the way to the end. Personality is fairly stable throughout life and most of what one sees in terms of the uses and abuses of money as people get older are the same as they always were. Examples of this are that stingy people remain stingy, openhanded people remain open-handed, people who use money to manipulate others continue to do so, and cautious people continue to be cautious about what they do and in what they get involved.

However, in old age, certain attitudes, sometimes the very same ones that have been present throughout life and which were not particularly bothersome, may become more and more prominent and, as the years go on, may become exaggerated to the point of caricature. One example of this is the person who tends to watch pennies. Such careful management of money may become more pronounced over the years and may cross the line into real miserliness. This becomes apparent when the aging person starts denying himself or herself necessities just to save money. We find people stinting on such things as food and new clothing, and priding themselves on finding restaurants that have early bird specials, serving dinners at much lower prices before 6 PM. This occurs even more frequently as one passes the 70-year mark, and these specials are prevalent in retirement communities or in other areas with large geriatric populations, so counting pennies is definitely a widespread personality trait. In the same vein, people with plenty of money may devote lots of time to collecting cents-off coupons on grocery items or may comparison shop a number of supermarkets to find which one sells a particular item for a few pennies less. There are other senior citizens who refuse to travel unless they can take advantage of special senior rates or can find some other bargain prices directed towards them. Saving money is a great idea and not spending more than you have to is also good judgment but there are those who distort their lives to conform to these special deals. Such attitudes in the elderly may be annoying to others, but are essentially benign behaviors and do not by themselves indicate severe personality problems or illness.

It is in the nature of being human to worry about money. For example even though you may have already worked out the problems of the retirement phase of life and adjusted to a slower pace of life, one worry that persists is how much money you will need to tide you over till the end. This dilemma may be based on a realistic examination of your finances or may represent an exaggerated fear which will stick with you until the end. Do you expect to live a long time on a limited amount of money or do you have a limited life expectancy with the problem of what to do with your money in the meantime? Even though your primary concern may be to find some way to protect yourself against winding up with no money at all to take care of your needs, many older folks also want to provide a significant sum of money for their heirs; they want to leave a legacy that their children will benefit from even when the children (and grandchildren) may have no shortage of money themselves. What we have here is a situation in which some of the elderly deprive themselves, not because they have to in order to ensure their future security but for the benefit of the heirs of their estates.

On the other hand, there are those who go overboard in their spending, not wanting anyone else to enjoy the fruits of what they so laboriously acquired over the course of a lifetime. At times, this overspending may serve as a denial of the fact that they do have limited means and it may be a revolt against constant and annoying restrictions on spending; they become angry at having to eternally watch every penny and they feel the need to go out and indulge themselves once in a while. Spending money in this way may in turn cause resentment in their children who feel that their inheritance is being wasted by foolish behavior on their parents' parts. This has fairly commonly led the family to call in physicians to determine whether spending money in this way might be a sign of Alzheimer's Disease and a reason to deprive the older person of the freedom to go about his or her own business.

Other elderly people believe that they are living on the brink of destitution and will run out of money in the very near future; they cut back on expenses enormously, being reluctant to spend on anything. There are, of course, some old folks who are very poor and who really don't have enough money to buy decent food, and they may subsist on dog or cat food. While this is sad, it's understandable because what they're doing is out of financial necessity; it's a bit more difficult to comprehend the same behavior when there really is enough money in the bank, and then we have to look for other explanations of this delusion (a false belief, contrary to reality) of poverty.

Intergenerational problems continue in relation to money and, where there have been family disagreements over money earlier in life, there is every reason to expect that these will continue into the older years. Not only do children keep an eye on how their parents spend money, but the parents too watch how and on what their children spend money. As a result, there may be burning resentments on the part of both generations, each seeing things from its own point of view. The older generation feels that its needs are deemed less important by their children who seem more concerned that their own immediate needs be gratified and their inheritance protected. The younger generation may feel that, because they have their lives before them, their needs should come first and that they should utilize to the maximum the fact that fate has dealt them a ready supply of money via their parents' savings. What has meant so much to the older person as he or she built up an amount of money in the bank doesn't seem to mean all that much to the younger person who may not see that parents continue to have needs and want to do things with their own money. From the parents' perspective, while they may be willing to help out, they often become outraged at the manner in which their children are spending money and they attack their children's priorities. "After all", say the parents, "it is our money and no one should have a claim on it except ourselves."

No matter how they may try to escape it, older people are victims of a widespread societal prejudice against them. In many places in the world and even in some places in this country, old people are treated with respect and admiration. They are considered to have accumulated experience and to have become wise, and they are viewed as the logical ones to pass on the traditions of their cultures. So, even as they begin to decline physically and intellectually, they are regarded as valuable members of society, and caring for them is seen as honorable and praiseworthy.

This view is much less common in our society which is oriented to the young and which often regards the elderly with a certain amount of indifference and irritation, if not actual disdain. They are seen, not only as interfering with their younger counterparts, but as impeding the progress of society, outdated fossils who are peripheral to what is currently going on and probably unnecessary. Expressed more strongly, some of the young wish that the old folk would hurry up and die to make room for the upcoming generation. However, this slant on the elderly is not without built-in contradictions and inconsistencies since many of them are loved and are considered intrinsic and cherished parts of their families. Unfortunately, in spite of what may be strong family affection, many elderly adopt the views that society at large has about old age, and begin to see themselves in the same light as ugly, unnecessary and uninteresting.

The elderly, as a group, control a considerable amount of the wealth of society. They have accumulated savings throughout their lives and also have huge investments in Social Security and in pension plans, and are definitely a financial force to be reckoned with. On the other hand, because few of them are actually working, some of the younger generation may regard them as drains on the public treasury which is forced to rely on younger workers to provide the work behind the income the old folks receive. This sort of feeling will probably worsen in the near future since, if we project ahead twenty or thirty years, there will be more and more old people on pensions and Social Security, and a smaller and smaller percentage of the population who will be actually working and paying for those pension payments.

The large amounts of money possessed by the elderly can be used to offset some of the problems of aging, beginning with what one looks like, to try to look and act younger to the extent that this is possible. We live in a country and an era where the best paid physicians are those who provide cosmetic or plastic surgery which wipes out the signs of aging and replaces wrinkles with smooth skin, removes fat from unsightly places and re-adjusts all sorts of body parts in order to help the patient (or should we say customer since the word patient suggests an illness), look younger and make her (men utilize these services somewhat less frequently) appear more vivacious and dynamic. This pursuit of youthful appearances is not limited to the goal of being sexually attractive but may be necessary to hold on to a job or to avoid some other prejudice visited upon the elderly. Although such treatments are undertaken mostly by the elderly, many of these remodelings are indulged in by much younger people who, for one reason or another, are in danger of being assigned to the elderly category, either by having premature graying of their hair, by having a genetic predisposition to wrinkles or by having some serious illness.

Many of the elderly and the elderly-appearing philosophically accept the facts of aging, and many are also quite realistic about the need to look younger for whatever reasons: to capture admirers, hold onto a job, deny aging. Others resent it and feel junked, thrown aside into the waste basket, and regard the fact that they are forced to undergo surgery as another insult dealt them by society. Depending on their financial means, some elderly people can afford operation after operation as well as maintenance therapies such as massages, expensive make-up and hair treatments and a wide range of personal training activities. Others can't really afford it but feel driven by their urge to look younger to spend their money on these procedures, being forced to cut back on other expenses, sometimes even going without proper nourishment. And there are others who cannot even dream of buying themselves more youthful appearances, having barely enough money to survive. As a result of monetary and psychological differences in the elderly, some enjoy the procedures, delighting in the fact that they have money enough to buy them and becoming experts along the way in styles and techniques of various schools of reconstructive surgery. Some resent them, some are jealous of those who can afford them, and some couldn't care less about the whole matter.

Plastic surgery is not the only way that people deny that they are aging. There are other tricks that are used but they rarely fool others. Depending on one's finances, one can buy whole new wardrobes in the latest fashion, wardrobes geared to young tastes and young bodies. Not so expensive are following other trends associated with youth, like going to youth oriented nightclubs and discos, following the latest trends in music and adopting currently trendy slang. These folk may also exercise great caution to be sure that they do not reminisce about events that occurred in their own earlier years because this may date them, and they limit their intellectual horizons to current day events. These tactics are not usually very successful, and the older person almost always looks exactly like what he or she is, someone who can't stand looking older but who is making every effort to reject age and look young. Imagine the distress of such individuals when they go to the movies and are automatically given the senior discounted ticket by the girl or boy in the ticket-seller's booth who takes one look and who would never even think to ask for proof!

Most people entering the older years come well furnished with spouses and children, with an extensive network of friends and with many interests. They do not lack for activities or for companionship, and they derive satisfaction from their stage of life. The problem is that, with the passage of time, there is frequently a series of events which results in a loss of loved ones, a reduction in the social network and in a restriction of activities. Spouses and friends pass on, other friends move away, and children have a way of pursuing their own interests and families with not too much attention being paid to the needs of their parents. Older people often have diminished energy to pursue interests and there is a consequent narrowing of horizons. As a result, some of the essentials for a happy life disappear and the elderly individual is faced with loss of companionship and sex, and with greater amounts of uncommitted time. Even worse, it becomes harder to satisfy the need to love and be loved, and to overcome a growing feeling of meaninglessness.

While some of the elderly see themselves in the same light that the rest of society has placed them, in negative terms, many do not and they do their level best to live normal lives, accepting and trying to overcome whatever limitations age may have imposed on them. Since they are not always welcome in younger communities, they often gravitate to special communities that are geared to their needs. These may include retirement communities in warmer areas in the country or may be special residences for senior citizens in the towns in which they live. Such communities, in addition to providing lots of same age companionship and activities, also offer services oriented to the elderly, making good health care readily available. These elderly must have adequate financial resources to take advantage of such places just as they must have sufficient funds to travel to seasonal resorts catering to their needs.

Poorer people who cannot afford this array of services turn to services that may be provided by their local towns and municipalities. I am referring to senior citizen clubs which meet daily during the week and which offer nourishing, well-balanced food, lectures, games, conversation and short excursions. Even when the elderly don't use these clubs, they feel great satisfaction in the knowledge that they are welcome there, and some even enjoy the luxury of deciding not to go, knowing that they have the choice of staying home or going; this means that life still provides them with choices and they are not completely dependent on the clubs. The fact that anyone can say "no" remains one of life's great pleasures, particularly when his or her surroundings have narrowed.

I mentioned that elderly have sexual needs, and this is clearly something society tries to ignore. Once you reach a certain age, you're supposed to lose all interest in that sort of thing unless you're a "dirty old man" or a sex-crazed old lady trying to make up for a wasted past. In point of fact, the elderly do have sexual needs even if the fires burn a good deal lower than they do in the young in terms of lesser frequency and intensity. However, the selection of partners is generally more limited for the elderly, particularly for women because there are fewer age-appropriate men around since men tend to die at earlier ages than women do. Older men have a larger choice of older women available to them since the numbers are in their favor, but many prefer younger women, reflecting the standards set by society that young is beautiful and old is ugly. Older women, too, may find themselves attracted by younger men rather than by the few older men around them, and it's not usually because these younger men are more sexually potent.

Indeed, not all reaching out toward the younger generation is sexually motivated. Most of the yearning is for companionship, to have someone to talk to and to go out to dinner with, to share interests and even to take vacations with. Some elderly are prejudiced against doing things with people of their own age, and a younger person may seem a more desirable companion. In terms of the competition that a lot of people feel throughout their lives, they may prefer to do things with younger individuals since greater prestige is attached to being with this generation than with people of one's own older generation.

Loneliness and the absence of companionship are among the most painful emotions known to humankind and it is only one short step for an older person to attempt to buy companionship and friendship from the younger generation if they can afford it. Most senior communities are staffed by young people with all sorts of motivations for taking these job. Some are dedicated to helping the elderly, seeing this as an almost religious calling to be useful to people who need them, while sometimes it's just another way of earning a living. Inevitably, there are a few who see this as a way to get rich. They, men and women, latch on to older people, shower them with affection and are available for social activities on an on-call basis. Gradually, the subject of monetary assistance, really a fee for service, enters the relationship. It may begin as a request for a loan by the younger person who then goes on to describe a difficult financial situation. The older person is touched by the story and wants to help a genuine friend. As time passes, the turning over of funds becomes an ongoing part of the relationship.

While not much money passes from one side to the other in the majority of cases, it raises the question of whether any relationship at all between the two would exist without money playing a part. In other words, if the elderly partner in the pair didn't have money or ran out of money as time went on, would the relationship vanish into thin air? But, if the older person in the relationship is truly wealthy, the question that comes up is how much money gets transferred before there is some sort of rupture; perhaps it will go on indefinitely or perhaps there will be some limit set by the older partner or by his or her family. While most people think in terms of this being a primarily sexual relationship, it is more often one of companionship with sex playing a secondary role, if present at all.

While all such arrangements may smell a little rotten to an outside observer, society generally regards such relationships as more acceptable if they involve older men and younger women. Somehow, the younger woman is considered wise and mature beyond her years for appreciating the personal qualities her man has acquired during his long lifetime even though there may be some snickering about her admiration for the size of his wallet.

When the situation involves an older woman and a younger man, a relationship, whether it be for sexual reasons or for companionship (and who really knows what goes on between two people?) is regarded with less approval and the older woman may be more openly laughed at for having to buy sex from her boyfriend (buying sex doesn't carry much prestige with it unless it can be used to prove that you're so rich that you have lots of money to spare), even though that may indeed not be part of the arrangement. Nevertheless, older women continue to date younger men with the emphasis being on having an escort for a social event, companionship and friendship. Words have been coined for the younger partner in both types of relationships, a woman being called a gold-digger and the man a gigolo. In any case, such relationships are rarely seen among poor people while occurring with regularity among the wealthy. The use of money to buy all sorts of desirable objects the older person can no longer obtain on his or her own is something that occurs again and again as one ages since it plays such a prominent role in overcoming or compensating for the problems of aging.

At times, the older person truly believes that he or she is helping a worthy, but charming, younger person who has had an unfortunate life. However, this does not mean that the older person is totally unaware that he or she may be in the position of being taken for a ride. The elderly may fear losing the relationship and decide that it's worth paying for or they may have some doubts but override them. While this usually involves strangers, the recipient of the money may actually be a child or some other younger relative who may want to help their older relative or who sees the loneliness as a good opportunity to make some extra money.

Things don't always work out the way these younger parties expect, though, because older people often continue to think in terms of costs for goods and services at the level they were accustomed to in their earlier years. They are shocked to the point of outrage to learn how much they have to pay for groceries and repair jobs and, when they speak of giving a lavish tip in reward for services, what they think of as lavish might strike someone younger as simply pathetic. Often enough, calculating juniors who spend a lot of time ingratiating themselves with the elderly find themselves the beneficiaries of a one dollar tip, sometimes only fifty cents.

The situation becomes more complex when the older person has a sizable amount of money and gets around to writing a will disposing of these funds after death. The younger generation, family or not, who is so inclined, tries to make sure that it gets its share in the disposition of the money after death and is often attentive to the older person with the specific goal in mind of being "remembered" in the will.

It's not always the elderly who get taken in such relationships; some of them quite coldly use the threat of exclusion from a will as a means of obtaining the services of some younger individual while rewarding those who do what they want by including them, or promising to do so in their wills. Everyone knows cases of elderly individuals who are constantly re- writing their wills to reward whoever is in their favor that month. Trying to manipulate the young by promising money and trying to coax money from the elderly in these relationships are rather cold-blooded approaches from both sides of the generational divide.

Matters may not always be so simple, however, as in the case of Harry and Jennifer. Harry was 68 years old when he retired to move with his wife, Dora, to a climate that would be less stressful for her chronic asthmatic condition. They were well-to-do, having jointly run an insurance agency for many years. In spite of the move, Dora died within two years and Harry was left alone to fend for himself in his retirement community. He tried hard to become interested in golf and in the activities offered to the senior residents but just couldn't get into it. With the other seniors, he was pleasant and cordial but he did not make any real friends, and he began to feel lonely and depressed. Then he met Jennifer, who was a 35 year old physical trainer at the senior community. They seemed to hit it off well and entered into a dating relationship. Harry became more animated and enthusiastic, and he soon proposed marriage to her. His three children were horrified by this May-December romance, and began to visit him, criticizing Jennifer and calling her a money-hungry viper among other things. They threatened to cut off communications with him if he went ahead with the proposed marriage but Harry ignored these threats because he said Jennifer was the best thing that had happened to him since Dora's death. Eventually, they married and Harry had two happy years with Jennifer before he died; they took three lengthy cruises and she nursed him attentively through his final illness. He left the bulk of his estate to Jennifer, who returned to her previous work, with only token amounts being left to his children.

This case raises many questions, one of which was Jennifer's motivation in hooking up with a man so much older than herself. Did she love Harry or did she see him as a rich man who could provide her with money for the rest of her life? Did she admire him for his personality and for the fun she could have with him? Was she one of the small number of people who find themselves attracted to the elderly? Did she pity Harry and try to help him overcome his sadness and loneliness? She was certainly not like many a gold-digger who marries, stays a minimal amount of time with her new husband, and then sues for divorce with a large settlement.

Another question that comes up is where Harry's children were during the two bleak years after Dora's death. Did they go out of their way to help him or to keep him company or to provide for him in some way, or did they just leave him to his own devices? Most people tend not to ask what was Harry's motivation in marrying Jennifer since it's pretty much taken for granted that older men like younger women. It's also taken for granted that Harry would expect her to nurse him when he fell ill.

I wouldn't say that Harry was exploited by Jennifer, but the fact is that, in this cold, cruel world, the elderly are frequently exploited by others. There are so many scams which take advantage of the situation of the elderly and their loneliness and feelings of emptiness. One reads almost daily in the newspapers of elderly people who receive phone calls promising them fantastic returns on investments if they only send in their money immediately. The callers are friendly, willing to chat, which is a great blessing to a lonely person, and seemingly very concerned about his or her well-being. Of course, once the money is sent in, these folks evaporate along with the money. There are innumerable other scams; indeed there are so many and the dangers of succumbing to them and losing one's life savings so great that police departments in metropolitan areas often visit senior centers just to give lectures to the seniors on whatever may be the latest scams.

Elderly people, as they become more frail with advancing age, are more frequently the victims of all sorts of crimes, and they know it. They can offer little resistance when mugged in the street and are more often robbed in their own homes than younger people, if not actually sexually attacked although that occurs too. At times, simply going out to shop for a few groceries looms as a frightening task with the very real possibility of just about any crime happening to them, from having a purse snatched or a piece of jewelry torn from them up to and including being raped or murdered. To be able to defend themselves, they often shop in groups and, if possible, arrange for police escort to protect them.

This state of frailty is just one of the very unpleasant conditions that are associated with very advanced old age. This is the time when illness catches up with one and there begin to be severe physical limitations such as loss of vision or hearing, diminished strength, and loss of function in various body systems. No longer can they continue the independent life style that is considered part of person-hood. Instead they must rely on others to do their shopping, their banking, their home or apartment maintenance, their laundry and even their food preparation. This loss of independence is sometimes called loss of autonomy and is usually accompanied by a loss of privacy as they fall back on others to help them. Inevitably what happens to them at this stage has a lot to do with money or family situations. When the elderly live in a family setting, their children gradually assume responsibility for these various activities, and handle all problems, at least in ideal circumstances.

That's what usually occurs. Just as the last few years have revealed that there's much more child abuse than anyone had ever imagined, there's also something called elder abuse. In this case, the elderly are physically abused by their children or by their caretakers for reasons that are hard to fathom; what pleasure can there be in hurting someone who is unable to defend himself or herself? Nevertheless, elder abuse occurs more often than we realize and, in some of the cases, there is a purpose that can be discovered; that is to obtain whatever financial resources the elderly person has. These may be in the form of savings but there is usually a social security check arriving every month and a rapacious relative or "friend" can beat the victim in order to have the funds transferred from the official recipient to the abuser. Most cases of elder abuse go unnoticed until he or she has to be hospitalized for treatment of an illness and, as is the case with child abuse, bruises and fractures are discovered.

When the elderly person lives alone and feels overwhelmed by needs and the inability to meet them, he or she is particularly vulnerable, not only to scams but to manipulations by others that are literally criminal. People may appear who assist them, not because they are health care professionals but because they see a possible opportunity to make a financial killing. They do things for the old person, help them with difficult situations and make themselves otherwise invaluable. It becomes only natural for them to be rewarded financially for their services which are interpreted, not merely as helping out but as caring for someone the world has pretty much forgotten about. Undue influence may be brought to bear at this time for a will to be written in the favor of such people, and the old person may be perfectly willing to reward anyone who has made life easier, either with small legacies or with large ones. Even when they are unwilling, the elderly may go along, recognizing that they are in no position to deny the helper.

More legitimately, money may be used to purchase help whether it be a live-in home health aide or a part-time assistant. Everyone has heard stories of wonderful health aides and everyone has heard stories of incompetent and uncaring individuals, and generally the more you pay, the better the situation. However, medical needs may progress to the point that staying in one's home is no longer possible. There is a large healthcare network which attempts to meet the needs of the elderly but as the ranks of the elderly grow and their needs become greater, it becomes harder and harder for society to meet these needs, and the elderly are collected in such institutions as nursing homes; to provide them with suitable health care, they must be removed from their homes and their belongings. This is one of the great dreads of old age, and people will use their last cent to put off such an option. Many have suicided rather than leave their homes.

Even when an old person has made his or her peace with the prospect of dying in the near future, there is anxiety concerning what comes after death, not in terms of heaven or hell, but in terms of whether the fact that they have died will be quickly noticed and the body disposed of rapidly. What the elderly fear is that they will die, no one will know, and their bodies will be left to rot or become food for rats and roaches until some neighbor complains about a peculiar odor coming from their home or apartment.

The problem is that serious needs exist at the same time that most other individuals in our society attempt to distance themselves from the elderly because they want no contact with illness and death, and don't want to be reminded that such things exist. We have all either heard the term geriatric ghetto or can well imagine what it means, the isolation of the elderly from the rest of society, usually in special retirement communities or in special resorts that cater to their needs when they are in good shape. For those who are sicker and poorer, there are nursing homes providing different levels of service and going by many names depending upon what they offer. Such locations have also been dubbed God's waiting room to indicate that, whatever the elderly may be doing in the meantime, they are waiting for death.

And finally, we come to that most dreaded condition, Alzheimer's Disease. This, as most of you know, is the condition formerly called senility and it strikes terror, not only into the hearts and minds of the elderly, but also into the hearts and minds of their families. Alzheimer's, which does not happen to everyone, involves a progressive loss of intellectual function and usually begins well after 70, although its age of onset is extremely variable. The condition is not well understood medically and its causes are unknown although there are suggestions that it might have something to do with your genes and that it comes about because of chemical changes in the brain. Its earliest sign is mild forgetfulness but this is no sure indication that the disease is present since virtually everyone forgets things from time to time. However, in Alzheimer's, the forgetfulness becomes progressively more severe beginning, for example, with not being sure what day of the week it is, something that has happened to everyone, to forgetting to mail in the rent check, something most of us remember to do, to forgetting that a spouse is dead or what one's name is, something that is far beyond normal experience.

While forgetfulness is usually the first sign, there may also be neglect of personal hygiene, loss of interest in the world, inability to manage personal and financial affairs (it is striking how frequently money and spending problems emerge as the first signs), and agitation and confusion. Since the afflicted lose their ability to deal with daily events, they feel frightened by new and strange situations, and react to protect themselves, often demonstrating rage and striking out at those who are closest. It is truly tragic to see how a formerly loving mother or father attacks verbally and physically an offspring who is trying hard to care for them. Medications are available to help control the agitation but there are no really good treatments for the loss of intellectual function. Generally, in its early phases, patients with Alzheimer's get along okay but their children and relatives know that they're in trouble when they find that the patient gets lost when going out of doors or forgets to turn off the stove, resulting in burned pots and food.

While Alzheimer's Disease has little to do with money, even in this chaotic condition we can sometimes see money playing a part. In the very early stages of the illness with some diminution in capacity to understand and handle monetary affairs, there may be greater carefulness about matters in order not to make mistakes. We may see, for example, that the individual tries so hard to keep up that he or she pays every bill that comes in, including every charity solicitation that arrives in the mail. It's not that they're more charitable; it's that they're afraid they'll make a mistake and not pay an important bill. Another trait that frequently occurs and drives relatives and care givers crazy is that money is squirreled away all over the apartment to "protect" it. The elderly person then forgets where the money is hidden and accuses those around them of stealing it. Children become insulted and care givers quit rather than be accused of theft.

Alzheimer's patients have some awareness that things are not as clear as they used to be and they may even be aware that they are forgetting things. They respond by trying to impose order on things around them, for one thing making lists of things to do or things not to forget. Alas, they then fail to remember that they have written these lists and are just as lost as before. At times, they try to use arithmetic to impose order on the chaotic situation and will count their money, both bills and change, repeatedly but with no practical purpose. One observes this counting over and over again in these patients, and it is a grim reminder of how significant a role money has played in people's lives that they choose to hold on to it in this way where it has no other meaning than to reassert some control over a vanishing mind.

One somewhat unusual case of Alzheimer's was that of Louise, a 75 year old woman who was married to a wealthy businessman and who was surrounded by caring relatives including three children. She had always been very attentive to her wardrobe and was known for her elegance in the social world she inhabited. Her children became concerned when she began to shop and tried to wear exotic items such as very short miniskirts and hot pants. She couldn't explain why she bought and wore them, and the question of a diagnosis of depression of old age was raised; the initial professional consultant suggested that she was rebelling against her past conservatism and was trying to make up for a poor sex life. This diagnosis and interpretation was rejected by her family with Louise simply going along compliantly with all her family's efforts. A second professional consultant determined that, while she retained good interpersonal skills, she was experiencing some memory deficits and could not explain simple proverbs, a deficit known as loss of abstraction ability or alternatively as concrete thinking, something that appears relatively early in Alzheimer's. This happens to be a good test of early Alzheimer's; just ask someone to define an abstract noun such as "charity" or "romance"; someone who is concrete will have trouble giving you a good definition. Similarly, ask someone to explain a proverb such as "you can't judge a book by its cover". An abstract explanation will be something like "you can't always tell what people are like from the way they look" while a concrete explanation is more likely to talk about a book or a cover.

In Louise's case, the diagnosis was made at the time of the second consultation but there was little that could be done and she entered a period of rapid decline with a whole spectrum of signs of Alzheimer's appearing. In spite of everything her family did to keep her home, she eventually became too difficult to manage there and was placed in a nursing home. Two years after the diagnosis was made, she passed away.

Even when the older person has sunk into Alzheimer's Disease, psychological problems with money are not over though the elderly themselves may no longer have any awareness of what is going on. These are the problems with money that get carried over into the next generation and may take many forms as relatives start to deal with the monetary issues that arise when someone is no longer capable of handling his or her own affairs. Here we see how the problems of a lifetime in families continue unabated even under these awful circumstances. Since the Alzheimer's patient can no longer manage routine personal affairs, it is best if the family designate one individual to take over all the financial management; in this way, it is clear who is responsible. Frequently, a family is not well organized and each child does things at random. As a result, there is likely to be confusion about what happened to money coming in and there may be double or triple payments of bills. At times, each child may assume that another has taken care of a problem only to learn that it was never handled at all.

With a dysfunctional family in which old rivalries continue, it is likely that each child will be watching to see exactly what everyone else is doing, both in terms of how much responsibility they are carrying in relation to each other (are they doing their share?) and whether they are taking away possessions while everyone else's back is turned. No matter how honest each one is and how sincere, there is bound to be resentment. Alzheimer's patients tend to forget the names of their children if they live with the disorder long enough and there will be serious jealousy problems if one child is still recognized by name while the others are forgotten. And there will be arguments, sometimes to the point of physical fights, over who can take what possessions, all this while the patient is still alive. Such combats serve to foreshadow what is likely to occur after the parent dies and the property, money and otherwise, has to be distributed among the children because, as we will see in the next chapter, money problems don't stop with death; they just move to another plane.

# 15

# To the Grave and Beyond

The subject of death (and the events that surround it, before, during and after it happens) is so painful that I thought long and hard before deciding to include it in this book. Virtually everyone is tremendously fearful about his or her own death and prefers not to think about it as if avoiding the idea has protective value and helps to defer the dreaded moment. Relatives and friends who are in danger of losing someone they love or who have just lost someone are usually so upset and overwhelmed by grief that they often can't think clearly at the time and, even afterwards, would rather not be reminded of one of the worst experiences in their lives.

Obviously, the pain attached to the process of dying, to death and to dealing with the loss of loved ones tends to bring out a wide range of emotions, some of which naturally (and some of which unnaturally) get expressed in monetary terms. In fact, there is probably more interpersonal trouble over money and possessions at this point in the life cycle than at any other. If I avoided talking about the interaction of money and feelings at such a stressful time, I would be doing the same thing that so many others do, pretending that death and its pain don't exist. I would certainly not be doing my job, part of which is to help readers handle this crucial phase in the life cycle, its end. Many books have been written about what goes on in the processes of grieving and overcoming, if possible, the loss but I will skip those emotional aspects surrounding death and dying that are not related to money issues. Nevertheless, it is difficult, if not impossible, to separate the normal sad feelings accompanying death and dying from feelings which are contaminated by psychological and personality issues, and the difficulty becomes all the greater when money is involved.

Most of us complain about having to take care of the bills every month or having to go through mountains of paperwork on a regular basis, but being forced to do so means that we are an active part of the world. Likewise, the person who is approaching death has been functioning until the terminal illness as a full fledged member of society, someone actively involved in the business of living. That means that he or she is a distinct financial entity with bank accounts and savings, and is obliged to pay taxes as well as monthly rent, electric and phone bills, buy food and clothing, and handle all the other day-to-day transactions necessary in this complicated, dollar- driven world. As they become ill, people may no longer be able to pay attention to business matters for a variety of reasons: mental infirmity, physical weakness, lack of interest, depression or some combination of these. Nevertheless, the bills must be paid or else! Furthermore, as illnesses progress, personal finances become even more complicated when you add on payments to doctors and arranging for appropriate nursing care as well as filling out innumerable forms for insurers and government agencies. Who does the job if the sick individual is no longer able to do so?

What most frequently happens is that close relatives gradually fill in the gaps and help with writing checks and balancing the books. When a family does not have major psychological problems and is, in psychiatric lingo, "functional" (in contrast to families where all you see are hangups and problems, something we label "dysfunctional"), these things are usually handled smoothly and without conflict, and the person who is dying is spared the additional headaches of figuring out and paying health care costs over and above writing the usual checks; there is, therefore, no need for an agonizing decision about who can be trusted to manage affairs honestly and appropriately. Furthermore, the sick person doesn't have to worry about losing his or her freedom of choice in making money decisions or allowing someone else to do it in his or her stead.

Usually, the closest person is the spouse and, when he or she assumes the burden of managing business affairs, this is absolutely the best solution from a legal viewpoint since the spouse is already legally regarded as a partner in virtually all affairs. When the spouse is out of the picture for whatever reasons, financial affairs are usually handled by a child and, if no child is available, then by a brother, sister or some other close relative. Much of the transition of the management of one's affairs from the sick person to someone else is done informally with the person who accepts the responsibility usually stepping in gradually and taking on more and more duties as the dying individual weakens and is less and less able to manage on his or her own.

However, things do not always run so smoothly and that doesn't always depend upon how much money there is. Relatives get all bent out of shape even when small sums are involved and matters may take on monumental significance when there's a lot of money and property. Things also become more complicated the larger the circle of potential substitute managers is (as in a large family or one with many managerial types). Also, the more problems that already exist among members of the family and between them and the sick relative, the greater the difficulty there will be in making appropriate arrangements as events unfold. In order to facilitate the handling of all these business affairs, the dying person may legally choose one specific person to serve as an agent or attorney-in-fact (not in the sense of being a lawyer but in the sense of being someone who is legally able to act in one's place). This is what is meant by giving power-of-attorney to someone.

Ideally, this should be done far in advance at a time when one is still healthy, when nobody can suggest that there are deficient intellectual abilities, rather than being done later under the pressure of events, when the decision may be challenged as resulting from impaired mental capacity. If done late while pressures and conflicts abound, legal proceedings may be necessary to validate power-of-attorney documents. The reason I say documents, using the plural, is that, while people generally write only one power-of-attorney, many financial organizations require that a person sign the organization's own special form indicating who the agent is. You can just imagine the situation when a terminally ill patient who has lots of bank accounts and other properties has to stop everything else and start filling in all these forms which almost always have to be notarized as well.

To give someone formal power-of-attorney means that a standardized legal document is filled out in which you state that this person can act in your stead in everything; he or she can write checks for you, can manage your funds, can arrange priorities in handling your business affairs and can sign your name to documents. Essentially this person can do everything monetarily and legally that you can do including giving the power-of-attorney to another person or even to more than one. The person whom you designate does have the right to refuse the responsibility or to bow out later on. Clearly, giving someone this assignment is something that should be discussed in advance and not come as a surprise. Since no one knows the date when such a document will be needed, it is usually effective at the time it is signed which means that, as of that moment, that person can represent you in everything. This is the flip side of the coin of doing it early since it means that, if the attorney turns out to be untrustworthy, he or she can rob you blind, and can empty out your bank and stock market accounts while you're still alive and active. If you are in pretty good shape health-wise, you can continue to supervise what's going on; if you're sick and likely to recover, you can still keep some control over your affairs, but when you're going fast, you really don't know what this person is doing and can't keep track.

On occasion, what is called a springing power-of-attorney may be used. This document makes it clear that the power-of-attorney will only go into effect when certain conditions are met; for example, it may become valid as of a specific date or under such circumstances as the writer's being out of the country for a prolonged period of time. It might also become operative if the writer is incapacitated with the presentation of a doctor's certificate attesting to the fact of the incapacity.

Most people, even when they recognize the need to have someone back them up in case of illness, don't like the idea of signing a legal document that makes the dreaded moment more real. It is frightening to make such arrangements for the same reasons that so many fear to write wills; they speak in a very definite way of terminal illness, loss of powers and imminent death. For those who are superstitious, it's an invitation to bad luck.

In addition, many don't feel total and implicit trust in anyone else, even a close relative. While there may be a general aversion to having a replacement available if you get sick, in some families, there are genuine psychological problems which make such documents all the more anxiety-provoking. There may have been conflicts over money between parents and children, and one or more children may have proven themselves financially irresponsible. Allowing someone who is not 100% reliable to have control over your financial resources is definitely something you don't want to do. Even when one child or some other relative is selected to be the attorney, things don't always work out the way you want since that child or relative has to maintain ongoing relations with the rest of the family, some of whom may be upset at the fact that this individual was chosen; they may have questions about his or her reliability or they may be jealous that you selected somebody other than themselves. As a result, your "attorney" may feel some need to make up to his or her siblings or other potential heirs and do things that you wouldn't have wanted done, like letting decisions about your affairs be made by a majority vote of all concerned. After all, he or she has to live with the others for a long time to come, long after you've departed the scene.

In some families, the children or other relatives are so full of conflicts and dislike each other so heartily that they can agree on nothing, and use every opportunity to fight and spite each other. Decisions may be made, not in the interests of the person giving the power-of-attorney, but rather to defy other relatives who may have strong opinions about what should be done. Obviously, giving even the nearest and dearest power-of-attorney carries with it potential problems although, in most cases, it works out fairly well since most families are constructive and well-intentioned, and really try to do their best.

Things get more complicated when the person signing the document has suddenly become ill and is acting under time pressure. Likewise, they are complicated when people have some degree of Alzheimer's Disease which is enough to influence their perception of others and to distort their judgment. Many elderly people literally feel that they are signing their lives away by giving someone this power-of-attorney and, if truth be told, many do it only under great family pressure without fully understanding the consequences; this lack of awareness of consequences applies as well to young people who are arranging for power-of-attorney. But, as I just mentioned, most families are loving and caring enough that there is little danger of stealing or of diversion of funds.

Something similar happens with health care proxies (also known as power-of-attorney for health care) in which individuals sign over to others the right to make medical decisions for them in case they are so incapacitated that they can no longer do so themselves. Usually, this deals with decisions concerning medical treatment and the giving of consent for various procedures. Many people are reluctant to sign such proxies for fear that others may make the wrong decisions and their deaths will be hastened as a result. Everyone has enough difficulty making decisions for themselves as it is, and it is scary to give that right to others, especially when there may be money-hungry relatives who want to get their hands on the loot sooner rather than later, or who may be so emotionally upset by the facts of the illness that they won't be careful enough in the decision-making process.

A word should be said about the writing of living wills which is yet another document in which someone who is approaching death writes down his or her wishes. Living wills essentially express what that person wants to have done or not done in the case of incurable terminal illness, specifically concerning whether life support systems will be utilized. In other words, should extreme measures be taken to continue life or should the individual be allowed to depart naturally, should every last desperate measure be employed or should the plug be pulled? Many hospitals request that people make their wishes known if such a document has not already been signed although, at times, a health care proxy may be stretched by the hospital or the treating physician to cover this situation as well. But, even when this form has been filled out appropriately and meets all legal requirement, there is no guarantee that the living will will be carried out if there is strong objection on the part of even a single relative, and if legal battles between family and hospital staff loom. At times, money is a consideration in what the family decides, particularly if the last will and testament has certain stipulations in it, such as if one dies before a certain time, the money goes one way or, after a certain time, it goes to someone else, although this is at present a rather rare event.

It may, however, arise more frequently in the future because, with changing laws concerning estate taxes, we may soon see a rash of people being kept alive into the following year if they happen to fall sick in the fall because inheritance tax rates for the upcoming year will be significantly lower than in the current year. One can only imagine the situation in 2009 when, all over the country, people will be kept alive into 2010 when the estate tax lapses. The situation will be even worse in 2010 because estate taxes are supposed to come back in 2011; one can imagine how many families will be in a hurry to lose their "loved one" in a non-tax year rather than have them survive into a year when the estate tax returns. A family can save itself a lot of money if the loved one dies in a non-tax year. Keeping someone alive for tax reasons has already been observed to a lesser extent when families want their dying relative to last into January rather than die in December so that he or she can be listed as a personal tax deduction for the new year.

A word should also be said about autopsies which are performed less frequently than twenty or thirty years ago. They are legally required in certain instances of sudden or violent death and are generally opposed by organized religion as a violation of the integrity of the deceased's body. Most of us don't like the idea of someone messing around with our bodies after we are gone and most of us prefer the idea of going to the grave intact or as intact as possible. On the other hand, some people want the causes of their deaths checked out as completely as possible and want their bodies autopsied. Nevertheless, no matter what our wishes may be, consent for autopsy may become a family battleground although money may not be at the root of this particular battle. One set of relatives, the "scientific" ones may want to know the details of the cause of death while others want to get on with the task of burial or cremation.

Along the same lines, if you're someone who wants to donate an organ to help a sick individual, you better make that fact known loud and clear to all, and have all your documents expressing this wish in order to be sure that what happens follows your plans. Doctors are most interested in organ donations from young adults who die in accidents rather than from older adults who die of illnesses, and it's just this group who usually doesn't have wills and hasn't expressed any thoughts about what will happen after they're gone.

This brings up the subject of dealing with the remains. Careful individuals have usually bought burial plots for themselves, reserved a place in a family plot or arranged for cremation, so there really should be no problem about what to do with the body. Furthermore, with such careful individuals, instructions concerning the style of ceremony have probably been discussed with family members or have been detailed in writing. Nevertheless, no matter what one's wishes may have been and no matter what may have been expressed in writing concerning the final disposition of remains, the situation is now in the hands of the family and what occurs is not always what the deceased would have wished. For example, someone may have expressed a wish to be buried next to a predeceased loved one but a relative may oppose that and proceed to make other arrangements. Verbal instructions to family and friends are not always considered at the time of the funeral and, after the fact, it is impractical to dig up the body so that such instructions may be carried out. When nothing has been arranged in advance and when nothing has been written down, the family has to make all decisions about handling the arrangements right then and there, hardly the best time and place to do so in view of the pressure they are under. Many funeral homes now urge prospective clients to pre-arrange their funerals so that things proceed just as the deceased wanted and so that there is a minimum of family discussion and argument. Nevertheless, just as people are reluctant to write wills, they are all the more so to pre-plan their funerals. Of course, there are some who like the idea and plan out, before they leave, every step of the funeral.

Some relatives also see the funeral as an occasion for show and expense in order to impress other family members, friends and business associates, and this may be carried out in spite of the deceased's wish for a simple affair. At other times, relatives may decide upon something terribly cheap in order to leave as much money as possible in the estate and they go against the deceased's wishes to have a large and ceremonious affair; funerals can cost in the tens of thousands of dollars. Even though one hears talk about the deceased's coming back to haunt relatives who flout their wishes, but I doubt that that happens. However, sometimes relatives do experience guilt if they do not honor their loved one's wishes. Everything that I have said about the burial might also be said about the selection of a tombstone; it may be big or little depending on the relatives' wishes and less so on the deceased's. Although the deceased may have had some opinion about the size and type of stone, this is rarely specified. People are usually too busy disposing of property as they write their wills and give final instructions to do much thinking about their tombstones.

Curiously, some of the oldest historical documents known deal with the disposition of property after death, archeologists having discovered wills carved in stone as they excavate sites of ancient civilizations. Property and what happens to it have clearly been major issues in humankind since the beginning of recorded history. These stone carvings include lists of important possessions, and sometimes specific wishes as to who gets what. So we know for sure that the writing of wills has a long history and is not something unique to recent times.

Ideally, everyone should have the right to determine the distribution of their own possessions after death, by the hands of a trusted executor, in the manner that they wished. After all, the property was theirs, they owned it and they could have done with it what they wished while alive. Things change, though, after death and, no matter what is written in the will, governments get into the act by having laws on the books concerning what happens to one's property, now called one's estate, even if they don't determine where every last cent goes. This is over and above whatever taxes are imposed upon the estate (or rather deducted from the estate) before anything goes to the heirs. Such governmental mandates may differ from state to state and may be different from one country to another, as for example, the United States and France. When someone has property in different geographic locations operating under different regulations, it may take years to work things out and the deceased's last will and testament may have relatively little to do with what eventually happens.

Not that everyone has a last will and testament. I've already mentioned that a large number of people don't like to think in any way of their own deaths; they never get around to writing a will and they die intestate, that is without a will. Property in the estate cannot be touched until the family or other interested parties bring the matter to a surrogate or probate court which then appoints an administrator who is usually a family member and who gets a small percentage of the value of the estate for his or her efforts. This administrator investigates the claims of the family as to their degree of relatedness and follows a formula in the allocation of assets which varies from state to state. In New York State, for example, the spouse, if there is one, gets the first $50,000 and one half the balance with the other half going to the children, if there are any. In the absence of spouse and children, other relatives may advance their claims but have to go through a fairly cumbersome process to do so since they have to prove their relatedness; at least it's cumbersome if the administrator is not a relative and doesn't know one person from another. If no relatives are identified after public notification (ads may be placed in local newspapers), and a designated period of time has elapsed, the money reverts to the state even though the deceased may have verbally expressed an intention to leave everything to a cherished friend or to some charity.

Even when there is a will, people who would inherit money when there is no will may make claims on the estate although they are not mentioned at all in the will. For example, a spouse who is not named in the will is, in New York State, automatically entitled to one third of the estate after taxes even if the couple hated each other and hadn't lived together for years. Minor children are also entitled to a percentage of the estate in some states but not in New York. As you can see, the deceased who had a spouse and children is denied the total freedom to allocate his or her property just as he or she wanted to do. No such rule applies, however, to adult children or to more distant relatives, and sisters and brothers, nieces and nephews, aunts and uncles, grandparents and grandchildren, and cousins have no special rights to any part of the estate although, in the absence of other, closer relatives and a will, they may make claims upon the estate. Even when the state intervenes to protect the claims of certain close relatives, as occurs in most states in the United States, one is still freer in this country to leave things as one wants than in many other places in the world.

In some circumstances, a couple may have a prenuptial agreement which is a contract signed by both parties before the marriage takes place in which it is stipulated very clearly what claims on each other's estate the spouse can make, if any. Prenuptial agreements became popular as arrangements between two older people each of whom wanted to leave his or her property to children from former marriages, marriages in which they spent most of their adult lives. Quite logically, they do not want their money to end up in the hands of the second spouse and his or her children, and therefore they sign an agreement to get around the usual rules regarding inheritance.

No prenuptial agreement is complete without the statement that the spouse surrenders all claims on the eventual estate.

Prenuptials have become increasingly popular in our complicated society where so many marriages end in divorce, and are now seen more frequently in younger people as well as older. Two individuals, each possessed of a certain amount of property, experience concern about what will happen to that property if the marriage fails or if one of them dies. Will the families from which they come still have some right to it, or will they have to share it with the spouse and ultimately the spouse's family? It seems like an unromantic way to enter a marriage, to plan for business matters in the event of divorce or death, but doing so does acknowledge reality.

Ideally, the deceased, even if not particularly wealthy, has left a detailed will behind which makes clear what his or her wishes are. The will is often supplemented by letters which are not legally binding or by codicils which may update the will or may allocate tangible personal property and personal effects such as cars, books, collections, furniture, clothing, mementos, jewelry and appliances.

Cash, for estate purposes includes stocks, bonds and notes, and life insurance benefits. These categories are considered to be distinct from real property such as land and houses. The writing of wills and the distribution of estate assets are one of the most common activities engaged in by lawyers who see to it that the transfer of property is done properly. They have little flexibility in applying the law, and cannot solve all the problems which the heirs may have in regard to the estate, especially when the deceased left no will, left a very complicated one, or had made no arrangements for the dividing up of personal effects. All of these situations may tie up the heirs in emotional knots and may drag out the final closing of the estate.

The initial words of a will state that the deceased is of sound mind and, therefore, is competent intellectually to know exactly what he or she is doing in writing the will and making decisions concerning property. The will then goes on to provide that all debts, including funeral expenses, be paid, including legal fees and executor fees. It then moves on to discuss who gets what. Distinctions between real property (land and houses) and personal property (other possessions) have significance in some parts of the world where a person can dispose of personal property as he or she wishes but has to follow the law of the country in terms of real property.

In France, for example, which follows a different code of law based on different principles than the law followed in the United States, the disposition of real property is determined by government mandate, and the individual has no freedom to choose otherwise in making a will. This Code Napoleon was formulated under Napoleon Bonaparte in the early 19th century and was based on principles laid down long before. The Code was exported to Spain which was under French control at the time, and went further afield to French and Spanish colonies including what are now the countries of Latin America. Even in the United States, it has contributed to the laws of Louisiana and of Puerto Rico. According to this code, family real property is divided with fifty percent going to the spouse and fifty percent being divided among the children. If there are no children, then it's fifty percent to the spouse and fifty percent to the family the deceased was born into. Citizens of these countries are accustomed to these regulations, but Americans are not and are often shocked when, after a death of a spouse, they find that half the real property they thought they owned there reverts to the spouse's siblings or parents when there are no offspring while the marital partner gets only the other half. What happens if someone doesn't hit it off with the inlaws and yet finds that they are now co-partners in the property? There is no way around this except not to own real property in jurisdictions that have such laws.

Let's get back to the law as practiced in most of the states. When the estate is small and uncomplicated with property left to next of kin, a simple will can usually do the job. Many people buy a standard general will in a stationery store and fill in the blanks, or even arrange for a will over the internet. However, if there is anything at all more complicated going on and that seems to be the case most of the time with such factors as a lot of money or special requests or an argumentative family, it is distinctly preferable to have the will drawn up by an attorney with all the contingencies dealt with very precisely and in detail. Remember, this is a legal document and its terms must be followed. Lack of clarity will only contribute to family battles if the family is so inclined, and it will certainly make life much more difficult for the executor who, like the lawyer handling the estate, has no option other than to adhere to the document. The only freedom an executor has is to set the time frame within which the estate is closed out, moving more or less rapidly; he or she, if so inclined, can drag it out for years. In some cases, the executor may have some freedom in the distribution of personal effects when they have not been assigned in the will but this is arguable. It is better for the person writing the will to leave all personal effects to one trustworthy relative with instructions on how to distribute them. Alternatively, they may be left to the executor or to the attorney with similar instructions. Legally and ethically, the executor has virtually no freedom of choice in the matter.

Often enough, a person changes his or her mind as death approaches and decides to make some alteration in the disposition of property as stated in the will. He or she may then write a codicil which is an addendum to the will. In the course of many changes of mind, it is possible that there may be many codicils written over a period of years, and that goes to make the overall wishes for the estate very confusing and sometimes contradictory. The situation winds up often enough worse than having no will at all. It is probably better to write a new will including all changes that one decides upon rather than go the route of codicils, certainly after there are one or two codicils.

One complicating feature of many wills is the setting up of trusts which is pretty much limited to large estates although it also has relevance when minors are involved even when the amounts are smaller. Here, the dying person doesn't exactly trust the heir, who may be very young and immature, and not able to appreciate what to do with the money. The money would usually, if the heir is under age, be managed by the child's parent or guardian. If the person leaving the money considers the parent or the guardian to be unreliable and fears that he or she may use the funds for purposes other than the deceased may have wished, the only alternative is for the will to arrange for the setting up of a trust to be managed by a trustee who may be another family member, a bank, some other financial organization or a lawyer. The trust will conserve and use for designated purposes the money and release it to the heir, at the appropriate time, as requested. In this way, the money is kept safe and will be distributed, even many years later, to the person for whom it was intended, even though no one can guarantee that it will be used wisely at that time.

There are, of course, people who attempt to control their heirs by setting up trusts and other restrictions in their wills. For example, the heir does not inherit till he or she is age 25 or married, has become a parent or fulfilled some other requirement. Obviously, this can be done and works for a while but control from beyond the grave doesn't work for too long since life events occur unpredictably and may render the trust more and more difficult to manage. The further into the future one attempts to control matters, the more details one has to consider; the trust becomes more and more complicated which will probably be more expensive as the trustees follow the deceased's directives over the years. There are any number of cases where so much money was spent in trustee services over a period of years or in legal wrangles that there was little residual estate for distribution when the time came to do so.

Not everyone in the family is necessarily willing to accept the will as valid, and there may well be a legal battle which can go on for years in which those who are dissatisfied challenge those who have been left what is felt to be more than their fair share of the estate. A well written will has the force of law and there is little that anyone can do about it unless he or she can prove that the writer of the will was not in his or her right mind and, in legal terms, lacked capacity. There are many disputes, both in law and in psychiatry, over what constitutes capacity, and this is reflected in many cases by legal battles after the will is read. But, in general, capacity means that someone knew he or she was writing a will, knew in general what was owned, and knew who were the natural objects of the will. In practice, lacking capacity may mean that they had Alzheimer's Disease or were so affected by their terminal illness as to no longer have good judgment.

Another complaint may be that the person writing the will was influenced to do so by someone who had so strong a position in relationship to him or her that this person's wishes could be imposed upon the dying person. One example that arises again and again is when a person is taken care of by a nurse or physician during a final illness, someone who is particularly good and helpful to them. When the will is read, it turns out this person has become the chief or a major heir of the estate. There are grounds for disputing the will but one must indeed prove that the writer of the will was indeed not able to resist the influence of the other even if he or she understood what was going on. This is extremely difficult to prove in a court of law. It was attempted by Harry's children in the case I mentioned in the last chapter where he left his entire estate to his second wife, Jennifer who was so much younger than he. As his wife, she was entitled to a significant share of his estate anyway but it was claimed that she exerted undue influence on him to obtain the rest. However, undue influence could not be proven, and the children lost the case.

I have reviewed the legalities relating to terminal illnesses and death at some length since it is important to understand what they are about in order to see where family and personal problems over money can influence matters and produce strife. As you can see, there is room for conflict at the time that someone takes over the affairs of the sick person, in the writing and carrying out of the power-of-attorney, in the use of the health care proxy and the living will, in burial arrangements, and in the implementation of the will, if there is one. Such issues as rivalry among siblings for a parents' love and respect with the wish for tangible signs of such preference, primary dislike between one sibling and another, needs for social and familial prestige, religious and philosophical considerations, doubts as to rationality of the deceased, and the desire for money all play their roles as the family deals with the crisis of death. Disputes over such issues often sour family relationships of the survivors for the rest of their lives although they were probably pretty sour to begin with. Let's look at a few cases where emotional problems complicated inheritance matters and either created bad feelings or further increased those that were already present.

Jessie was a woman who died at age 85, leaving her estate to her three daughters. She had been widowed at a young age and raised her children with the help of some inherited money and a small income from doing housework for others. She was a rather romantic individual who named her three daughters after heroines in operas by Richard Wagner: Elisabeth, Elsa and Eva, and she liked to see each of them in very different terms. Elisabeth was the serious one, Elsa the beautiful one and Eva the romantic one, descriptions the three did not agree with. Once her children were raised and on their own, she began to invest in the stock market and, with good advice and good luck, was able to build up a tidy amount of money. As she entered advanced old age and could no longer maintain her independence, she moved in with Elisabeth who accepted the responsibility and provided for her mother at her own expense. Since Elisabeth was the "serious" one, her mother gave her power-of-attorney, something the two other daughters didn't mind too much because they didn't want to be bothered, except that they did periodically ask for information about Jessie's current business affairs and expressed concern about what was happening to her possessions. When Jessie passed away, naturally Elisabeth was the executor appointed in the will; she strived very hard to be totally scrupulous about dividing up her mother's property, both real and personal, although she harbored the thought that she was really entitled to more than the other two because of all the expenses of Jessie's care over the previous several years and because of all the work she put in, first while her mother was alive and then in managing the estate. Even though she did not take one penny extra, both Elsa and Eva were convinced that they had been short-changed by Elisabeth and kept on asking about the location of certain items of jewelry, whether the investments were handled wisely, and whether there weren't more bank accounts. It was obvious that they thought that Elisabeth was holding out on them in some way. There had been considerable sibling rivalry among the three over the years but there was an explosion of anger on everyone's part after Jessie's death which continues to this date, ten years later.Furthermore, Elisabeth was extensively criticized by her two sisters for not seeing to it that her mother had better health care even though she was treated by outstanding doctors in her frail years and in her final illness; they also criticized Elisabeth for her choice of attorney to supervise the carrying out of the will, believing that she had chosen someone who would favor her. It would be a mistake, though, to think that Elisabeth was the only object of suspicion in this family. Both Eva and Elsa distrusted each other and, at one time or another, thought the other was in league with Elisabeth to rob her by taking more than their fair share of the property. This case illustrates how sibling rivalry plays its part in a number of ways in the terminal illness and dying process: the selection of an attorney, arguments over health care responsibility, and the handling of an estate. These issues do not arise all of a sudden in a solid family background but are the outcome of years of covered-over strains in family relationships.

Another case which reveals the stresses of terminal illness on a family and its monetary consequences is that of Ernestine who had a several year struggle with cancer before she passed away. She was the mother of two sons and two daughters, and had been widowed about ten years before the diagnosis of cancer was made. Everyone in the family knew that her favorite was Vivian who had moved away from her parents' home when she went to college and never returned. She was a struggling actress who didn't quite make it and had little to do with the family over the years. In spite of that, Ernestine never stopped trying to get her to come and visit, and obviously was more concerned about Vivian's successes and failures than about what happened to the other children. Because Vivian was so far removed from family activities, she wasn't even considered as an agent or as an executor. However, when Vivian learned that her mother had entered the final stages of her illness and was sinking into coma, she did return to be with her. Almost immediately, she began to criticize everything that the others were doing and, when the time came to remove life support systems, something that Ernestine had clearly specified in writing that she wanted done, Vivian refused to accept that option. She not only fought with her siblings over this but argued with the doctors and the hospital administration, requesting additional consultations and threatening legal action if care was terminated. The hospital was reluctant to act for fear of a suit and the four siblings had screaming bouts in the hospital to the point where hospital security had to be called. Eventually, Ernestine did pass away, not in the way she wanted, and it turned out that her will was biased in favor of Vivian, with Vivian getting half the total amount and the other three splitting the rest. Also included in the will was a statement that Vivian needed the money more than the others did because of the uncertainties of her profession.

The question that arises is why did Vivian fight so to keep her mother alive, was it out of sheer orneriness toward her siblings or did guilt about neglecting her mother all those years play a part?

You may have noticed that the two examples so far are of elderly widows, and there's a reason for that. Women tend to marry men who are a bit older than they are and then live longer than their spouses. When men die, their wives generally take over the estate and there is usually little conflict about that. However, when the women die, their estates usually go to their children, and that opens the door to greater conflict depending upon the accumulated stresses and problems in the families over the years, particularly sibling rivalry.

The case of the death of a young man, Joshua, demonstrates other problems. He died at 30 from rapidly progressive AIDS. He was born into a poor home and worked hard from an early age to improve his lot and look after his mother and brothers, he being the oldest. He managed to put aside some money and, out of the goodness of his heart (in contrast to many such situations, he did not receive payment for doing so), in order to help her stay here, he married a young woman who was an illegal immigrant in this country. They never lived together; indeed, she continued to live with her husband from the old country and a son who was born in the United States. When Joshua became ill, he knew that he had to write his will in order to see that his estate be disposed of as he wished. He used an attorney who did volunteer work at the hospital and who drew up a simple will, making sure that Joshua's gay partner got 50% and Joshua's family got 50%; this was not actually what Joshua wanted but was forced on him by the lawyer writing the will who believed that gay partners should be protected. When he died, the "wife", who was nowhere in the will, initiated a claim on the estate for herself and for her son; the family, however, threatened to report her case to the Immigration and Naturalization Service, and she promptly totally disappeared from the scene. The estate was finally distributed according to the provisions of the will although some of the personal effects meant for family members had vanished while in the custody of the room-mate. In this case, we see how a hastily drawn will, written under pressure, does not carry out the real wishes of the deceased and we also see how a wife, no matter how far removed from that role, can make a claim which, if pursued, must be granted over and above the intentions detailed in the will. It was only her fears of being deported unceremoniously from the United States to her native country that made the "widow" disappear and give up her claims.

Ellen was another elderly woman who died in her 80s. She had never married, but had four nieces and nephews with whom she maintained cordial but distant relationships. In her will, she left them nothing but did leave her money to specific charities. Although the amount was not large, one of her nieces did not want to accept the will and began a suit to cancel it out because she claimed that her aunt lacked capacity. The suit did not go very far since the will was several years old and, during those years, Ellen had handled her own affairs with skill, proving that she was fully competent and knew what she was doing when she wrote her will. Just not liking a will on the part of a family is hardly sufficient grounds for throwing it out.

Phil died at the age of 75, leaving a small estate but no will. He had never married and had a small but successful business which provided him with sufficient funds, in addition to his social security and pension, to enjoy life during retirement. He stated many times that he wanted to enjoy what he had and really didn't care what happened after he was gone. When he knew he was dying, he started to collect sedative pills so that he could do himself in before he lost control of his life and became a "hospitalized cripple". Unfortunately for him, he went into coma before he could do the job himself and lingered for several weeks before he died. His nearest relatives were cousins who had to prove their relatedness to him, no easy matter since all were born in Europe and the records, whatever there may have been, were destroyed in the Second World War. Eventually, the relationship was proven and the cousins shared Phil's remaining property.

Erica was a professional woman who had made great contributions to her chosen field and had accumulated an estate of several million dollars when she died of cancer at the age of 65. Her will left the money in equal shares to the two sons and one daughter of her first marriage. What makes her case so striking is that her second marriage was to an enormously wealthy man who was the president of a retailing empire that was global in scope. He also had been married before and had children by his first wife. At the time they were wed, they signed a prenuptial agreement which included a provision that, if either of them started divorce proceedings, he would immediately transfer 20 million dollars to her account and that would presumably be the end of any claim she could make on his billions. In her last few days before death, at a time when he was recovering from cardiac bypass surgery, she started divorce proceedings against him, probably in an attempt to swell her own estate and leave considerably more money to her own children. He was horrified by what he felt was Erica's callousness and refused to comply with the transfer of funds either then or after her death. Her two sons took him to court to obtain the money, and the case drifted on for a while to the delight of the scandal sheets which published all the details. While Erica was motivated by mother love for her children and concern for their welfare, her actions produced the opposite outcome, tying them up in legal matters for years and using up in legal fees and court costs all the money that she had left them. One can only wonder what would have happened if she let matters be and trusted to the generosity of her husband and whatever good will there was; perhaps he would have been kinder to them and they would have wound up with more.

I could go on with stories illustrating the problems of death and dying, and their financial implications, particularly in troubled families, but you see the point I'm making: financial problems don't stop just because one is in the hospital or even in the grave. They go on and on, especially the ones accompanied by emotional problems although it's now other people than the deceased who have to deal with them.

# APPENDIX A

# *How Much is Enough?*

As you've observed both in your life and throughout this book, there are people who always want more and more, both of money and of the things it buys. They ignore considerations of personal happiness and satisfactory relationships with others as they try to get all they want, and seem to feel that no amount is enough. They justify this to themselves by advancing all kinds of reasons and they blind themselves to what their psychological motivations might be in their pursuit of material goods. Such behavior raises first the question of just how much is really enough and second, the related question of why do people want more than enough, being motivated by psychological needs rather than realistic ones.

If we check out what's been said about these questions by a number of well known people, it only goes to show how frequently the questions have been asked and how diverse the answers are but they do not really provide us with much guidance. Responses range from the most minimal to "the sky's the limit". For example, when asked how much land a man needs, Count Leo Tolstoy, the great Russian novelist and philosopher who yearned for the simple life, answered in words to the effect that a man needs just enough space to be buried in. Contrast this with the Duchess of Windsor's famous comment that "one can never be too rich nor too thin"! The "never too thin" part sounds like the battle cry of an anorexic but the "never too rich" part is at the opposite pole from Tolstoy's viewpoint and tells us something about the Duchess' personal view of the world. Mae West, a sex symbol of the middle years of the past century, stated that "too much of a good thing can be wonderful", her sultry delivery of that line suggesting that she was talking more about sex than about money. More recently, we have the "the material girl", Madonna, singing that she wants more.

I'll try to answer the two questions myself. Let's start out by looking at the first one. Just how much is enough? What gets included here depends to a very great extent on who you are and where you come from, but would always have to include enough money and material goods to keep you well fed and adequately clothed and housed, at a minimum. These basics, however, might look different in different places in the world; for example, different countries have different diets and rely on different foods. They also have different requirements for housing and clothing, and what works on a tropical island would not be at all suitable for Eskimos in the far North. However, the real problem in defining "how much is enough?" occurs, not when we compare the basics, but when we add things to them.

We would have to start off with the fixed expenses of living and add such other items as whatever money is necessary to pay for medical and dental costs, both now and in the future. We would also have to add into the answer some money squirreled away to take care of expected future outlays like education for our children and for their wedding expenses as well as help in starting them out on their own lives as independent adults once they have completed their separation from us. We also need some savings for any emergencies that might come up as well as for retirement. Let's not forget that we also need money to maintain a sense of safety and security in a high-crime, sometimes dangerous, society, as well as money to pay for the occasional vacation. We are also entitled to some entertainment.

This country has been a land of plenty except for only occasional periods in its history, and is currently near its peak of prosperity with its citizens having enormous buying power. We share this tremendous buying power with the citizens of a number of other industrialized nations, in all of which having enough of the basics is a fact that everyone takes for granted. What else do we take for granted as part of that "enough"? At least one car per family, at least one color television, a high quality stereo, air conditioning and lots of other things that weren't even thought of a generation or so ago. Of most recent vintage are such new necessities as computers, the internet, and cell phones, which were initially used to facilitate business but have gradually entered the general marketplace, crossing the line from luxuries to necessities. People in middle and upper income groups use these new technological wonders as if life couldn't proceed without them and now even poor people are acquiring them.

In addition to your national and economic background, your age also plays a part in how you regard what is enough, with lots of older people feeling strongly that cell phones, for example, are luxuries while younger people see them as necessary to survival in today's world. Since the older generation got along for most of its existence without these modern trimmings, it knows that life can be lived without them but younger people have grown up with them and can't understand how people managed before they were discovered. With all this technology, we have moved pretty far from the basic elements of what's required for a simple life. However, we shouldn't forget that, in most other parts of the world, what constitutes "enough" is much less than it is in the United States and what we require would be regarded as too much. Our enough might be regarded as horrible greed elsewhere and those who pursue it as incredible gluttons. Even in this country there are people and subcultures who look critically at what most of us take for granted as essentials of the good life.

The real problem, though, with defining "enough" is the personal component since, even in the same society, any one person's enough may be another person's not enough as well as yet a third person's too much. When any of us wants money or objects that are more than what most people have and that more than provide us with the basics of a reasonably good life, then we most likely have a situation where there is too much, these things having taken on a value of their own. In other words, they have assumed psychological importance and fulfill some emotional need for that person. Depending upon what this value is for him or her, the usual enough is no longer sufficient and that person tries to get more and more.

For example, if money takes on the meaning to someone that the more you have, the longer you're going to live, he or she will keep on trying to accumulate more, not wanting to face the prospect of death. If you look a little more closely at the idea that money brings you immunity from death, you might be forced to agree that a lot of money can buy you the very best medical care and, in a pinch, that might make the difference between life and death. However, even with the best medical care, when you reach the point that your body can no longer go on, you will give up the ghost and no amount of money can save you. So, while there may well be a germ of reality in the wish for more money, it is exaggerated beyond all reason to support one's urges to have more.

Other people use money to gain power over others. They may be reacting to an earlier time in their lives when they were victimized by others and felt attacked, belittled and worthless because they couldn't defend themselves. For them, as long as the threat of further attack is still something that persists in their minds as a possibility, they will want more money in order to buy a more strongly defended position. As a result, there can be no such thing as enough for them and they will always want more.

Over and above defending themselves from feared attacks, yet others will use their wealth to get revenge on people who hurt them in the past and to inflict pain and suffering on them because of their own previous pain and suffering. They feel that, if they have enough money, they can destroy those who hurt them and made them suffer. For such people, money is no longer just something that provides the basics of life, a number of luxuries and a feeling of security. It is also used to punish others and, as a result, there never is enough because the need to punish continues no matter how much is spent.

Money may also be used as a means of controlling others and forcing them into submission. This is an important motivation for those who need that sense of power over others since having lots of it definitely enhances one's feeling of being important and reinforces one's self-esteem. Others who keep getting into competitive relationships also need more money to let them always come out ahead. There are also those who define their success by being able to outdo their parents and, for them, having more is one way of demonstrating their superiority. It also is a way of overcoming boredom by enabling the moneyed individual to do more things than he or she could do if strapped for funds.

Of course, these motivations for having "more" indicate that the individual who never has enough is showing evidence of psychological problems which drive him or her to acquire more money and, along with that, more possessions. While it may sometimes be difficult to draw the line between enough and more than enough, it usually can be done. If you go on to examine the situation a little more deeply by getting to know someone well, it should also be possible for you to find the reasons why more and more is needed by that person.

During the last year or so, we have learned about executives who get their companies to pay thousands of dollars for such items as umbrella stands, shower curtains and trash cans. Such excesses outrage the average person who believes that this lavishness is more than enough to the point that it reveals itself to be greed or gluttony. Why are the needs of these people so great, what psychological forces motivate them to such extremes? There certainly is a need to compete with each other and to acquire more than each other, to impress with the size of their incomes, the expense of the objects they can buy and the casualness with which they can spend large amounts of money. Most of what they bought brought them little actual pleasure except for the knowledge that they could buy these items and have more than their "friends" or at least be the first in their group to acquire them. The greed shown by these individuals only goes to prove that, for some people, as the Duchess of Windsor stated, there is never enough.

There is obviously no simple, universal answer to the question how much is enough. Each of us is different in our needs, and the distinction between necessities and luxuries is a blurry, changing one. What can be answered more definitely is whether your own personal psychological needs are pushing you into the too much category. You have to do some real thinking about what enough means to you and whether or not you are going far beyond that and why.

# APPENDIX B

# *Becoming Rational About Money*

Reading this book makes you more knowledgeable about the many things that money means to different people and how these are expressed throughout life. Interesting as that may be, what could be more important to you is to figure out what money means to you, where your own real needs end, and where your emotional needs begin. These emotional needs are better dealt with directly and not through the symbolic use of money.

Your attitudes towards money have been shaped by your personal experiences, but that does not mean you have to be stuck with those attitudes for the rest of your life, particularly if they hurt you and those you love. You can learn new attitudes through contact with others whose experiences and attitudes are different from yours. Realizing how they use money can make you more aware, by contrast, of the role it plays in your own psychology. With greater awareness comes greater control over the direction of your life and the power to use money more effectively.

One good start to answering the question of what role money plays in your life is to ask yourself some questions, a self-assessment.

Did you see yourself from time to time as you went through the book? Did you find yourself in agreement with my definition of how much is enough? What does enough mean to you? Do you never have enough money and the things it buys? Do you try to get too much? Does money have meanings to you besides being just money? When I ask you to look at your own attitudes towards money and what they've done to help or harm you, it may prove more difficult than it at first seems. People who are sensitive to criticism and protective of their egos often blame everyone around them for causing problems in order that they themselves can feel totally innocent. On the other hand, some people with low self-esteem tend to blame themselves for everything that goes wrong in their vicinity. Neither extreme is likely and it may be hard to quantify what your contribution to the strife consists of if you are in either of those categories. Even if you are not at an extreme, it is not all that easy to examine yourself critically and come up with some answers about where you fit in.

Unless you have very serious problems with money such as being an out- of-control gambler or a severely compulsive shopper who literally can't stop till you drop, the chances are that you don't need to consult a mental health professional but are capable of helping yourself. What I suggest you do is to attempt a process of self-treatment following your self-assessment, this treatment being modeled after psychotherapy with a therapist but with two changes. You have to be your own objective observer, hard as that may be, instead of having a therapist do the job, and you are looking at money issues exclusively, a much narrower focus than if you undertook a total personality examination.

Because being objective about oneself is so very difficult, it would be ideal to have a calm, reasonable friend with whom you can discuss these things, somebody without an axe to grind as far as you're concerned. Be warned though that it is extremely difficult to find objective people. So many of those who surround us have their own difficulties in relationship to money and they're usually more eager to have a sounding board for their problems than to listen to someone else. They may also have hidden agendas in relation to you which will color their advice. Certainly, if you've ever had a money dispute with someone, that person is absolutely not the right one in whom to find objectivity.

For a proper self-examination, you have to sit back in a quiet moment or hour when you are not under stress and are consequently more capable of objectivity, and review your life, your money attitudes and your interpersonal transactions in order to come up with some correct answers. To begin self-treatment, it's a good idea first to ask yourself just who you are and what influences have made you the person you are today. Start with the sort of approach to dealing with money your family had, whether there was general agreement between your parents in money matters or whether they had ongoing conflicts which spilled over into their children's thinking and dealing with money. Even in the same family, there can be vastly different attitudes to life, different personalities and different relationships to money from one child to the next since each one was treated individually by their parents. Where did you fit in?

What influences did your more extended family (your grandparents, aunts, uncles, and cousins) and your friends have on you and did they build your self-confidence or did they make you doubt yourself, leaving you with a greater need for money to strengthen your self-esteem? When you started going to school and expanding your educational and social horizons, did your experiences in these new surroundings tend to confirm what you learned at home or did they contradict those ideas, attitudes and behaviors? Also ask yourself about the prevailing attitudes, both idealistic and in actual practice, towards money in your community, ethnic group and social class, and whether your standards are close to them or far away.

By the time you got around to a romantic life and to marriage, were there problems with your partner over money and, if so, what kind of problems? Did these problems repeat themselves with partner after partner if you had a number of them along the way? If the same problem keeps coming up, it may mean that it is part of your emotional baggage. Either that or you had the bad luck to run into a series of people who just happened to do things differently from you, one after the other, a possible but not very likely situation.

I'm not trying to tell you who's right and who's wrong, and I wouldn't want you to think in those terms since that's not the real issue; we are all the inevitable products of the forces working on us since we were born, superimposed on factors that came with our genes, and in that sense we're always right since we couldn't have turned out any other way. However, now that we have a chance to look the matter over, we do get some choices.

Once you can identify something that you feel is an error in your approach to money, then you have to ask yourself what is the rational, reasonable thing to have done in those circumstances and why did you go in the opposite direction. Then comes the hardest part of all, making a considered decision to junk the old way and use a new, more thoughtful, one. Changes like this don't happen overnight but require repeated examination and review (a process called working through) to make sure that you are indeed following a course of action that you decide upon clearly and thoughtfully, and are not slipping back into old habits and coming up with rationalizations for staying with these old habits. It's anxiety-provoking to give up familiar ways of dealing with things, no matter how much trouble they may cause, and to start using new and untried approaches.

I have, throughout this book, presented examples of the many diverse problems that people have with money; these examples are drawn from my contact with patients as well as from history and literature, and from my own acquaintances, sometimes from my own family. I have provided you with these brief case studies not only because they are interesting and illustrate the points I am making but also because they give you some idea of how other people deal with money issues. It makes it easier to see your own problems when you can compare what you are doing with what others have done. Learning about others who are not that different from yourself makes it possible for you to recognize more easily what you yourself are doing and helps to provide some objectivity.

Another source of personal pain that arises in every therapy, whether done by a therapist or by yourself, is the realization that you haven't always been dealt with fairly. It is easy to become angry at those who hurt you and to express that anger towards them, but that means that you are still locked into the situations that they helped create. Far better to not only rid yourself of the problems but to recognize that these others (your parents, for example) have suffered their own hurts and then transmitted their problems to you. Once you are truly free of their malign influence, you can afford to be philosophical and charitable towards them, and that also makes for a saner and happier way of life, in dealing with people about money and about almost everything else.

In addition to maintaining a private practice for over forty years, Dr. Lowenkopf has taught at several medical schools in New York City. He is a Distinguished Life Fellow of the American Psychiatric Association and a Fellow of the American Academy of Psychoanalysis and Dynamic Psychiatry. He has worked with people with emotional problems about money and has lectured widely in the United States and abroad on the subject.

Money was invented about 5000 years ago and has proved essential to civilization. It has also become so charged with emotions that it dominates events throughout life and looms large in all interpersonal transactions. This book looks at all aspects of the money/mind relationship from the viewpoint of a psychiatrist who has dealt with the problems that money produces and the problems that it supposedly resolves. There are chapters dealing with important stages in the life cycle such as childhood, adolescence, marriage, maturity, retirement, old age and death as well as chapters concerned with special topics such as divorce, poverty, wealth, gambling, stealing, philanthropy and hoarding. The author illustrates these issues with cases drawn from his professional work and from history, literature, current events, and popular culture and personalities. He shows the reader how many of their personal psychological problems can be remedied by more realistic attitudes to money and activities dealing with it, which in fact is how psychotherapy works.

CPSIA information can be obtained
at www.ICGtesting.com
Printed in the USA
BVHW080941140123
656261BV00002B/54